European Studies

A A Scott

PITMAN
PUBLISHING

PITMAN PUBLISHING
128 Long Acre, London WC2E 9AN

A Division of Longman Group UK Limited

© A A Scott 1992

First published in Great Britain 1992
Reprinted 1992 (twice), 1993

British Library Cataloguing in Publication Data

A catalogue record for this book is available from the British
Library

ISBN 0-273-03813-3

Typeset by Avocet Typesetters, Bicester, Oxon
Printed in England by Clays Ltd, St Ives plc

Acknowledgement
Paul McGregor, for writing
Part Five Contemporary Issues.

Contents

1 Introduction to Europe

Objectives
1 Introduce the main areas of study – Europe, the European Community and the Single European Market.
2 Find out what are the motivations for studying Europe.
3 Complete an audit of existing knowledge and skills.
4 Construct a catalogue of information sources.
5 Organise a filing system for notes and material gathered.

The boundaries of Europe

Living in Britain we think that Europe begins with the Channel, and it is true that the countries on the other side are mainland Europe. However, we must not forget that Britain is a part of Europe, and so is Ireland.

The Scandinavian countries – Norway and Sweden – are often thought of as being somehow different, the strip of water that separates them from Denmark and Germany affects our thinking just as much as the Channel affects our thinking about the 'Europeanism' of Britain and Ireland.

We have no hesitation in saying that Morocco, Algeria and Tunisia, located on the Southern shore of the Mediterranean, are part of Africa rather than Europe, despite the fact that Algeria belonged to France until just a few years ago. How do we react to the news that they would like to join the European Community? What about Madeira and the Canary Islands? They belong to Spain, but lie in the Atlantic, off the coast of Africa.

Political boundaries, as well as physical boundaries, are important. We hardly hesitate before deciding that Greece is part of Europe, but we think for a moment before accepting Yugoslavia, Bulgaria or Albania, even though they are geographically closer to us.

Similarly, Poland, Czechoslovakia, Hungary and Romania, together with Latvia, Estonia and Lithuania, are countries that were considered 'a million miles away'; behind the 'Iron Curtain'; or part of the 'Eastern Bloc', until quite recently.

In some countries, regional areas are striving for independence, and may in the future become European countries in their own right.

In the main, this book will concentrate on the countries that are closer to Britain geographically and culturally, and those which have major economic significance.

Activity 1.1   **1** Make a copy of the map (Figure 1.1). Mark on it the countries that you believe are definitely part of Europe and, in a different colour, those which are not, in your opinion, part of Europe but are worth studying in this unit. Be prepared to justify your choice.

Figure 1.1 What constitutes Europe?

2 Compare your map with those of other European Studies students. Choose a range of countries that is representative of them all.

The European Community

On 9 May 1950 the then French Foreign Minister, Robert Schuman, proposed a scheme that would end the disagreements over coal and steel production that had gone on for years. In 1951 an agreement was signed setting up the European Coal and Steel Community (ECSC).

In 1957 Treaties were signed establishing the European Economic Community (EEC) and the European Atomic Energy Community (EURATOM).

There were six founder members: Belgium, Germany, France, Italy, Luxembourg and the Netherlands. Denmark, Ireland and the United Kingdom joined in 1973. Greece followed in 1981 and Portugal and Spain, in 1986.

By this time the aims of the Community were widening. The 12 nations had historical and cultural differences but they all wanted to live in peace, to assert themselves on the world's political and economic stage, to improve the living and working conditions of their citizens, to offer support to the developing countries throughout the world, and to set a good example of democracy and justice.

To help achieve these aims a number of institutions were set up, notably the European Commission, the European Parliament and the Council of Ministers. Through these institutions policies are formulated and legislation introduced. The more controversial of these policies concern agriculture, the monetary system, regional and social affairs.

The success of the European Community can be judged by the seriousness with which the world's most powerful trading nations – Japan and the USA – take notice of its policies. Other countries, some of which you might not think as being part of Europe, are keen to join and share in the benefits.

This is the cause of a major dilemma. Should the EC admit more countries to membership, or should it concentrate on progress towards closer links between existing members? At the time of writing this is a major issue.

The Single European Market

1992 is a major year in the history of the EC. This marks the creation of a single European market, in which there will be full freedom of movement for goods, persons, services and capital.

The Single European Act 1986 provided the framework for a radical and comprehensive approach to remove all internal barriers and achieve a truly

The Commission
Makes proposals

The European Parliament
Gives opinions and proposes
amendments

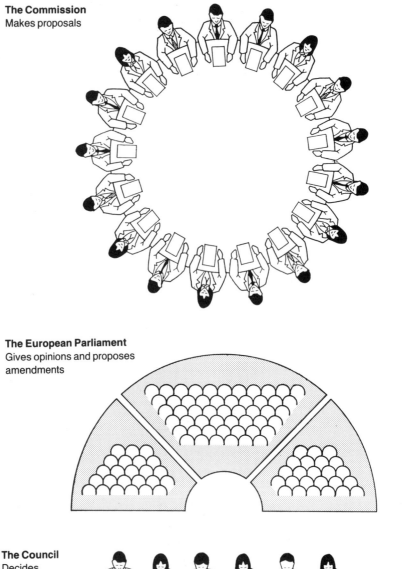

The Council
Decides

Figure 1.2 European Community institutions
Source: Department of Trade and Industry

common market. A date was set to achieve this of 31 December 1992.

Because all the publicity urged businesses to be prepared for '1992' there was an implied urgency for them to be ready by the beginning of the year. In fact this allowed 12 months before the last barrier had to be removed and the Act was fully effective.

Why is it so important to learn about Europe?

In the past, most UK citizens lived and worked in the UK. They often took holidays in other European countries, but these were relatively short and were in tourist areas which didn't give a true impression of local people and culture.

With the removal of barriers to living and working in other EC countries it will be much easier for you to move to a country that is more attractive to you, either because it has a better standard of living, a better climate, a shortage of people with the job skills you have, or for any other reason.

Conversely, you may find yourself competing for a job with someone from another EC country, in the UK.

As the EC becomes more and more of a common market, companies will find it easier and more attractive to trade with other European countries. Therefore, a knowledge of Europe will make you a more valuable employee.

EC regulations already affect you. The Common Agricultural Policy, and Policy on Competition affect the prices you pay in the shops. Regulations on Health, Safety and the Environment improve the environment in the UK, as well as in the rest of Europe and other parts of the world.

Policies that affect the economy will determine whether you are paid in pounds or a common European currency; what interest you get on your savings; and what interest you pay on a mortgage, or a loan to buy a car.

Acquiring a knowledge of EC institutions, will assist you in making informed choices when voting in the elections to the European Parliament.

Europe isn't just the European Community. There are many countries outside the EC that we visit, do business with, and whose policies, economies and defence strategies have an effect on us. You should bear this in mind, so that when gathering information for this course you cover a wide perspective. Throughout your studies, issues will arise and be discussed that affect the future shape of Europe. Recent examples are the development of the Channel Tunnel, the unification of Germany, and the break-up of the USSR. The final chapter describes how you should, together with your fellow students, collect and analyse material about such issues so that you can offer an informed opinion on them.

Starting points for studying European countries

From studies of geography you may know something about European countries – where they are, what climate they have, whether they are mainly agricultural or industrial, the population, and so on.

A study of history may have taught you something about their constitution and government, what their relationships have been with other countries and what cultural heritage they have.

You may be familiar with one or more European languages in addition to English and be able to translate articles and television/radio programmes.

Other studies may have given you some special awareness of European countries.

If you have been on holiday to a European country you will be familiar with the principal tourist areas, the currency, food and some of the air, sea and road routes to and through that country.

Activity 1.2   **1** Make a list of all the experiences you have had which have contributed to your knowledge of other European countries.

2 Write down all the skills that you have that might help in building up further knowledge of the countries.

3 Compare your knowledge and skills with other European Studies students. You may need to form groups to carry out some of the later activities. When you do, make sure that each group has the appropriate mix of skills.

Sources of information

Your college and public libraries will have information that will be of use to you during your studies. Sometimes books are classified under 'Europe' but there will be many more books that are classified according to subject areas.

The European scene is changing rapidly and books become out of date. Take care to check the date of any book you use and quote the source and date of any data you use in assignments. Always use the most up-to-date figures available.

The European Commission produces a lot of statistical and policy documents, many of which are free. Your library should be able to get these without difficulty.

Table 1.1 shows the classifications of library materials to be found in one Further Education College Library, in the Decimal Dewey system.

Activity 1.3   Liaise with your local librarians to obtain up-to-date lists of the classifications of resource material on Europe.

Most libraries are able to arrange to borrow further books, periodicals and videos from the main County Library.

Table 1.1 College library material on Europe

Non-Fiction Section		COEC Report on the Activities of the EC	382
Finance and Taxation	332	Dictionnaire Commercial et Financial	403
Taxation in Europe	336	Language dictionaries	433–463
Economy	337	Facts on File	904
Foreign Trade/Exporting	382	Europe year-book	910
Doing Business in the EC		Chambers World Gazetteer	910
Marketing	658, 659	Handbook for Europe	940
Mind your Manners			
European Policy on Agriculture	338.184	**Restricted Loan**	
European Community	337, 338, 382	Europe in Figures	314
1992 Single Market	338, 382, 658	European Campaign, Projects for the Countryside	333
European Parliamentary Law	341–347	Croner's Europe	338
Europe – History		COEC Panorama of European Industry	338
Germany	914.3	Tourism and Europe	338
France	914.4	British Overseas Trade Board	
Spain	914.6	– Hints for Exporters	338
Europe – Geography			
France	944	**Periodicals**	
Italy	945	*The European* – weekly	
Spain	946	*CEDEFOP* – vocational training in Europe	
Belgium & Luxembourg	949	European Parliament – *EP News*	
Languages:		*Euroreporter*	
German	431–439	*Economic Progress Report* – monthly	
French	440–448	*Economic Review* – quarterly	
Italian	450–458	*The Economist* – weekly	
Spanish	465–468	*The Spectator* – weekly	
Tourism – European aspects	338.47	*The Listener* – weekly	
Careers information/Working abroad	371.425	*Single Market News*	
		1992 – Single Market Community Review	
Reference section			
British Humanities Index		**Folders**	
– European Report (twice weekly)	016	European Single Market – Exporting	338
What's what in the 1980s	032	The European Parliament	341
Economic terminology		Europe's Parliament – Information for Students	341
– German/English, English/German	330	EC Policies	382
World Bank world tables			
Britain and the EC	337	**Videos**	
The Times 1000 – World's top companies	338	*Dial 010 for Europe*	
The EEC – A guide to the maze	338	*Our Europe*	
The EC Background Reports	338	*1992 and Education*	
A dictionary of the EC	341	*Europe Open for Business*	
Multi-lingual comercial dictionary	380	*1992 – What's That?*	

Attached to the County Library there may be a Business Resource Centre with an extensive stock of up-to-date information on Europe. Clwyd's main library, for example, houses a European Information Centre which stocks books and magazines related to business matters and a wide collection of European Community literature, and offers (for a charge) an information retrieval and consultancy service to businesses. These organisations are more likely to co-operate with colleges than with individual students.

Far better than any books or videos are personal contacts with people in other countries. You may have your own contacts, via relatives or friends, and your college may be part of a network of links with other colleges in Europe.

If you have friends or relatives, or penfriends in a European country you will be able to ask them for information about that country.

If you have friends or relatives that have business, or other connections, with European countries they will also be able to provide you with information about those countries.

Activity 1.4   Ask your relatives and friends, when you next meet them, what connections they have, and what they know, about other European countries.

Getting information often takes a long time. If you write to an organisation it may be a while before they reply or they may not reply at all. Leave yourself time to find another way of getting information if your first choice does not work out, or to do the task in some other way.

It takes longer for post to get to destinations that are outside the UK. If you write in English the recipient may have to translate what you have written, and perhaps translate the reply into English. On the other hand, if you try to short-cut this by writing in the recipient's language, is it understandable?

Telephone calls are much quicker. However, unless you know exactly who you are trying to contact it can take a long time to establish the link and, again, there may be a language barrier.

An alternative to consider, one that is both fast and cheap, is sending a fax (facsimile). You can write out your message just as you would in a letter and then transmit it. The cost is only that of a short 'phone call. Remember to include your name and address and the 'phone or fax number to which you want the reply to be directed.

Activity 1.5   Locate a fax machine and make arrangements to use it and pay for the calls.

ORGANISING   During this course you will find that you get into the habit of looking for
MATERIAL   information about European affairs.

The amount of information will grow quickly. Unless you are well-organised, before long you will have a mountain of paper. If it gets to that stage the information will be of no use to you, for two reasons.

Firstly, you won't be able to easily find the information you want on a particular topic. Secondly, you won't be able to easily replace old information with new.

Therefore, it is essential that you set up an efficient filing system.

Try to file everything in the right place as you obtain it. That way the filing will take just a minute or two each day – hardly noticeable. Wallet folders are useful for filing documents. They can hold quite a lot and don't cost very much.

This book is organised into five parts – Infrastructure of Europe, European Community, Living and Working in Europe, Doing Business in Europe, and Contemporary Issues. These could provide starting points. Number your folders 1 to 5.

If you find that a folder is getting full, think about how you can divide it up. Community Policies, for example, in Part Two could be split into the individual issues Agriculture, Regional policy, Social policy, Research and technology, Monetary policy and Foreign affairs.

Some of the information will be easy to file – leaflets, cuttings from newspapers, photocopies from books, and so on. Always write the source and date, for example 'The Times, 11/12/92'.

To save money on photocopying it might be better to include just the reference to a book so that you can get it out of the library to look at it when you need it. Make a note of author, title, publisher and the date it was published, and the Dewey decimal library code which will make it easy to find again. Note also the relevant page number(s). You should also include a heading and a few words to explain what the book is about.

Activity 1.6   Purchase wallet folders, label and number them.

How do I plan my studies?

A possible timescale based upon four to five hours per week (three hours with a tutor and one to two hours of independent study) is given below. You may want to give more emphasis to some of the topics than others. If possible, right at the beginning, make a plan of what you intend to study and the sequence in which you are going to do it.

Table 1.2 Timetable of studies

Weeks	Topics
1	Introduction to European Studies
2–7	Infrastructure of Europe (Part 1)
8–11	European Community (Part 2)
12–17	Living and Working in Europe (Part 3)
18–25	Doing Business in Europe (Part 4)
26–30	Contemporary Issues (Part 5)

If you find you want to exceed the planned time on a topic look ahead to see what can be cut down unless you are in the fortunate position of having time to spare.

It may be that you do not have the freedom to plan your own learning schedule. Your tutor may have arranged something that you have to fit in with. If you are working with others in a group on a topic you will all have to agree the timing.

Activity 1.7   **1** Prepare a learning schedule, showing week by week what you will study and what you will achieve. Your achievements should be accompanied by a 'deliverable' – that is something tangible such as a report, an audio or video tape, a file of newspaper cuttings, etc.

2 Agree the content and sequence of the schedule with your tutor.

Assignments

At the end of the chapters of this book you will find assignments. These are intended to be substantial pieces of work that help you to assess how much you have learned and to develop your knowledge and skills further.

Don't wait until you have completed the chapter before looking at the assignment. It may be that you have to carry out some research before you can complete it, and research takes time.

Read the assignment before you begin the chapter and make a start on collecting the information for it.

The final assignment, at the end of Chapter 12, is special. It asks you to prepare a file of information on contemporary issues concerning the European Community. You will need to collect this information throughout the course, so start now!

Assignment 1   **HOW EUROPEAN ARE WE?**

Background

In 1990, MORI carried out a survey on behalf of the British subsidiary of a large Japanese company – Epson (UK) Ltd.

It found that there was much ignorance about Europe, that businesses were in a poor state of preparedness for the Single European Market, and that there was a suspicion towards all matters Eurpean amongst the British population and even in the realms of government.

It also found that, while many companies were of the view that 1992 would be very significant, few appreciated the potential impact it would have on their business, and even fewer understood the implications of the changes in Eastern Europe.

Activities

Construct a questionnaire and carry out a survey of local businesses.

Choose a sample that is representative of the whole busines population, including manufacturing, retail, service and public sector organisations.

Analyse the results and compare them with the findings of the MORI survey.

Write a short report for a local organisation, such as the Chamber of Commerce, outlining the situation and making recommendations on what businesses should do to maximise European awareness.

HOW EUROPEAN ARE WE?

This was the result of a survey carried out in 1990 (remember that changes occur; for example Germany is now united):

Question	Answers	% correct
1 Who is Britain's European Commissioner?	Leon Brittan/Bruce Millan	53
2 Is Britain a member of the EMS?	Yes	22
3 What does ERM stand for?	Exchange Rate Mechanism	23
4 What is the currency of Portugal?	Escudo	69
5 Who is your MEP?	–	17
6 Within 500, how many lira are there to a pound?	2065	27
7 What is the CAP?	Common Agricultural Policy	43
8 Where is the headquarters for the European Commission?	Brussels	37
9 Which was the last country to apply for EC Membership?	Austria	
10 Who is Jacques Delors?	President of the European Commission	48
11 What is the capital of West Germany?	Bonn	–
12 What is the Blue Angel?	West German symbol for environmentally sound product	6
13 Which Western European country has the highest population?	West Germany	43
14 Which is Europe's biggest retailer?	Albrecht (WG)	6
15 What is an ECU?	European Currency Unit	60
16 Approximately how many ECUs are there to a pound?	1.4	6
17 What is the capital of Italy?	Rome	95
18 How many MEPs does Britain have?	81	6
19 How would you say 'Good morning, my name is . . .', in German?	'Guten Morgen, ich heisse	31
20 How many full members are there of the EC?	12	33

Part One
Infrastructure of Europe

2 Geography and transport

EC countries

Over a period of 30 years the European Community has grown to include
12 countries. These countries have decided to build their futures together.
However, they have a tremendous range of cultural and historical differences.
Some have even been at war with one another, not very long ago.

Activity 2.1   List the 12 countries that form the European Community, in alphabetical order.

With all their different structures and traditions it is difficult to believe that
the 12 can work out common goals and devise policies that are acceptable
to all.

The Community pronounced its aims in the Treaty of Rome (1957).
These were to live in peace, assert itself in the world, improve living and
working conditions, encourage improved human rights and justice
throughout the world, tackle problems such as unemployment,
environmental pollution and regional deprivation, and develop new
technology.

The road to 'Community Europe' is not smooth. Each country has a
different perception about what the goals and policies should be. These
differences arise from the geography of their country, the people and culture,
their economy, and their constitution and system of government.

Geography (and travel) are covered in this chapter, while the other aspects
are the subject of later chapters in this part. Sources of statistics are provided,
so that you can obtain more recent ones. The changes over a period of
time may be as significant as the actual figures.

At the time of writing few statistics on the united Germany are available,
nor are there many on the German Democratic Republic (East Germany).
Most of the information is, therefore, on the Federal Republic (West
Germany).

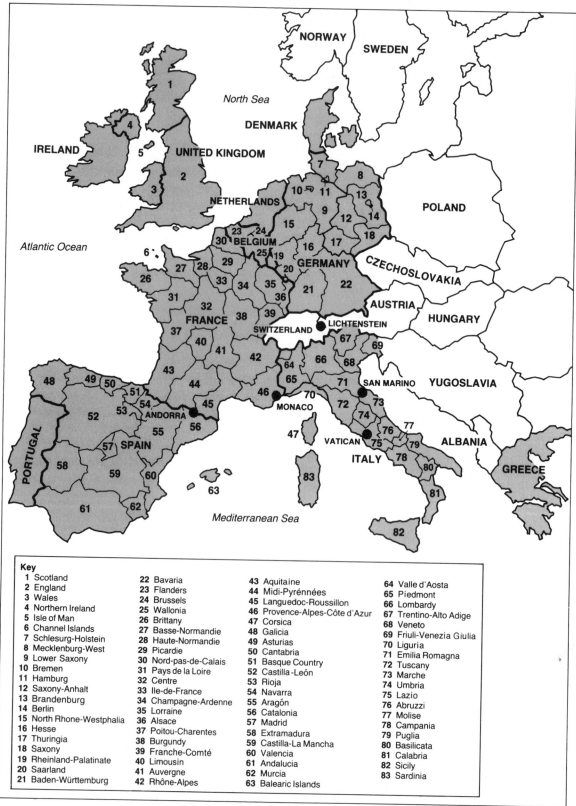

Key

1 Scotland	**43** Aquitaine
2 England	**44** Midi-Pyrénnées
3 Wales	**45** Languedoc-Roussillon
4 Northern Ireland	**46** Provence-Alpes-Côte d'Azur
5 Isle of Man	**47** Corsica
6 Channel Islands	**48** Galicia
7 Schlesurg-Holstein	**49** Asturias
8 Mecklenburg-West	**50** Cantabria
9 Lower Saxony	**51** Basque Country
10 Bremen	**52** Castilla-León
11 Hamburg	**53** Rioja
12 Saxony-Anhalt	**54** Navarra
13 Brandenburg	**55** Aragón
14 Berlin	**56** Catalonia
15 North Rhone-Westphalia	**57** Madrid
16 Hesse	**58** Extramadura
17 Thuringia	**59** Castilla-La Mancha
18 Saxony	**60** Valencia
19 Rheinland-Palatinate	**61** Andalucia
20 Saarland	**62** Murcia
21 Baden-Württemberg	**63** Balearic Islands

22 Bavaria	**64** Valle d'Aosta
23 Flanders	**65** Piedmont
24 Brussels	**66** Lombardy
25 Wallonia	**67** Trentino-Alto Adige
26 Brittany	**68** Veneto
27 Basse-Normandie	**69** Friuli-Venezia Giulia
28 Haute-Normandie	**70** Liguria
29 Picardie	**71** Emilia Romagna
30 Nord-pas-de-Calais	**72** Tuscany
31 Pays de la Loire	**73** Marche
32 Centre	**74** Umbria
33 Ile-de-France	**75** Lazio
34 Champagne-Ardenne	**76** Abruzzi
35 Lorraine	**77** Molise
36 Alsace	**78** Campania
37 Poitou-Charentes	**79** Puglia
38 Burgundy	**80** Basilicata
39 Franche-Comté	**81** Calabria
40 Limousin	**82** Sicily
41 Auvergne	**83** Sardinia
42 Rhône-Alpes	

Figure 2.1 Regional map of Europe

Physical geography

BELGIUM
Belgium extends 230 km from north to south, and 290 km from east to west and has a 66 km North Sea coastline. Inland from the coast are lowlands – fertile polders (reclaimed land), the sandy Flanders plain, heaths and woodlands of the Kempen. In the south are wooded Ardennes and Belgian Lorraine – an area that extends into France and Germany. Between the coast and southern areas lies an alluvial, fertile plateau. The country's highest point is the Signal de Botrange (694 m) in the Haut Fagnes.

The river Scheldt originates in Northern France and flows through Ghent and Antwerp into the Netherlands. The Meuse also flows into the Netherlands, rising in the French Vosges mountains and passing through Namur and Liege in eastern Belgium.

Some coal is mined in the Meuse-Sambre and Campine fields.

The Grand Place in Brussels, Belgium's capital, is famous for the beauty of its Gothic town hall and its seventeenth-century guild houses. Many Belgian towns feature buildings dating from the Romanesque, Gothic Renaissance, Baroque and Neo-classical eras. In the fifteenth and seventeenth centuries Jan van Eyck and Peter Paul Rubens were the crowning glories of the great school of Flemish painting.

DENMARK
Denmark consists of the Jutland Peninsula, 100 inhabited islands, and 383 islands which aren't inhabited. At the southern end of the peninsula is a 67-km border with Germany. Its coast is 7300 km long bordering the North Sea, Skagerrak, Kattegat and Baltic Sea. Denmark is a fertile country, famous for its dairy products and bacon. It is a flat country, its highest point is only 173 m above sea level.

Its longest river is the Gudena, which flows from central Jutland to the Randers Fjord.

Copenhagen, the capital, is the largest city in Scandinavia. It lies on the islands of Sjaelland and Amager. Whitewashed village churches and Romanesque cathedrals are preserved alongside castles and palaces of the Renaissance and Baroque periods.

FRANCE
France has coastline bordering the Channel, the Atlantic, and the Mediterranean, a total of 3120 km. Its 2170-km land frontiers are almost all mountainous barriers – the Pyrénées in the south-west, the western Alps in the south-east, the Jura and the Vosges in the east. France offers a wide range of landscapes, ranging from flat farmland north of Paris to the volcanic remains in the Massif Central.

There are four principal rivers: the Seine which flows through Paris into the Channel, the Loire (famous for its chateaux) and Garonne which flow into the Atlantic, and the Rhone which flows into the Mediterranean.

Wheat, maize and oats are grown extensively but the traveller through the farming areas is more likely to notice the sunflowers. Fruit and vegetables are grown, particularly in the south, but France is best known for its vines, especially in Languedoc, Burgundy, and Bordeaux. There are iron ore

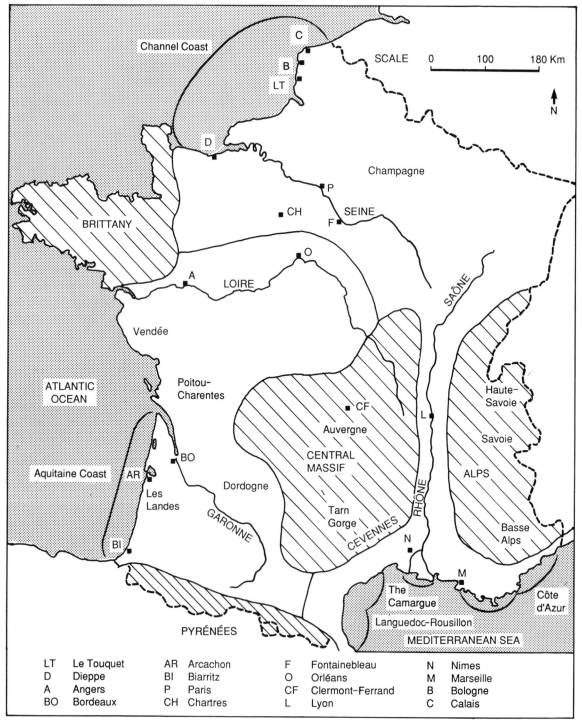

Figure 2.2 Geographical regions of France

deposits in Lorraine, coal in the north-east, natural gas in the south-west, potash in Alsace, and Bauxite which originally got its name from Les Baux, a town in Provence.

Paris is not only the capital but a focal point of France with roads and railway lines converging on it from all directions. It has a rich cultural heritage with famous landmarks like the Eiffel Tower, Louvre, Notre-Dame cathedral, Arc de Triomphe and church of Sacré Coeur.

GERMANY

To the north, Germany is bounded by the North Sea and the Baltic, to the south by the Alps, Lake Constance and the Rhine. It is made up of mountain areas, uplands (1500 m) and plains. The highest mountain is the Zugspitze (2963 m) in the Alps.

The main rivers are the Rhine, which forms the country's south-west boundary, the Danube, the Elbe, the Weser and the Moselle.

Its mineral resources include lignite, coal, iron and copper ores, and potash.

The capital is currently Bonn, a relatively small city, but a decision has been taken to move it back to Berlin, now the German Democratic Republic (East Germany) and the Federal Republic (West Germany) have been united. There are 16 states of 'Lander' which have their own administration, policing, culture, education and judiciary – all the functions that are not specifically allocated to central government.

GREECE

Greece's 2000 islands stretch from Kastellorizo in the east, as far south as Crete, and as far west as Corfu, and account for about 20% of the total area. Only 134 of them are inhabited. Greece has a coastline of 15 021 km. Agion Oros on the Athos peninsular is a self-governing part of the Greek state. The northern frontier which separates the country from Bulgaria, Turkey, Yugoslavia and Albania is 1212 km long. It is mainly mountainous, its tallest peak being Mount Olympus (2917 m). There are no major rivers.

Greece is very much a farming country, producing fruit and vegetables, raisins, tobacco and olive oil for export. It has deposits of lignite, bauxite and iron ore. Oil has been discovered in the Northern Aegean.

The capital is Athens, famous for its links with ancient civilisation, symbolised by the Acropolis.

IRELAND

The Republic of Ireland is 486 km from its northernmost to its southernmost tip, and is 275 km from east to west at its widest point. The country is divided into four provinces, Connacht, Leinster, Munster and Ulster. There are central lowlands with a fringe of hills and mountains, the highest of which is Carrantuohill (1040 m).

The Shannon (370 m) is the longest river and there are many lakes.

Ireland manufactures base metals and uses its plentiful supply of water, peat and natural gas to produce energy.

Dublin, the capital, is located on the east coast at the mouth of the River Liffey. Ireland is famous for its Celtic culture.

ITALY   Two independent states, the Republic of San Marino and the Vatican City State are surrounded by Italian territory. The familiar 'boot' shape extends from the fringe of the Alps in the north, which rapidly gives way to the plain of the River Po, to the southern 'toe', off which lies Sicily, and on which is Europe's biggest volcano, Mount Etna (3326 m). To the west lies Sardinia and smaller islands like Elba, Ponza, Capri and Ischia, mostly mountainous. To the east is the Adriatic Sea. Down the 1000-km peninsula runs the 130- to 250-km wide Apennine range of mountains. The highest peak is Gran Sasso (2914 m). Italy has other volcanoes, Vesuvius near Naples and Stromboli on the Lipari islands.

The longest river is the Po (652 m) running from the Cottian Alps through a delta to the Adriatic. The Arno which passes through Florence, and the Tiber on whose banks Rome is built, both arise in the Apennines.

Italy has few minerals, the only significant ones being sulphur, bauxite, lead ore and marble.

Rome, the capital, is the home of many famous buildings, temples and forums, some of them 2000 years old.

LUXEMBOURG   Luxembourg is a tiny, inland country, bounded by France, Germany and Belgium. It is hilly and rich in woodland. The Oesling, a 450-m high plateau is part of the Ardennes.

The main rivers are the Our, the Sure and the Moselle. The Moselle valley is famous for its wines – Reislings, Auxerrois and Sylvaners.

There are deposits of hematite in the south which have resulted in a large-scale iron and steel industry.

It has an excellent network of motorways linking it with France, Germany and Belgium and has always been the 'crossroads of Europe' settled by Celtic, Germanic, Roman and Frank peoples in past times.

NETHERLANDS   The Netherlands extend roughly 300 km from north to south and 200 km from east to west. Behind the North Sea coast are polders, as in Belgium. The islands of Zeeland and South Holland are linked by dikes to prevent the recurrence of flooding caused by storms. Over half the country is below sea level and the land is criss-crossed by lakes, rivers and canals. Only in the south-east is there higher land.

Minerals such as coal, oil and natural gas are found in the Netherlands.

The capital is Amsterdam although the centre of government is the Hague. Rotterdam is the world's largest port. Canals, windmills and the typical Dutch gabled houses make the Netherlands visually distinctive.

PORTUGAL   Portugal is longer north to south (560 km) than east to west (220 km). Its only land frontier is with Spain (1215 km); its Atlantic coastline is 837 km. The nine islands that make up the Azores are in mid-Atlantic, 1500 km from the coast of Portugal. The two islands of the Madeira group are off the African coast, 1000 km south of Lisbon.

The River Tagus separates the mountainous north from the plains and plateaux of the south. The coast has alternate sandy beaches and rocky headlands. The country has three important trading ports – Lisbon, Oporto and Setubal – which stand at the mouth of the rivers Tagus, Douro and Sado respectively.

As well as being rich in woodland oak, eucalyptus and pine, Portugal has large mineral deposits, e.g. tungsten, iron pyrites, tin and uranium.

Lisbon, the capital, on the banks of the Tagus, has been a trading city for centuries and it is from here that many explorers set out.

SPAIN Spain has a total of 3904 km of coastline with the Atlantic and Mediterranean and a land frontier of 5849 km with France and Portugal. It is the second most mountainous country in Europe (after Switzerland). Mountain ranges alternate with river valleys. The centre of Spain is a plateau, the Meseta, which is arid but pierced by the Douro and Tagus rivers which flow from east to west, into Portugal. The Guadiana and Guadalquivir cross Andalusia where sub-tropical areas alternate with permanently snow-capped peaks. It is here that Mulhacen, the highest mountain on the Spanish mainland (3481 m) is located. However the Peak of Tenerife in the Canaries (3718 m) is the highest point in Spanish territory.

The rivers Ebro, Turia, Jucar and Sequa flow east into the Mediterranean where there are many fine beaches. The Navia, Nalon, Nervion and Bidassoa are short rivers rising in the Cantabrian Mountains; they irrigate the green coastal strip which extends west from the Pyrenees and forms one part of the north of the Iberian Peninsula. The other part, Galicia, north of Portugal, has humid weather and green countryside, through which the Mino flows. Its climate is more typical of countries further north.

Madrid, the capital, is a city of museums and art galleries, notably the Prado.

UNITED KINGDOM The Channel, which separates Great Britain from mainland Europe, contributes a great deal to its sense of independence from the rest of Europe. There is now little dense woodland in Britain but there are large areas of heaths and moorland.

The Pennine range running from the Cheviot Hills on the Scottish border to the Midlands has been a significant boundary between west and east. Scafell Pike (977 m), in the Lake District in north-western England, is the highest mountain in England. In north Wales, Snowdon is higher (1085 m) but the highest peak in the UK is Ben Nevis in the Scottish Grampians (1342 m).

The most significant river is the Thames on the banks of which lies London. Ports are situated at the mouths of major rivers, for example Bristol on the Avon, Liverpool on the Mersey, Glasgow on the Clyde.

The UK has four capitals: London is the capital of England, Cardiff the capital of Wales, Edinburgh the capital of Scotland and Belfast the capital of Northern Ireland. Some English cities such as London, York and Chester are of Roman origin but many date from the Middle Ages and from the Industrial Revolution.

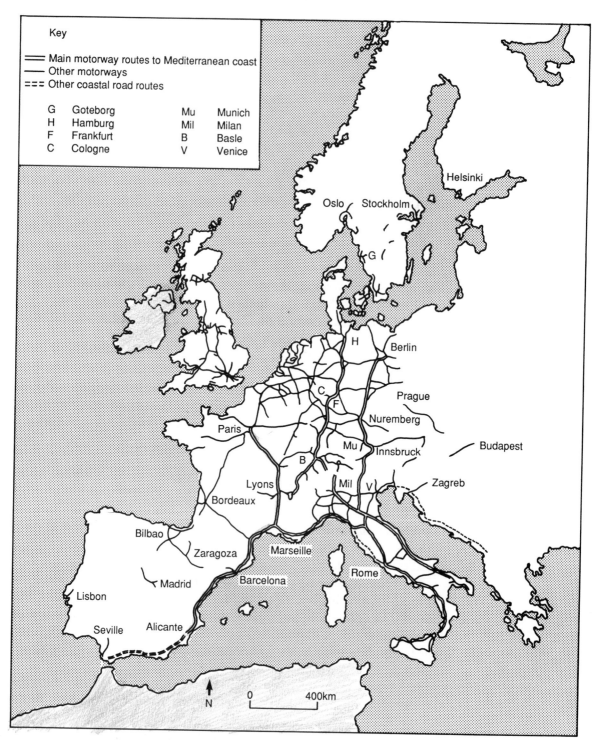

Figure 2.3 European motorway routes

Activity 2.2   The European Commission has identified the principal dangers in EC countries as tornadoes, avalanches, landslides, tidal waves, floods, earthquakes, volcanic eruptions, forest fires, dam bursts, industrial accidents, and accidents from the transport of chemicals.

Consideration is being given to setting up a rapid reaction unit to be deployed in an area suffering a disaster.

For each hazard, identify the countries that you consider to be at risk.

Travel in Europe

BY ROAD   The northern countries of Western Europe all have excellent motorway systems and there are good routes in some other areas too. It is possible to drive from Dover to the south of Italy by motorway, except for about 20 miles, the only trouble-spots being the Alpine tunnels. The Mont Blanc Tunnel, for example, has an excellent approach from the French side but only a two-lane road on the Italian side which can easily be blocked by traffic.

Many major cities have orbital motorways but some, such as Zurich, Lyon and Munich have yet to be by-passed by motorways. However, a fast journey is not guaranteed even when there is a by-pass. The M25 around London is notorious, and the Périphérique around Paris is just as bad especially on Friday afternoons.

Organisations such as Germany's ADAC and the UK's AA and RAC issue regular bulletins on European road conditions.

Activity 2.3   Find out which mountain passes are closed, where major roadworks are situated and what delays can be expected when driving in Europe by consulting the AA Eurowatch in *The European* newspaper.

Computer packages are available that will select a route based on a choice of motorways or ordinary roads, intermediate towns, and the average travelling speed. Lap-top computers that will operate in a car, together with car-phones linked to up-to-date information sources, are now available.

When planning a route it is important to consider the time of day. Commuter areas have to be avoided in 'rush hours'. Germany has long periods of heavy traffic – from 6 am to 10 am and from 4 pm to 8 pm. Greece has four periods to be avoided: morning, evening and either side of lunchtime. However, French, Spanish and Italian roads are quiet from 12 noon to 2 pm, during siesta.

During public holidays roads are busier than usual. In almost all of Europe there is a national holiday on 15 August (Assumption Day). In the UK, our August bank holiday is later than this.

Traffic varies with the season, too. In France cities empty for a month at the time of the *grande vacance* in August. The *Autoroute du Soleil* from

Paris to the Mediterranean is packed with traffic on the day of the *grand départ* in late July and it is common for traffic to come to a standstill for up to 10 hours on this motorway. In most countries the peak holiday time coincides with the school summer holidays. In Italy this is from mid-June until late-September. Spanish school holidays begin early in June, and in Portugal they begin in early July.

Improvements to the road systems are often made in advance of special events. For example, in Italy for the World Cup, and in Spain for the 1992 Olympics and World Fair.

In France, Italy and Spain, over 90% of motorways are toll-roads with 'pay-as-you-drive' systems. There are also stretches of road in Austria, Greece and Portugal which are toll roads. In 1991 the UK gave consideration to introducing its first private toll-road, on a 30-mile stretch north of Birmingham.

Environmentalists have, for a long time, called for road-pricing as a means of 'traffic calming' on congested roads.

Motorists do not automatically shun roads that have tolls. In France, for example, the ordinary roads in the north are relatively traffic free, despite being straight and in good condition, whereas the péage (a motorway on which tolls have to be paid) is used extensively.

Accident records vary. Particular roads, such as the N620, the main route across Spain between the Portuguese and French frontiers, has a bad reputation and the N340 into Madrid is nicknamed the 'highway of death'. Greek drivers have the worst driving record. In 1990 road deaths in Greece averaged 6 per day, caused by flouting of speed limits, ignoring stop signs, (illegally) not wearing seat belts, etc.

The wearing of seat belts is compulsory in all European countries except Gibraltar, and the majority of EC countries including the UK now insist on the wearing of rear seat belts.

BY RAIL It is amazing that rail technology dating from the nineteenth century, and developed separately in the various countries of Europe should be sufficiently standardised for trains to be able to cross Europe without hindrance. The potential for variation can be seen by studying the history of the railway in the UK, where different track widths, different signalling systems, and different rolling stock evolved from the various railway companies and required massive investment to achieve the universal system that is British Rail.

The traveller will see differences. For example, platforms in Europe are usually lower, so that there are several steps up to carriages. In France, railway stations are usually on the edge of towns, whereas in the UK they are more commonly in the centre.

The conditions under which the trains operate vary around Europe. The services in southern Europe, for example, have to cope with much higher temperatures so that air conditioning is a must on long distance journeys and highly desirable on shorter routes. In the Alpine areas, tunnels and bridges have taxed the engineers' skill to the utmost, and it is still the case that gradients are more severe than anywhere in the UK.

In general, except for commuter services, trains in Continental Europe travel further between stops than in the UK. There has been a greater incentive, therefore, for the development of high-speed trains.

When goods have to be transported over long distances the railway has a distinct advantage over road transport, and is environmentally preferable. On shorter journeys, such as are found in the UK, the overhead of assembling a viable-sized number of wagons to go to the same destination, and the distribution from the rail-head, means that road transport is more convenient.

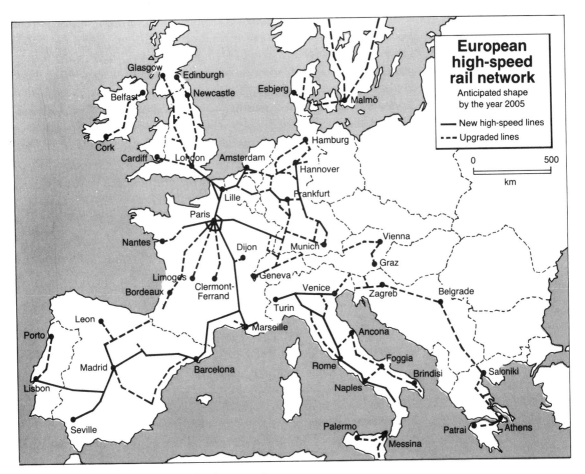

Figure 2.4 European high-speed rail network

**BY SEA
CAN THE EC FLAG
RULE THE WAVES?** This is a crucial question when we consider the fact that in the ten years from 1980 to 1990 the EC countries' share of world shipping tonnage dropped from 30% to 14%. Leading companies like Royal Dutch Shell and British Petroleum had already changed to 'flags of convenience' (*see* over) when P & O considered making the same move with its 200-strong fleet

in 1991. In 1980 there were 1500 ships flying the flags of EC countries; by 1990 there were just 300.

Ships which are registered in countries like Liberia and Panama – the main 'flag of convenience' countries – are able to undercut the competition because they are subject to fewer restrictions and are able to employ cheap third-world crews.

Norway and Denmark have protected their national fleets by offering incentives to shipping operators.

Plans for a European Register of Shipping (EUROS) are contentious because they would involve subsidies and interfere with the tax-gathering policies of individual EC countries. Taxation is still organised on a national basis and is therefore connected with 'sovereignty'. The EUROS scheme involves tough safety standards and guaranteed levels of jobs for European nationals. Cargo ships must have 100% European officers and 50% European ratings and passenger ships must be entirely European-crewed. Minimum crew sizes are stipulated. The Greeks are very much in favour of EUROS as it would increase their country's tax revenue.

BY BUS, TRAM AND UNDERGROUND

Different types of bus transport are clearly differentiated in the UK. On the one hand there are the long-distance coaches, the equivalent of the inter-city trains. Although they cannot compete with rail in speed they are very competitive on price, and offer comforts like television. Some people argue that they are safer for an unaccompanied traveller.

Other bus services cater for commuters in both rural and urban areas.

The pattern is similar elsewhere in Europe. However, differences arise as to whether governments choose to maintain state or local government control or to deregulate services, as happened in the UK. If it is accepted that buses are a public service, rather than a purely profit-making venture then some element of control has to be retained.

Some routes are profitable (urban, rush-hour) while others cannot be financially viable (rural). Licences to operate are usually granted on a 'mix' of routes so that bus companies cross-subsidise.

Many cities in Europe have trams as an alternative to, or as well as, buses. The routes are less flexible, and there is a capital cost of laying track, but they are better environmentally than buses.

Underground systems of transport operate in many of the larger cities of Europe. The London Underground is well-known, as is the Metro in Paris. However, other cities such as Barcelona have similar systems.

Activity 2.4   Prepare a catalogue of towns and cities that have tram or underground systems.

BY AIR   There is a trend toward air travel around Europe becoming more common.

The European Commission intitially gained the agreement of the member countries for a removal of price-fixing on EC routes, making it easier for new operators to get routes. The third stage, to be implemented by 1996, is to remove the right of national airlines to dominate routes in their 'own' airspace.

Critics of the scheme fear that European routes will be dominated by a few large carriers as happened when deregulation in the USA resulted in a free-for-all that ousted smaller airlines from major routes. In Europe, however, small operators using aircraft with fewer than 80 seats will have protection against big competitors.

Traffic Commissioner Karel Van Miert said in 1991 that, 'the proposals should lead to lower tariffs on at least some routes, where fares are too high'.

The Secretary General of the Association of European Airlines argued that 'The story of cheap air fares is the biggest lie I have ever heard. Not a single piece of EC legislation has helped airlines to reduce costs'.

Sir Michael Bishop, chairman of British Midland (an independent UK airline) disagreed: 'Business travellers are paying falsely inflated fares to Europe because of lack of competition. Twelve of the 15 busiest air routes out of Heathrow are only operated by the two respective national carriers, providing similar frequencies and identical fares'. He continued: 'Since we have entered service on the Heathrow to Paris route, Europe's busiest with 2.3 million passengers per year, previously operated only by British Airways and Air France, business travellers have been able to save over £100 per trip'.

British Midland claim that businesses are paying up to 30% too much for flights to Europe. It claims that £236 million per year could be saved on the top 15 routes out of Heathrow when the legislation comes into force.

The key issue is the level of profit. If operators are forced by competition to reduce profit, but can still achieve acceptable returns, then it will be good for consumers.

However, increase in services will need better air traffic control in some countries, such as Greece, so that there is the capacity to handle more aircraft. Ultimately the only solution seems to be to have a centralised air traffic control system. This is unlikely before AD 2000.

Activity 2.5 Tourism is a major industry in many parts of Europe.

Identify the 'tourist' areas and say what the main attractions are in each case.

Most people live and work around the cities and industrial areas. Trace the routes they would follow to reach the tourist areas and compare these with the road and rail networks, and airports and air routes.

Summary 1 The 12 countries of the EC are Belgium, Denmark, France, Germany, Greece, Ireland, Italy, Luxembourg, Netherlands, Portugal, Spain, UK.

2 The EC countries are diverse in terms of:
- geography and natural resources;
- people and culture;
- economic wealth;
- constitution and government.

3 The countries of the EC share common aims:
- to maintain peace;
- for the EC to have a world profile;
- to improve the living and working conditions in the EC;
- to support human rights and justice worldwide;
- to tackle the problems of unemployment, the environment and deprivation;
- to develop new technology and industries.

4 Europe has a good road and rail network. Its cities suffer from commuter congestion. Deregulation of air travel is planned for 1996.

Assignment 2   **GETTING TO KNOW THE EC COUNTRIES**

Background

This chapter has briefly outlined the characteristics of the countries in the European Community.

It may be that at some time in the future you may consider going to live or work in Europe. If so you will need to know more about the area. For example, it would be useful to know which are the principal cities and towns in that area and something about them. What the climate is like, whether it is an industrial, agricultural or tourist area, whether it has its own airport, what are the places of interest, and so on.

Activity

Choose five areas (within or outside the EC) that you might go to live or work because of your chosen career (not for a holiday).

Negotiate with your fellow students so that you each are studying different places.

Collect information on the area.

Prepare a summary of the facts that you have gathered. Write notes on what is attractive to you about the place, and what you don't like about it.

3 Economics and government

Objectives
1 Contrast the business environments of the European Community countries.
2 Compare their constitutions and systems of government.

Business environment

Activity 3.1
1 Table 3.1 gives statistics on the 12 EC countries for 1983 and 1987, obtained from Eurostat. Obtain the latest figures.

2 Prepare pie charts to clearly show the differences between each country's size, population, and Gross Domestic Product (GDP).

3 Prepare bar charts to compare the population density of the countries, and to compare the per capita GDP.

Size, population and GDP are significant factors in that the countries with the greatest of these will have more 'weight' in European affairs. However, these factors do not necessarily demonstrate the wealth of the countries. Population density and per capita GDP give some indication of this, as do the balance between exports and imports, and the per capita final consumption figures.

Activity 3.2
1 Prepare suitable charts to compare the exports, imports, balance of trade, and final consumption figures of the countries.

2 Which countries are the wealthiest? Are these the largest?

 ECONOMIC INTEGRATION
The differences between EC countries in economic performance and government policies are likely to reduce in the future. If they do, it will be easier for the EC to make progress on integration and harmonisatoin in other areas.

At present, each country has its own industrial structure and business traditions reflecting historical circumstances, geographic conditions and government decisions. Integration does not mean the structures and traditions

Table 3.1 Europe in figures

EUROSTAT 1983	Belgium	Denmark	France	Germany	Greece	Ireland	Italy	Luxembourg	Netherlands	Portugal	Spain	UK
Area ('000 sq km)	30.5	43.1	544	248.7	132	70.3	301.3	2.6	41.2	92.1	504.8	244.1
Population (million)	9.9	5.1	54.3	61.4	9.9	3.5	56.7	.4	14.3	10.1	38.4	56.4
% change by AD 2000	1.2	-3.4	7.2	-3.7	6	17.5	1.9	1.9	9.3	13.9	13	2.7
Population per sq km	323	119	100	247	75	50	188	141	349	110	76	231
GDP ('000 million PPS)	110.1	61.6	641.1	735.7	56.7	24.7	517.3	4.1	153.7	47.7	290.3	577.2
per capita GDP (PPS)	11176	12053	11776	11977	5759	7040	9102	10500	10702	4828	7616	10238
per capita Exports (ECU)	5719	3574	1876	3100	511	2765	1441	6719	5122	516	582	1854
per capita Imports (ECU)	6112	3618	2159	2798	1103	2938	1591	6112	4808	906	856	2025
per capita Final Consumption (PPS)	9265	9846	9477	9204	4918	5578	7465	9310	8370	4192	6220	8423

EUROSTAT 1987	Belgium	Denmark	France	Germany	Greece	Ireland	Italy	Luxembourg	Netherlands	Portugal	Spain	UK
Area ('000 sq km)	30.5	43.1	544	248.7	132	70.3	301.3	2.6	41.2	92.1	504.8	244.1
Population (million)	9.9	5.1	55.6	61.2	10	3.5	57.3	.4	14.7	10.3	38.8	56.9
% change by AD 2000	-2	0	4.5	-3.1	4	17.1	0	0	4.1	8.8	5.2	1.6
Population per sq km	319	119	102	245	76	51	190	133	356	111	77	233
GDP ('000 million PPS)	145.2	85.2	887.4	1014.7	79.3	33.2	874.2	6.8	233.7	76.5	419.7	873.9
per capita GDP (PPS)	14712	16606	15951	16580	7928	9381	15242	18313	15258	7838	10807	15383
per capita Exports (ECU)	6986	4449	2227	4163	565	3951	1757	6986	5730	772	813	1983
per capita Imports (ECU)	7049	4413	2453	3231	1126	3371	1887	7049	5655	1131	1038	2350
per capita Final Consumption (PPS)	9465	9015	9712	10250	5324	5446	9303	10027	9291	5186	6873	9637

EUROSTAT 1991	Belgium	Denmark	France	Germany	Greece	Ireland	Italy	Luxembourg	Netherlands	Portugal	Spain	UK
Population (million)	9.9	5.1	54.3	78.5	9.9	3.5	56.7	.4	14.3	10.1	38.4	56.4

Notes
GDP = Gross Domestic Product at market prices
ECU = European Currency Unit
PPS = Purchasing Power Standard

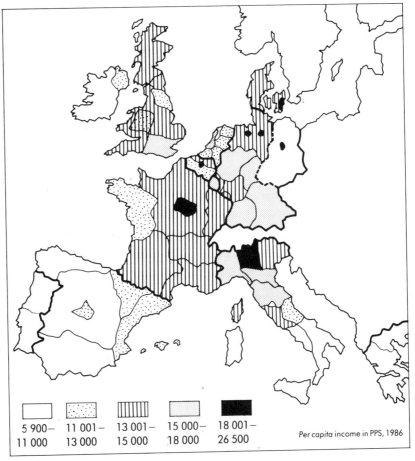

Figure 3.1 GDP in purchasing power standards per region, 1986

Source: Eurostat, European Commission

will become identical. A single market may lead to countries specialising even more in what they do best and benefiting from economies of scale.

Five countries are by far the most important in the Community, in terms of Gross Domestic Product (GDP) and population. They are France, Germany, Italy, Spain and the UK. In 1990 they accounted for 87% of its GDP and 84% of its population. *See* the following section on European economies for in-depth information on the five.

Progress towards integration has been hampered by individual countries being reluctant to give up power to the European institutions. In the 1960s it was France that held back. In the 1970s and 1980s, the UK was the reluctant participant.

Enlargements to the EC have also hampered progress. They shift political attention to the membership issue and make negotiations on common policies more complicated.

The economic crises of the 1970s and early 1980s created an unfavourable climate for free trade. National governments were inclined to adopt policies that protected national interests and supported their own country's industries.

During the 1980s it became clear that Europe was losing ground to its main competitors, Japan and the USA. To overcome fragmentation of the European economies, the Single European Act (1986) made a commitment to remove internal barriers by the end of 1992.

The final goal of an economically united Europe can, arguably, only be achieved by Economic and Monetary Union with a European Central Bank (Eurofed). As this requires the surrender of some powers to European Community institutions from individual national government control there needs to be closer political integration. The word 'federal' has been used to describe this but there are different interpretations of this word which have to be explained and resolved.

European integration is based on a market-orientated approach. Most policies are designed to achieve a large, free, internal market characterised by strong and fair competition.

The EC is one of the three largest economic blocks in the world. In 1990 its GDP surpassed that of the USA and was more than twice that of Japan. The EC also has the largest population, 345 million in 1990 against 251 million in the USA and 124 million in Japan. However, the 'average' US citizen is by far the richest in the world, with the Japanese second and Europeans third, although the latter two are catching up. Japan's strong economy is also demonstrated in its low unemployment rate and inflation figures.

The growing gap between the EC and its two rivals in high-technology industries has been a powerful stimulus to the European nations striving for integration so that they can tackle the deficit.

EUROPEAN ECONOMIES

European countries have a wide range of characteristics. Some are mainly agricultural, while others have a large industrial base. Some have a major tourist industry. Figures given are for 1991.

BELGIUM

Belgium is an industrialised nation, heavily dependent on international trade. Metal processing is highly developed accounting for 38% of industrial employment. Electronics (14%) and chemicals (13%) are also important areas of employment. The traditional industries are Flemish textiles and Venetian glass.

Major exports are machinery and vehicles (26%), iron and steel products (13%), textiles and clothing (7%) and chemicals (6%).

Main customers are: EC (73%), USA (5%), Switzerland (2%) and Sweden (2%).

DENMARK

Denmark's main industries are agriculture, tourism, oil and natural gas extraction. It is shifting away from agriculture to service and modern, light industries.

Major exports are foodstuffs (especially meat, dairy products, fish, etc.)

(27%), furniture, clothing, etc. (26%), machinery and transport equipment (25%) and chemicals (9%).

Main customers are: EC (53%), Sweden (11%), USA (9%) and Norway (8%).

Activity 3.3   Denmark was very quick to recognise the Baltic states when they became independent of the Soviet Union in 1991.

What do you think are the advantages to Denmark of their independence?

FRANCE   France suffered from a severe recession in the early 1980s with high unemployment and inflation. A major shift in policies in 1983 towards free market approaches, together with an improvement in world trading conditions resulted in a speedy recovery. France still, however, lacks strength in any specific sectors of industry.

There are very close links between the ministries responsible for the economy, the professional civil servants, and the leaders of the business community (especially banking, insurance and large business conglomerates).

Relatively few employees in the private sector belong to trade unions. There are, however, government regulations imposing minimum wages and restricting redundancies.

France tends to be 'inflation-prone'. Since 1986 the competitive environment and stringent public spending restrictions are highlighted as factors that have kept inflation down. Salary restraint, a relatively high level of unemployment and lower raw material and oil prices have also been contributing factors.

Personal income tax is highly progressive, takes into account family size, and exempts a large proportion of the population by having a high threshold. In 1988 only just over half of the population paid income tax. Social insurance contributions are high. An average production worker would expect to pay 7% of his/her income in tax and 17% in social insurance (1988 figures).

An expansion of public ownership in 1982 was reversed in 1986 with a policy of privatisation. In 1988 a neutral policy was adopted – an end to privatisation but no re-nationalisation.

French banks are amongst the largest in Europe. (Indeed Crédit Agricole is fourth largest in the world.) As well as the private banks there is a nationalised bank, the Banque de France, which manufactures and distributes bank notes and supervises the banking system, amongst other functions.

Oil price shocks in the late 1970s and a lack of natural energy sources (such as coal) spurred the French to develop nuclear-powered electricity generation plants. It is the second largest producer in the world, after the USA, supplying over 50% of France's energy needs. France is the EC's largest energy exporter. The UK is its biggest customer, followed by Switzerland and Italy. France generates electricity at a cost 45% lower than the UK and 54% less than Germany.

Although France's economy has only shown signs of strength since 1987 the policies that led to it were put in place some years earlier. Radical changes would be needed to the taxation system to harmonise it with other EC countries. There is a sense of unease about this in France because such changes could destabilise the economy and adversely affect some public services, notably education. There is an underlying sense of nationalism that could come to the surface under pressure although mainstream political sentiment is very much in favour of progress toward Community integration.

France is the largest agricultural country in the EC and the second largest wine producer (after Italy). It also has a large industrial sector, producing steel, motor cars and manufactured goods. Its main industrial areas are around Paris and Lyon.

Major exports are machinery and vehicles (35%), manufactured goods (28%), foodstuffs (12%) and chemicals (11%).

Its main customers are: EC (58%), USA (7%) and Switzerland (5%).

GERMANY   Germany is by far the largest of the EC countries. Even before reunification its GDP was more than 25% higher than France, the second largest. Clearly Germany will continue to be the leading economic force in the EC.

Germany's economic success has been attributed to its social market economy. It is intended to achieve a balance between market efficiency and social interests.

Public sector decision-making is delegated to the lowest possible level and federal involvement takes place only where local authorities are unable to cope. This offers the advantages of autonomy and flexibility but it is difficult to co-ordinate.

There is a large body of legislation protecting consumers and competition and regulations governing such things as transportation, mail, telecommunications and utilities. There is a strong guild tradition in which tradespeople have to undertake special training and gain formal qualifications.

The central German bank is largely independent from the government.

Germany's economic growth is close to the EC average but starts from a higher than average base.

Germany has the highest labour costs in the world but these are partly compensated for by the growth in productivity. German products are renowned for their quality and reliability.

The working week is the shortest in the world, 31.2 hours per week on average. However, Germany also has the lowest number of hours lost through strikes and absenteeism.

One of Germany's major strengths is its highly developed transport and communication system, facilitating mobility and distribution. However, traffic congestion is still severe in some areas . Housing is expensive throughout Germany.

Germany's economy is heavily dependent on exports.

Major exports are machinery (20%), road vehicles (18%), chemicals (13%), electrical appliances (9%), iron and steel (6%), food, beverages and tobacco products (4%).

Main customers are: EC (51%), USA (11%), Switzerland (6%), Sweden (3%) and [former] USSR (2%).

GREECE   Until the 1960s, most of Greece's businesses were family owned, reflecting a preference for trade rather than long-term industrial projects.

Greece's major industries are agriculture, merchant shipping, and tourism.

Major exports are industrial products (44%), farm products (including tobacco, raisins, cotton, wine, olive oil, citrus fruits) (29%), ores and metals (6%) and textiles and chemicals (3%).

Main customers are: EC (64%), USA (7%), Egypt (2%), [former] USSR (1%) and Yugoslavia (1%).

Activity 3.4   Greece is a relatively poor country by the standards of other EC countries. While tourism is growing, there is a decline in shipping as an income earner.

Industry is sometimes classified as 'sunrise' or 'sunset' reflecting its future. Which of the existing industries are in each of these categories, and which other 'sunrise' industries does Greece have the capability of supporting?

Can Greece derive any advantage from its position at the east of the Mediterranean and its trading past?

IRELAND   Ireland has a very high-profile scheme for promoting outside investment in new technology. As well as an important agricultural industry and a great deal of tourism, Ireland is a promising territory for oil and gas extraction.

Main exports are machinery and transport equipment (30%), food products (especially meat and dairy products) (23%), textiles and other manufactured goods (21%) and organic and other chemicals (13%).

Its main customers are: EC (72%), USA (9%) and Canada (1%).

ITALY   Italy experienced considerable economic growth in the 1980s. In particular the Milan region boomed. Italy has many small to medium-sized businesses and these formed the basis of that growth. The gap between the northern and southern regions continues to widen.

Italy also has problems in the form of high inflation and an inefficient public sector.

During the late 1960s and early 1970s many Western countries had significant levels of industrial and social unrest. Price increases originating from the cost of oil and raw materials hit the Italian economy at a time when conflict was at its height. An agreement was reached to link wages to inflation, thus protecting the workers' real incomes. This, however only put off the problems because of the rising level of public spending on social security and health care.

In 1983 the link between salaries and inflation was changed by the government, and major employers took a much tougher stance in industrial relations. During the years that followed profits and investment improved and by the late 1980s a great deal of industrial modernisation had taken place.

Figures for Italy's GDP must be treated with suspicion because of the extensive 'black economy' in which, for example, people have two or three jobs but only register, officially, in one.

When Italy joined the European Monetary System in 1979 it was forced to abandon the practice of devaluing the lira as a way of protecting its economy. Consequently inflation fell from 16% in 1982 to under 5% by 1988. A notable feature of the present period of development in the Italian economy is the strength of the currency, due to high interest rates. The lira traditionally was thought of as being weak and, linked with high inflation, making it the butt of jokes.

Tourism made a major contribution to the economy in the past but is progressively less important. Increasing affluence has encouraged Italians to take their holidays abroad, and the cost of living has deterred foreign visitors.

Unemployment, especially in the south, is considered to be one of the reasons why organised crime in Camparia, Calabria and Sicily is so high, although the cause and effect relationship is difficult to prove.

Italy is being transformed from an agricultural to an industrial nation. There are significant differences between the north (industrial) and the south (agricultural).

Major exports are machinery and vehicles (34%), textiles and clothing (18%), chemicals (7%) and food products (5%).

Major customers are: EC (54%), USA (11%), Switzerland (5%) and Libya (1%).

LUXEMBOURG Luxembourg is, for its size, a major producer of heavy engineering products.

Steel and machinery account for 90% of exports. Other exports are chemicals and agricultural products.

Major customers are: EC (70%), USA and Switzerland.

NETHERLANDS The Netherlands has a wide range of industries. There are major chemical, electrical engineering and motor industries. Agricultural products are an important sector. The oil and gas extraction industry is growing rapidly.

Major exports are minerals (24%), textiles and other finished goods (21%), food and beverages (including dairy products, fresh meat, canned and bottled products, fish, cocoa, chocolate) (17%), vehicles and electrical appliances (19%) and chemical products (15%).

Its main customers are: EC (76%), USA (5%), Sweden (2%) and Switzerland (2%).

PORTUGAL Portugal has a weak economy, and persistent balance of trade deficit.

The climate, topography and soil are not favourable to agriculture. Inadequacies in transport and equipment add to the difficulties. There are many small firms in traditional industries such as textiles, footwear and food processing.

Portugal's exports include textiles and clothing (30%), electrical machinery and equipment (16%), wood, wood products and paper (14%) and food and drinks (8%).

Its main customers are: EC (68%), USA (7%), Spain (7%) and Portuguese-speaking countries (4%).

Activity 3.5   Identify which countries are 'Portuguese-speaking' and explain why so much of Portugal's trade is done with them.

SPAIN   Spanish GDP per head of population was still the lowest of the five major EC countries in 1990 but was rapidly catching up. During General Franco's rule it had a closed, protected, regulated and monopolised economy. During the 1980s Spain suffered high unemployment, interest and inflation rates. However the governments were quite successful in preparing Spain for full integration into the EC in 1993. The economy is now much more competitive and investment is very high, much of it financed by foreign capital.

Two years are of special significance in recent Spanish history. In 1978 a democratic system, suspended since the 1936–39 civil war, was re-established. In 1986 Spain was accepted as a member of the EC.

Spain has followed a policy of decentralisation since 1984, passing public sector responsibility from state control to the autonomous committees and local authorities.

Despite a sharp increase in public expenditure, Spanish levels are still low compared with other EC countries. While most European countries built up their welfare state during the period of economic expansion after the Second World War, Spain has had to attempt this task during a recession.

A major feature of the transition taking place between joining the EC and full integration is the dismantling of its protectionist policies. It had a complex set of tariffs, quotas and restrictions aimed at limiting imports. Exports received very favourable tax concessions, effectively providing a hidden subsidy that in some product areas amounted to 'dumping'.

The future of Spanish agriculture is full of uncertainties now that Spain is part of the EC. Spain has severe natural deficiencies (climate, altitude, etc.); farms that are too small in the north and too large in the southern and central regions; and a poor distribution system. However, the products are distinctive compared with those of northern Europe and competitive, especially in quality, with the other southern European countries.

Towards the end of the 1980s Spain suffered a major crisis in its large and economically vital tourist trade. It appears to arise from a shift in demand from Spain to other Mediterranean countries rather than an absolute reduction in demand. Provided Spain can overcome the disadvantages that arose from unplanned growth and its 'bad press' the tourism trade is still thought to have great potential in the regions where it is concentrated.

The largest industries are agriculture and tourism.

Major exports are motor cars (31%), iron and steel products, machinery and fruit.

Spain's main customers are: EC (61%) and USA (9%).

UNITED KINGDOM

In the 1960s the UK performed badly compared with the EC average. In the 1970s it had improved but was still below average, and in the 1980s it had crept ahead. A particular strength is the financial sector. Like Italy it has strong regional differences in its economy and has suffered high interest rates and inflation.

The high degree of centralisation of power and control in the UK, and the essentially two-party system, gives the governing party very extensive powers. Thus the governments of the 1970s and 1980s were able to introduce laws drastically changing economics and industrial relations.

When the UK decided to join the EC in 1973 it had to consider its special relationship with the Commonwealth countries, for some of whom the UK was the biggest market.

The years that followed entry were difficult in terms of inflation, unemployment and adverse balance of payments. Dealing with inflation was the major goal of the Conservative governments of the 1980s. Cuts in personal income tax, especially the higher rates were intended to stimulate work effort. They were paid for partly by restraints on government spending. Legislation was passed to curtail the power of the trade unions and social security reforms were introduced. Wage and price controls were removed and bank lending liberalised. Subsidies to industry were reduced and measures such as deregulation aimed to increase competition. There were many transfers of nationalised industries and public corporations of the private sector.

The 1980s were characterised by growth in the service sector, a rise in both the number and proportion of females in the labour market, and the increase in part-time working. In contrast the number of people employed in manufacturing fell dramatically.

In the 1960s and 1970s governments favoured large enterprises and mergers were encouraged through the Industrial Reorganisation Corporation. In the 1980s the emphasis was on encouraging the formation and growth of small firms.

Most large firms operating in the UK are multinationals with extensive activities overseas. Among the 100 largest manufacturing firms, 20 are foreign-owned. Fifteen hundred manufacturing firms, about 1% of the total but accounting for 20% of total sales and 14% of employment, were foreign owned in the mid-1980s. American, Japanese, EFTA and Far-Eastern organisations are all concerned to have access to the EC market after 1992.

Three areas of weakness could be identified in the UK business environment in the late 1980s. Investment in research and development was only half that of Germany, and much of the UK's spending was on defence-related projects.

The UK also had a poor record of investing in education and training. Innovations and new technologies cannot be exploited unless management and the workforce have the appropriate skills. In 1990 the UK was placed twenty-second out of 23 industrialised countries in the overall quality of its workforce. UK firms commit only 0·15% of turnover to training compared with 1–2% in Japan, Germany and France.

While an integrated high-speed rail network is taking shape in mainland Europe the UK is lagging well behind. Increasing congestion on the roads is a reflection of the comparatively low investment in public transport compared with France and Germany.

Industry is undoubtedly 'leaner and fitter' in the 1990s than it was a decade earlier due partly to the recession of the early 1980s and partly to government policies. Paradoxically this made it more difficult for business to survive in the recession of 1990–91.

The United Kingdom was the world's first industrialised country. Older industries such as coal, iron and steel, heavy engineering (such as shipbuilding) have declined.

Britain is currently almost self sufficient in oil and gas.

New industries such as communications, robotics and computing have been encouraged.

Main exports are machinery and transport equipment (34%); manufactured goods (27%); oil and gas (22%); and chemicals (11%). There is also a large 'invisible exports' sector comprising banking and insurance.

Main customers are EC (48%), USA (14%) and Commonwealth countries (such as Australia, Canada, New Zealand) (over 5%).

Activity 3.6

1 Table 3.2 gives us figures on agriculture, industry, energy and unemployment.

2 Which countries are most dependent and least dependent on agriculture?

3 Which are least dependent on imports for their energy?

4 Which have the best and worst unemployment figures?

Activity 3.7   Use Table 3.3 to determine which countries are best and worst in the EC 'league table' on growth, employment and inflation. Knowing the answers to these questions will help you to understand why countries have different priorities when EC policies are being decided.

Constitution and government

Activity 3.8   Britain should:

a Become a republic.
b Have an elected upper chamber.
c Adopt proportional representation.

Study the following section so you can make comparisons with other countries, then discuss each of these propositions with your fellow students and take a vote on each.

Table 3.2 The European Economy (1987)

	Belgium	Denmark	France	Germany	Greece	Ireland	Italy	Luxembourg	Netherlands	Portugal	Spain	UK
% agricultural land that is utilised	46.00	66.00	57.00	48.00	70.00	81.00	58.00	49.00	54.00	48.00	54.00	76.00
Industry as % of GDP	34.40	27.70	35.80	49.90	28.50	36.50	39.10	35.40	34.80	37.70	50.00	40.80
Agriculture, forestry & fishery as % of GDP	2.50	6.30	4.10	1.90	18.50	10.10	5.20	3.20	4.60	8.20	16.70	1.70
% of energy imported	71.30	79.60	54.00	50.20	64.50	54.00	83.90	99.00	5.20	90.00	60.60	15.10
Unemployment as % of labour	12.60	7.60	10.80	8.10	7.50	18.40	13.80	1.50	12.40	8.50	21.50	12.10

Table 3.3 EC growth, unemployment and inflation

Growth rates (%)

	Belgium	Denmark	France	Germany	Greece	Ireland	Italy	Luxembourg	Netherlands	Portugal	Spain	UK
1989	4.2	1.7	3.2	3.8	2.5	5	3.5	3.6	3.7	4.7	4.8	2
1990	3	1.9	3.1	3.8	1.5	4.5	2.9	3.2	3.5	4	3.9	1
change	-1.2	.2	-.1	0	-1	-.5	-.6	-.4	-.2	-.7	-.9	-1

Unemployment rates (%)

	Belgium	Denmark	France	Germany	Greece	Ireland	Italy	Luxembourg	Netherlands	Portugal	Spain	UK
1989	9.2	7.5	9.5	5.5	8.5	16.7	10.5	1.7	9.9	5.2	17.5	5.9
1990	8.2	8.4	9	5.2	11.5	16.7	10.4	1.6	8.3	5	15.5	6.2
change	-1	.9	-.5	-.3	3	0	-.1	-.1	-1.6	-.2	-2	.3

Inflation rates (%)

	Belgium	Denmark	France	Germany	Greece	Ireland	Italy	Luxembourg	Netherlands	Portugal	Spain	UK
1989	3.2	4.7	3.5	3	14.3	4.2	6.2	3.3	1.5	13	6.7	7.5
1990	4.3	2.7	3.8	3.3	22.3	2.7	6.8	4.2	2.9	14.4	7.1	10.2
change	1.1	-2	.3	.3	8	-1.5	.6	.9	1.4	1.4	.4	2.7

EC trends

	1986	1987	1988	1989	1990
Unemployment (millions)	15.9	15.8	15.6	14.1	13.8
Inflation %	3.5	3.4	3.9	4.7	6.3

EUROPEAN POLITICAL SYSTEMS

BELGIUM

Belgium is a hereditary monarchy and a parliamentary democracy. Legislative power is exercised jointly by the King, the Chamber of Representatives, and the Senate. Each can take the initiative. The 212 Representatives and a number of the 178 Senators are elected for a fixed term of 4 years by proportional representation. The other Senators are selected by elected provincial councils or co-opted by the elected senators. The central government controls 90% of the total budget. It consists of equal numbers of French-speaking and Flemish-speaking ministers.

Belgium's 9 provinces – Antwerp, Brabant, East Flanders, Hainaut, Liege, Limburg, Luxembourg, Namur and West Flanders – are each administered by a provincial governor, assisted by some of the members of the elected provincial council.

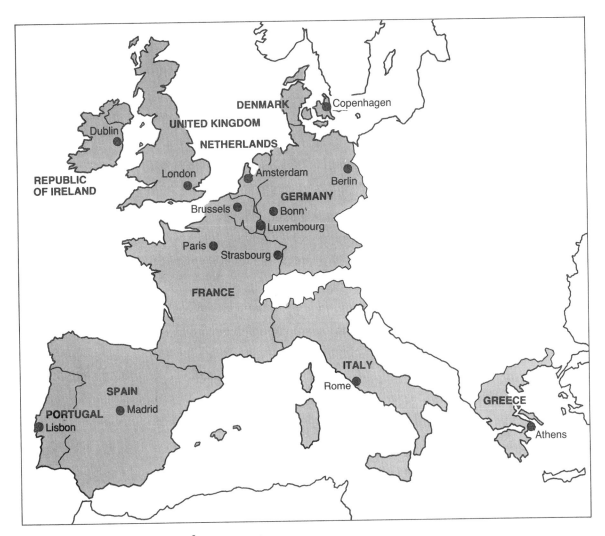

Figure 3.2 European centres of government

Belgium also has a number of regional bodies to tailor policy to specific needs. Councils are elected by each community and each region. Executives are elected from these. The executives and councils legislate by decree.

Polling day is on Sunday. Voting is compulsory for Belgians from the age of 18. They may stand for election to the Chamber of Representatives at 35 and to the Senate at 40. Currently 14 political parties are represented in the Chamber of Representatives.

Belgians prefer compromise to confrontation. For example, when the King felt that his conscience would not allow him to consent to abortion legislation, passed by parliament in April 1990, he abdicated for a day.

Military service is compulsory.

DENMARK   Denmark is a constitutional monarchy and a parliamentary democracy. Legislative power lies jointly with the sovereign and the single chamber parliament (the Folketing). There are 179 members of the Folketing, elected by proportional representation for a term of 4 years. The Faroes and Greenland each elect two members.

The country is divided into single seat constituencies. Additional seats are allocated to parties in the Folketing to ensure proportional representation. There are currently nine parties represented in the Folketing.

Denmark is divided into 14 counties. There is also a metropolitan region, comprising Copenhagen and Frederiksberg. The Faroes gained home rule in 1948 and are not part of the EC. Greenland obtained home rule in 1979 and withdrew from the EC on 1 February 1985.

Polling day is normally on Tuesday. Danes may vote and stand for election when they are 18.

Military service is compulsory.

Activity 3.9   Some EC countries such as the UK, Netherlands, and Denmark, are monarchies. To what extent should the royal family become involved in politics or make controversial comments, such as those by Prince Charles on architecture?

FRANCE   France is a republic in which power is shared between the President, the Government, and Parliament. The President is directly elected by the people for a period of seven years. He appoints the Prime Minister and, on the Prime Minister's recommendation, the other Ministers. He presides over the Council of Ministers, can dissolve the National Assembly, and organise referenda for major bills.

Parliament comprises two chambers. The 577 Deputies of the National Assembly are elected by a system of two-round majority voting (until 1986 there was a single ballot from departmental lists). The 317 Senators are elected for nine years by an electoral college comprising the Deputies, Councillors from the departments, Major and Municipal Councillors. One third of the Senate is replaced every three years.

The separation between left- and right-wing parties is greater in France than in many European countries and can bring about what business people most dislike – uncertainty.

Metropolitan France is divided into 22 Regions and 95 Departments. The Regions are: Alpes-Côte d'Azur, Alsace, Aquitaine, Auvergne, Brittany, Burgundy, Centre, Champagne-Ardenne, Corsica, Franche-Comté, Ile-de-France, Languedoc-Roussillon, Limousin, Loire Valley, Lorraine, Midi-Pyrénées, Nord-Pas-de-Calais, Lower Normandy, Upper Normandy, Picardy, Poitou-Charentes and Provence-Rhône-Alpes.

Polling day is on Sunday. The French are entitled to vote at the age of 18. They can stand for election as a Municipal Councillor at 18, a mayor at 21, a Deputy at 23 and a Senator at 35.

Military service is compulsory for men.

GERMANY

The Federal Republic of Germany is a parliamentary democracy with a federal constitution.

It is made up of 16 *Lander*: Baden-Württemberg, Bavaria, Berlin, Bremen, Hamburg, Hesse, Lower Saxony, North Rhine-Westphalia, Rhineland-Palatinate, Saarland, Schleswig-Holstein, Brandenburg, Mecklenburg, Saxony, Saxony-Anhalt and Thuringia. The last 5 were reformed from the original states abolished in the former East Germany.

The basic law of the German federal constitution states that federal states are responsible for all matters that are *not* expressly allocated to central government. Central functions include foreign affairs, defence, currency, customs, air transport, and the postal service.

The Bunderstag is the supreme legislative body. Members of the Bunderstag are elected for four years by a combination of proportional representation and plurality. Each *Lander* has three, four or five members in the Bunderstag, depending on population. There are currently five parties represented in the Bunderstag.

A federal convention comprises all members of the Bunderstag and an equal number of members elected by the Land Parliaments. The Federal Convention elects a President whose term is five years. The President represents the German Federation in international law, concludes treaties with foreign states, and implements new laws. The President is also responsible for nominating a Chancellor, usually from a majority party in the Bunderstag, who is acceptable to the whole Bunderstag. He (or she) chooses ministers to form the federal government.

Polling day is on a Sunday or public holiday. Germans may vote and stand for election from the age of 18.

Military service is compulsory.

GREECE

Greece is a parliamentary democracy. Power is exercised by the President and the Vouli (parliament). Members are elected by proportional representation. There are also 12 State Deputies, making up the total of 300 representatives in parliament. These are designated by the political parties in proportion to the number of votes cast for each party.

The President is elected by Parliament for five years. He appoints the Prime Minister and, on the latter's recommendation, the ministers. There are currently three political parties represented in the Vouli.

Greece is divided into 52 Nomi (prefectures) and 13 Regions which are: the Northern Aegean, the Southern Aegean, Attica, Crete, Epirus, Central Greece, Western Greece, the Ionian Islands, Central Macedonia, Eastern Macedonia and Thrace, Western Macedonia, the Peloponnese, and Thessalae.

Voting is compulsory. Greeks may vote at 18 and stand for parliament at 21.

Military service is compulsory for men. It is voluntary for women.

Activity 3.10   Voting is compulsory in many countries, including Greece and Belgium. What are the advantages and disadvantages of forcing people to vote?

IRELAND   Ireland is a parliamentary democracy. The Oireachtas (National Parliament) comprises the President, the Dail Eireann (House of Representatives) and the Seanad Eireann (Senate).

For the Dail, 166 Members are elected for a period of up to 5 years by proportional representation.

There are 60 Senators. Eleven are nominated by the Taoiseach (Prime Minister), 43 are elected by the Members of the Dail, the previous Seanad, and local authorities. Panels of candidates, representing five key areas – education, agriculture, labour, industry and commerce, and administration – are proposed for this election. The remaining six Senators are elected by the country's university graduates.

Bills that would alter the Constitution require passing by both chambers and a referendum.

There are 115 local authorities (county councils, county borough councils, borough councils, urban district councils, and town commissions) responsible for local administration.

The Irish may vote at 18 and stand for election at 21. European Community citizens, resident in Ireland, may vote in local elections and European Parliamentary elections.

There is no compulsory military service.

Activity 3.11   Select a country other than the UK and find out what are its main national political parties.

Try to discover the differences between the policies of these parties. (If you choose a country that is about to have a general election the British press will usually have some information on this.)

ITALY   Italy is a parliamentary republic comprising two chambers – the Senate and the Chamber of Deputies – which have equal powers.

The 630 Deputies and the 315 Senators are elected for 5 years by proportional representation. Senators are elected regionally.

The President, elected by the Parliament, appoints the President of the Council of Ministers (Prime Minister) and, on the Prime Minister's recommendation, the other Ministers.

Italy is divided into 20 administrative regions. Five of them – the Aosta Valley, Fruili-Venezia Giulia, Sardinia, Sicily and Trenrino-Alto Adige – have more autonomy than the other 15 – Aburzza, Apulia, Basilicata, Calabria, Campania, Emilia Romagna, Latium, Liguria, Lombardy, Marche, Molise, Piedmont, Tuscany, Umbria and Veneto.

Polling is normally on Sunday and Monday morning. Italians are entitled to vote at 18 and stand for election at 25. The current Parliament has representatives of 15 political parties.

Military service is compulsory.

LUXEMBOURG   Luxembourg is a constitutional monarchy and representative democracy. The Grand Duke has executive power, delegated to the members of the government, co-ordinated by the Prime Minister.

The Chamber of Deputies is directly elected by the people. After the last election 5 political parties were represented in the Chamber.

Polling is on Sunday and voting is compulsory. Luxembourgers must vote from the age of 18, and may stand for election at 21.

Military service is not compulsory.

NETHERLANDS   The Netherlands is a hereditary monarchy and parliamentary democracy.

The sovereign and cabinet constitute the government. The States-General (Parliament) comprises two chambers. The First Chamber has 75 members nominated by the Provincial Councils. The 150 members of the Second Chamber are elected by proportional representation for a period of four years. There are currently nine political parties represented in the Second Chamber.

The Netherlands is divided into 12 provinces: Drenthe, Flevoland, Friesland, Gelderland, Groningen, North Holland, South Holland, Limburg, North Brabant, Overijssel, Utrecht, and Zeeland. Each province has a Provincial Council and a Provincial Executive, both chaired by a Queen's Commissioner appointed by the central government.

Polling is on a Wednesday. Dutch citizens may vote and stand for election when they reach the age of 18.

Military service is compulsory.

PORTUGAL   Portugal is a parliamentary republic. Parliament has 1 chamber of 250 Deputies, directly elected by proportional representation (the d'Hondt system) and hold office for 5 years.

Continental Portugal comprises 18 districts: Aceiro, Beja, Braga, Braganza, Castelo Branco, Coimbra, Evora, Faro, Guarda, Leiria, Lisbon, Oporto, Portalegre, Santarem, Setubal, Viana do Castelo, Vila Real and Viseu.

SPAIN   Spain is a hereditary monarchy and parliamentary democracy, under a constitution established in 1978. The king is head of state and commander of the armed forces.

The Cortes Generales (Parliament) comprises two houses. The Senate (upper house) comprises 225 Senators. Many are elected by plurality from each of the provinces and the others are appointed by the legislatures of the Communities. The Congress of Deputies (lower house) is made up of 350 members elected by proportional representation.

Elections take place every four years. Spaniards can vote and seek election at the age of 18.

There are 19 provincial communities. Four have considerable autonomy. They are Andalusia, Basque, Catalonia and Galicia. The others with some degree of autonomy are Aragon, Asturias, the Balearic Islands, the Canary Islands, Cantabria, Castille-La Mancha, Castille-Leon, Estremadura, Madrid, Murcia, Navarre, La Rioja, and Valencia. Ceuta and Melilla are also to be given special status.

Military service is compulsory for men.

UNITED KINGDOM   The United Kingdom is a hereditary, constitutional monarchy and parliamentary democracy. There are 2 chambers: the House of Lords and the House of Commons.

The House of Lords has approximately 1000 members, comprising hereditary peers, life peers, the senior law lords, the two archbishops, and the senior bishops of the Church of England.

The House of Commons has 650 members. They are directly elected by majority voting in single-member constituencies, for a term that must not exceed five years.

Although the UK has a unitary administrative system, many powers are delegated to Scotland which has a distinct legal and education system. Wales also has some degree of delegated power. There is a secretary of state, a cabinet minister, and an established regional administrative organisation in Edinburgh and Cardiff. Until 1972 Northern Ireland had a regional parliament at Stormont, but this was suspended and Northern Ireland is now administered directly by the Northern Ireland Secretary, a cabinet minister responsible to parliament.

England is divided into 46 counties, Wales has 8, and Scotland 12 regions for local government. There are 26 districts in Northern Ireland.

The British can vote from the age of 18 and stand for election from 21.

Military service is not compulsory.

Activity 3.12   British generals are against the introduction of conscription in the UK. In Switzerland everyone has to do military training every year.

British forces have been at war several times in recent years whereas several hundred years have passed since Switzerland was at war.

What are the advantages and disadvantages of having compulsory military service?

Summary
1 There is a contrast between the industrialised and agricultural regions of Europe. Tourism is of major importance and is still a growing industry.

2 There is extensive trade between the countries of the EC. External trade is often based on the links between the member states and their traditional trading partners elsewhere in the world.

3 There are profound differences in economic wealth between member states. Germany is the richest, and Greece and Portugal are the poorest.

4 Economic and monetary union, aimed at integration of European economies, arose out of a need to consolidate the position of the EC as one of the three largest economic blocks in the world, the other two being the USA and Japan.

5 All the member states are democracies, although Greece, Portugal and Spain were dictatorships until only a few years ago. Most have central and regional governments elected by proportional representation.

6 The governments of Germany and Spain are to a large extent decentralised. Government in France and the UK is very centralised.

Assignment 3   **PRESSURES TO MOVE**

Background

Some areas of Europe are attractive, and have a net inflow of people from within and outside Europe. Others are being depopulated.

The reasons are complex and only some of the factors are outlined in this book.

Activities

Task 1

Identify two areas of population gain and two areas of population loss.

Explain the particular reasons why each area is gaining or losing people, where they are coming from or going to, and what the effects are on the economy and culture of the area.

Task 2

If you were a resident in one of these areas, decide what view you would take – would you support the population movement or oppose it?

If your local and central government had policies that were contrary to what you believed they should be, how would you go about gaining political power to change things? Explain fully.

4 Demography and culture

Objectives
1 **Identify differences in lifestyles and living standards across Europe.**
2 **Explain the significance of demographic trends.**
3 **Differentiate between the people of Europe in terms of language and culture.**

Demography of Europe

Healthier, wealthier, but lonelier – and fewer of us. That is what statistics indicate about today's Europeans, according to an article in *The European* 26 July 1991, which drew on a survey of social trends in the EC conducted during 1990.

BIRTH AND MARRIAGE

There has been a 25% reduction in the birth-rate since the boom of the 1950s and 1960s. It began in the northern countries of the EC but the average number of children per woman is now 1.3 in both Spain and Italy – a drop of over 70% in the last 30 years. Even in Ireland, where the birth-rate is now 2.1 children per woman, it has dropped from 4.0 in 1960.

The average age, throughout the EC, at which a woman has her first child has risen from 24 in 1970 to 26 in 1990.

The birth-rate is currently only three quarters of what is needed to maintain the existing population. By contrast, the populations of USA and Canada, China, and the USSR will continue to grow.

As well as smaller families, there are more working wives (although mainly part-time) and more births outside marriage now than there were 30 years ago.

If the present low birth-rate continues, the population of the 12 countries will be cut by 4 million by the year 2020.

Activity 4.1   Discuss with your fellow students whether you think the birth-rate will continue to fall.

The number of births outside marriage has risen from 5% in 1970 to over 17% in 1989. During this period an increasing number of couples chose to live together and start families without getting married. In 1989 almost one half of Danish babies, 28% of French babies, and 27% of British babies were born to unmarried parents.

However, after the decline in the mid 1980s, the number of weddings has increased except in Italy and Ireland (where the decline had been less). Many of the weddings involve remarriages where one or both of the partners is divorced.

Divorce is at the highest level ever, four times what it was 30 years ago. It is now legalised in Italy and Spain, though not in Ireland. Of over 538 000 divorces in 1988, nearly 167 000 were in the UK and almost 129 000 in (West) Germany.

Activity 4.2   Read the sections on standard of living and mortality and then discuss with your fellow students where, in the EC, you would choose to live on the basis of these factors alone.

STANDARD OF LIVING   Living standards have improved since 1970 but there are significant differences between the member states. The figures given in the prevous chapter show that the Gross Domestic Product, adjusted to take account of differences in the cost of living, suggest that the Luxembourgers are most affluent, and the British, Danes, Germans and French are about twice as well-off as the Greeks and Portuguese. The differences are changing, though. The Portuguese and British have shown greatest improvement in the last three to five years while the Danes and Greeks have had the lowest improvements.

Another way of assessing affluence is to look at gross average monthly earnings. This indicates that Luxembourg is ahead of Denmark, Germany, the Netherlands, Belgium, Ireland and France.

However, if tax, social security contributions, and family allowances are considered the picture is different. A married couple with two children living on one average salary would have a better income in Belgium, Germany and the UK than in Denmark or the Netherlands. A single person is comparatively well-off in Belgium, Spain and the UK.

Averages can be misleading, so it is a good idea to look at the differences between rich and poor.

The highest level of poverty is in Portugal, using the EC definition of poverty which is an income of less than half the average income for the country. It is also high in Ireland with 19% of the population, and in the UK with 18%. Belgium, Denmark and Germany have less than 10% poverty.

In 1988, over 50% of the female population of the EC was either employed, in training, or unemployed but looking for a job. This compared with 78% of the male population. Denmark had the highest proportion of women in 'economic activity' with 76%, compared with 63% in the UK, and the lowest levels of 38% in Spain and 39% in Ireland.

From 1983 to 1988 the male workforce increased by 2 million to 128.5 million. During the same period, the female workforce increased by 4 million to 49.4 million. Service industries accounted for 60% of employment, manufacturing industries employed over 32%, while agriculture, forestry and fishing employed less than 8%. The proportion of part-time jobs had increased from 12% to 14%.

The number of primary school children dropped from 29.1 million in 1971 to 22.7 million in 1987, due to the falling birth-rate. However, in the last 16 years the number of students in tertiary education has risen from 3.5 million to 6.6 million. Of these 3 million are university students. Women students outnumber men in Portugal and France, and there are roughly equal numbers of male and female students in Denmark and Spain. In the remaining countries there are more male than female students.

The number of students studying arts subjects such as literature has declined but there are now twice as many social science students than there were 16 years ago. Business studies and computing are now very popular subjects. Over 69% of British and Danish and almost half of other EC young people (under 21 years) can use a computer.

Over 75% of school children in Denmark, Germany, France and the Netherlands study English. The same proportion of pupils study French in Flemish-speaking parts of Belgium, Luxembourg and Britain but French is studied by fewer than half of pupils in other EC countries. German is the third most popular language.

Home ownership is most common in Ireland, Spain, and Greece. It is least common in Germany and the Netherlands.

There is one car on the road for every three Europeans. Forty per cent of Germans have a car, but fewer than 13% of Greeks own a car.

Leisure now accounts for 10% of spending in British, Danish, Irish and Dutch families, and 6% in Belgian and Greek ones.

More than 60% of British, Dutch, Danish and Germans go to other countries for their annual holiday, compared with fewer than half of the inhabitants of Greece, Spain and Portugal. Does this indicate a lack of cash or a wonderful climate? Probably the latter because most Spaniards and Portuguese, and Italians, do take holidays, but in their own country.

MORTALITY   EC males can now expect to live past the age of 70, compared with about 64 in the 1950s. Spanish men have the best life expectancy – 73 years. Life expectancy for women has risen from 68 to 78 in the last 40 years. In the UK women can expect to live to 77.5 but in France the figure is 80!

Heart disease and cancer account for 45% of all deaths. Lung cancer is most common in Scotland, northern Italy, Belgium and the Netherlands. Breast cancer kills most often in the UK, Ireland, Denmark and the Netherlands, while the UK, Denmark and Germany have the highest death-rate from cervical cancer.

Out of almost 29 000 AIDS sufferers diagnosed by the beginning of 1990, just under 4000 were women. Forty-seven per cent were homosexual or bisexual men and 30% were drug addicts. More than 5% were attributed to heterosexual sex. France reported 30% of the EC total, with the next highest rates in Spain and Denmark.

There are now more than half as many AIDS sufferers as there were road deaths in 1987 – 45 000. While the number of AIDS deaths is rising, annual road deaths are declining – from 54 500 in 1980. France still has the worst record for road deaths but has achieved a 25% reduction since 1970. In Germany there were 8000 deaths in 1990, less than half the 1970 figure.

Suicides are uncommon in the EC. They most often occur in France and Belgium; the fewest occurrences are in Greece and Spain.

Activity 4.3   Longer life, improving living standards and a spectacular dive in the birth-rate are turning Europe into a wealthier but ageing community.

By 2020, less than 20% of the population of the EC will be under 20 years, and more than 25% will be 60 or over.

The combination of a lower birth-rate and longer life-expectancy means there is a prospect that fewer working people will have to finance an increasing number of pensioners.

What would you do about this if you were an EC policy-maker?

People and culture

WHAT MAKES A
EUROPEAN?

Table 4.1 European values

Percentage of people claiming 'very strong' attachment

	Denmark	France	Germany	Italy	Spain	UK	Overall
Free enterprise	26	56	57	54	58	49	54
Europe	27	44	55	67	61	18	48
Money	25	43	42	41	53	40	43
Religion	15	34	28	59	54	25	38
Solidarity	61	72	65	85	84	32	66
Marriage	58	54	64	64	74	66	64
The nation	74	53	44	63	76	50	56
Democracy	72	69	75	74	78	65	72
Work	58	71	61	81	81	57	69
Culture	40	69	62	88	86	47	69
The family	86	91	83	91	91	85	88
Freedom	84	91	84	93	78	81	86
The rights of man	82	83	84	88	85	73	82
Equality	63	80	68	84	83	67	75

Source: The European, 21 June 1991

Activity 4.4   Look through the list in Table 4.1 and answer 'yes' if you have a strong attachment to each of those things; 'no' if you do not have a strong attachment.

Compare your answers with those of your fellow students and calculate the percentages of 'yes' for each question. Compare your results with those in Table 4.1 which were obtained from a survey of 2400 people, 400 in each of Denmark, France, Germany, Italy, Spain and the UK.

If the percentages of 'very strong' attachments are close to the overall figures from the survey then you can claim to be 'European'. It may be, however, that your answers fit more closely with those of a specific country. If you have any skill with statistics you may wish to carry out a correlation test on the figures.

The results of the survey, featured above indicate significant differences in attachment to the so-called *European values* among the member countries of the EC. Other issues surveyed are defence, monetary union including a single currency, a common foreign policy, and federalism.

The scores for France are closest to the average for the 12 on European values. The French also indicate the highest level of support for common policies. Seventy-eight per cent of French people want a policy for a European common currency and 75% favour a common defence policy. For years the French government advocated both. Unemployment is the chief concern of the French and 49% are concerned about immigration. Unlike the other two Catholic countries in the survey only 34% have a strong commitment to religion. Opinion is split on the election of a European president.

The Danes are the least European of those surveyed. They are strongly nationalistic and are pessimistic about the effects of the single market. They anticipate more unemployment, more inflation, greater inequality, more racism, an increased number of AIDS sufferers and more urban crime. Half of them favour a common defence policy but only 11% want a European president.

Germans care about freedom and the rights of man more than they care about the family. Germans have no doubt that home-produced industrial goods are best and they worry that their high standards might be jeopardised by the common market. They are less concerned by the problem of AIDS than other nationals.

A huge majority of Italians want a single currency and expect the common market to solve many of their country's problems. However, there is a strong sense of Italian nationalism and a strong commitment to both religion and culture. They are very concerned about AIDS.

Spain is committed to a single currency and the single market. They also believe strongly in marriage and the family.

Europeanism is gaining ground only slowly in the UK and is still not strong. The British think of Europe only in terms of economics and politics. They are strongly nationalistic.

Activity 4.5 Germany, the USA and pre-1991 USSR are all examples of 'federal states'.

Could Europe ever become a federal state and should it?

EUROPEAN CULTURES Although the EC recognises only 9 languages for its 12 countries, it acknowledges and encourages the retention of minority languages and cultures.

Activity 4.6 Read the following sections, then answer these questions.

1 Identify the 9 official languages used by the 12-country EC.

2 Use the latest population figures for the countries to prepare a bar chart that shows clearly the number of people officially using each language.

3 Identify at least 5 minority languages.

BELGIUM Belgium is a nation of two languages. About 5.5 million of the population live in the northern part of the country, Flanders, and speak Flemish, which is similar to Dutch. In the southern, Walloon, area, the language is French. Most Walloons cannot speak Flemish and most Flemings won't speak French.

Nowhere else in the EC are there such distinct ethnic and linguistic communities. However, the different Belgian groups do not have separatist aspirations like the Welsh and Scottish in Britain or the Basques in Spain.

Over 9% of the people living in Belgium are foreigners. Of these nearly 35% are from Italy and another 30% from other EC countries.

Belgium is predominantly a Roman Catholic country.

Belgians spend a large amount of their income on their home. They are third in the EC in consumer spending on home furnishings and top spenders on tableware, cutlery and food processors. They also are close to the top for purchases of home computers, but near the bottom in purchases of video recorders. They prefer to buy foreign clothes but Belgian-made cars and durables.

The Belgians are the third largest consumers of meat in the EC; the preferred meat is pork. They drink more mineral water per capita than any other country, and more beer than the British.

DENMARK Danish is the principal language. There is a German-speaking minority in South Jutland.

Almost all Danes (98%) belong to the Evangelical-Lutheran church.

Denmark is a liberal-minded, tolerant, compact nation with a low crime rate and a deep sense of social welfare. Danes tend to react with stubborn resistance to outside pressure.

Danes insist on stylish, well-made products and prefer to buy Danish-made products. They spend heavily on home furnishings and electrical goods. They prefer clear, bright colours in articles they buy.

Pork products are popular, and fish is also a common choice in food.

FRANCE The official language is French but other languages including Breton, Alsatian, Basque, Corsican and Catalan are spoken in some of the provinces.

About 8% of the population comes from other countries. About 3% are from other EC countries, half from Portugal.

Over 90% of French people are Roman Catholics.

The French are traditionally very nationalistic.

The French have a strong attachment to their own region, but Paris has a special status not shared by any other city. There is a distinct difference between the north, where the Germanic influence is strong, and the

Mediterranean south. There are also major differences between the west, on which the Atlantic has a strong influence, and the east which is Continental. It is in the north and east that industry is concentrated, around the coal and ore deposits close to the River Rhine.

Activity 4.7

1 People who share the same culture and language are sometimes separated by national boundaries. Can you identify any?

2 It is also the case that minority groups want to retain their own ethnic identity. The Welsh and Scottish are examples of this in the UK. Can you identify others who might want some degree of autonomy?

GERMANY

The peoples from what used to be the Federal Republic and those from the Democratic Republic are still two different communities. West Germany (FDR) was one of the richest countries in the EC while East Germany (GDR) was a centrally-controlled communist country with all that implies in scarce, poor quality, consumer products, low prices and low wages. It will be years before the two 'cultures' are reconciled.

Over 7% of the population of the FDR were foreign residents. Of this 4.4 million, almost 1.4 million were from other EC countries, including 565 000 from Italy and 292 000 from Greece.

Forty-three per cent of the population are Protestants and 43.3% Roman Catholics.

The stereotype of Germany is an efficient, conscientious and formal nation. In the north (Hamburg, Bremen, Hanover) there is an ethos of hard work but there is some truth in the idea that Germans have become more relaxed. The German worker does 20% fewer working hours than 15 years ago. The working week is 20% shorter than the Japanese and they have longer holidays than the British. Germans are concerned that the work they do is of the best quality.

Germans have the highest level of dual language proficiency of the EC nationals.

Germany is the EC's biggest spender on consumer goods. They have the highest spending on electrical goods (except stereos where they are second to the UK). More cars and bicycles are bought than in any other EC country.

Germans are top of the 'league' in drinking beer, spirits, orange juice and coffee, and second to the Belgians in drinking mineral water. There is a high preference for meat products and pork is the favourite meat.

Germans are very environmentally aware. They are very health conscious with an emphasis on exercise, rather than careful diet.

GREECE

Ninety-six per cent of Greeks belong to the Greek Orthodox church, the official state religion.

Greeks are proud of their history and their country's role as the first centre of European civilisation. They are fiercely independent, seeing the state as a foe to be outwitted.

Purchases of household equipment is one of the lowest in the EC, except for cookers, fridges and deep freezers.

Greeks have one of the highest levels of consumption of mutton, lamb and goat; fish is also very popular and is eaten as much as the total of beef, veal and pork combined. More cheese is consumed in Greece than in any other member state, although France is not far behind. Consumption of bread and pasta is second to Italy.

Greeks spend very little on clothes, and are the second lowest EC country in car purchases.

IRELAND   Over three-quarters of the 90 000 foreign residents in Ireland come from other EC countries.

The official languages are Gaelic and English.

Ninety-five per cent of the population is Roman Catholic.

Refer to Ireland, or the Republic of Ireland, when writing or speaking. Do not use Eire (which is the Gaelic name for it and is used only when the whole letter or conversation is in Gaelic).

The Irish spend less per capita than most EC states on durables, food, etc.

They consume almost the highest amounts of potatoes and beer. Tea is drunk more than in most other EC countries. They rank sixth in meat consumption, eating equal amounts of all the main meat products. Relatively low amounts of cheese are eaten, but they are second highest in consumption of butter.

Sales of cars are very low in Ireland. Japanese cars have over 40% of the market. Clothes are also a low spending priority.

Activity 4.8   Climate and rainfall are specially important to agriculture, and to leisure and tourism.

Choose 5 places in different parts of Europe and obtain temperature and rainfall figures for them.

Prepare bar charts to show how the temperature and rainfall is spread throughout the year.

What effect does the climate have on people's lifestyle and spending?

ITALY   The national language is Italian. Other languages are spoken in some of the regions: French in the Aosta Valley, German and Ladin in areas of the Alto Adige, and Slovene in Trieste and Gorizia.

Almost all Italians are Roman Catholic.

Italy has a strong cultural history with museums, art galleries and many historic buildings, particularly in Rome, Florence and Venice. Italians have traditionally had a stronger regional loyalty than a national one.

Italians prefer to spend on food than on the home, but the latter is increasing. Spending on clothes, especially by men, is amongst the highest in the EC.

The Italians consume more pasta and bread than any other EC country.

They have the highest per capita consumption of fish and eat equal amounts of beef, veal, pork and poultry.

Italy produces a large quantity of wine. Domestic wine consumption is second only to France. By comparison beer consumption is low.

The Italians are second highest in purchases of cars, with preference to their own companies. Fiat has over 60% of the home market.

LUXEMBOURG Over 25% of residents in Luxembourg are foreigners. Although Letzeburgesch is the national language, French and German are the administrative languages.

About 95% of Luxembourgers are Roman Catholic.

Historically Luxembourg had closer ties with Germany than its other neighbours but today it is more and more associated with France. Its location in the heart of Europe makes it ideal as an administrative centre despite its tiny size.

Luxembourgers spend a great deal on furnishings and appliances for the home. Their preferences are for eating pork in various forms.

NETHERLANDS Dutch is the official language. There is a small Frisian community in the north-east of the country, speaking its own language. However, nearly 32% of Dutch people speak 2 languages, and over 10% speak 3.

Thirty-six per cent of Dutch are Roman Catholic and 32% are Protestant (mainly Dutch Reformed Church).

The Netherlands has had a commercial relationship with the UK since the sixteenth century. The Dutch share many tastes with the British. They spend a great deal on furniture and household appliances. They dine out more than most nations.

The Dutch have shown a willingness to undertake daring massive projects such as the blocking off of the Zuider Zee and reclaiming of 20% of the country from the sea. It is a country of massive multinational companies and technology-based agriculture.

The Dutch have a reputation for being 'straight laced' and conservative, in a bourgeois nation of clean streets, tidy buildings, order and conformity. On the other hand, they have followed radical policies with regard to drug control and penal reform.

PORTUGAL Over the last 20 years, over 2 million Portuguese have emigrated, about half a million of them to other EC countries.

The official language is Portuguese.

Most Portuguese are Roman Catholic.

Portugal's recent history is dominated by the revolution in 1974, which transformed the country from a dictatorship into a democracy. It remains to be seen whether Portugal will become more like Spain and follow, some years behind, a road from autocratic rule to a socialist government. Traditionally a trading country, Portugal may come to rely more on tourism. However, it will remain distinct from its neighbour, since Portugal faces the Atlantic Ocean, while Spain is predominantly influenced by its Mediterranean aspect.

Portugal is the poorest nation in the EC. For this reason consumption of home and household appliances is low by comparison with other countries, but is comparable with many when measured against disposable incomes. Their spending on meat is the lowest in the EC, and is mainly on poultry.

There is a growing clothes industry; domestic spending on beer and wine is greater than that on clothing.

SPAIN

In 1984 there were 227 000 foreign residents, more than half (134 000) from EC countries – mostly from the UK (28 537), Portugal (23 000) and Germany (23 609).

The official language is Spanish (Castillian) although Catalan, Basque and Galician are officially recognised in their respective autonomous communities.

Many cultures, including those of the Romans, Visigoths and Muslims have influenced Spain. The predominant religion is Roman Catholic.

Spain has the most pronounced regional dissimilarities of any of the EC countries. Spaniards are a proud nation.

Spaniards desire beautiful homes and spend a great deal on furnishings. They tend to buy products made in Spain because of the price and availability.

Spaniards consume more meat per capita than the British, preferring pork and poultry. Although Spain produces a lot of wine, more beer is drunk than wine. Spanish consumers have the highest preference for alcohol-free drinks in the EC. There is also a strong preference for additive-free and low-fat foods.

UNITED KINGDOM

Of the UK population 80% are English, 9% Scottish, 5% Welsh, and 3% Northern Irish. There are approximately 2.3 million immigrants from the Commonwealth, of whom almost a third live in the London area. There are almost 400 000 migrant workers from the EC, over 66% from Ireland.

The official language is English but there are sizeable communities in Wales who speak Welsh, and in Western Scotland and the Hebrides where Gaelic is spoken. There are large ethnic communities in many of the larger cities, notably from the Indian and Asian continents.

The Protestant (Anglican) church is the official religion in the UK with the Queen as its head. In Scotland the Presbyterian Church of Scotland is the established church, governed by the Moderator of the General Assembly.

The UK has the highest level of ownership of leisure electrical equipment in the EC, with the highest purchasing level of video recorders and home computers, and the second highest (to Germany) of stereo equipment.

Spending on furniture is lower than the other Northern European countries, but domestic appliances are a high priority.

Only the Belgians and Germans drink more beer per capita than the British. The British are still the greatest tea drinkers in the EC. More milk is consumed than in any other EC country and the consumption of other dairy products (home produced and imported) is also high.

Consumption of meat and fish varies greatly from region to region. Britain ranks third in the purchase of cars. Unlike France and Italy there is no preference for domestic models. There is an awareness of environmentally friendly products but this doesn't match that of Germany.

Summary

1 The EC has a falling birth-rate and an ageing population. An increasing proportion of women are involved in economic activity (paid work).

2 Living standards vary greatly between the member states. Standards are improving throughout the EC with many of the poorest states improving fastest.

3 Germany and France have the greatest commitment to the Community. The UK and Denmark are most nationalistic.

4 Those committed to further development of the EC want to see a single market, a single currency, a foreign policy and a defence policy. They want more co-operation on crime, unemployment, immigration and AIDS.

5 The nine official EC languages are Danish, Dutch, English, French, German, Greek, Italian, Portuguese, and Spanish, although minority languages and cultures are recognised.

Assignment 4   **THE INFRASTRUCTURE OF EUROPE**

Background

Many of you will eventually work in organisations that have close links with other European countries. The EC, and in particular the removal of barriers by the end of 1992, is likely to have extended trade between the EC countries and political changes in Eastern Europe will increase the trade with those countries.

It is a distinct possibility that students will at some stage in their career live and work in another European country.

This assignment's aim is to develop a framework of knowledge and understanding of European countries, including all the EC 12, plus some non-EC and Eastern European countries. It is also a preparation for Parts three and four of the book, entitled, Living and working in Europe, and Doing business in Europe.

Activities

You will be preparing dossiers on a number of countries. The aim is to describe the infrastructure of each country and to highlight any similarities and differences between them.

1 Negotiate with your fellow students to:
- form groups of three to four students;

- select three to four countries (the same number as there are students in the group), different from those of other groups;
- identify the topics to be investigated (*see* Checklist of topics below);
- determine the structure of the dossiers.

2 Prepare a written schedule to complete the work within the set timescale. Report progress to your tutor, in writing, at weekly intervals.

3 Work in your groups to prepare a dossier on each of the selected countries.

The group will agree, amongst its members, and with the other groups, what topics should be investigated and what should be the format of the dossiers. To achieve this it is essential that the members of a group consult closely with one another. It is also essential that there is liaison between the groups.

4 Each group will prepare and give presentations on its countries, using appropriate visual aids to an audience comprising the other groups and interested 'outsiders'.

Checklist of topics

The following ambitious list of topics was identified by a group of students in 1991, to be investigated for inclusion in a dossier on each country:

Taxation	Environment	Imports and exports
Time zones	Government services	Terrorism
Stability	Leisure	Financial standing
Racism/equal opportunities	Health services	Politics
Physical geography	Fashion	Military influence
Population/demography	Housing	Social affairs/problems
Principal businesses	Employment/unemployment	Culture/lifestyle
Cost of living	Language	History
Trade and industry	Climate	Religions
Disposable income/poverty	Monetary systems/currency	Economy/economic wealth
Transport (road/rail networks)	Telecommunications	Attractions (inc. tourism)
	Attitude to EMS	Media
Inflation	Membership of	Socio-economic structure
Police	international bodies	Education/training

Suggested approach

The students organised themselves into teams. Each team chose to investigate four countries:

Team 1	Team 2	Team 3	Team 4
Britain	Denmark	Germany	Belgium
France	Switzerland	Portugal	Sweden
Holland	Spain	Ireland	Austria
Turkey	Italy	Greece	Luxembourg

Each team's list contains a 'high profile' country which is relatively easy to research and a 'low profile' one for which data is less readily available. *Note*: Not all the countries are in the EC.

Part Two
The European Community

5 European Community institutions

Objectives 1 Identify the principal European Community institutions.
2 Describe the legislative process and distinguish between the types of legislation.
3 Explain the structure of the European Commission and the functions of a Directorate General.
4 Describe the procedure for electing a Member of the European Parliament and the duties performed by MEPs.
5 Distinguish between the European parliamentary political groupings and their policies.
6 Identify the function of the European Court of Justice.
7 Describe the democratic process and methods of influencing European decision-making.

Background to the EC

The European Community is unique among international organisations because its member countries have agreed to share a degree of sovereignty in order to develop common policies where joint action offers benefits for all.

Activity 5.1   What do you understand by the word 'sovereignty'?

The Treaty of Paris, signed on 18 April 1951, created the European Coal and Steel Community (ECSC). This experiment in co-operation proved successful and the member states decided to deepen and widen it, embracing their whole economies. On 25 March 1957 the Treaty of Rome created the European Economic Community (EEC) and the European Atomic Energy Community (EURATOM).

It became clear that progress towards unified economies was made difficult by the barriers to the movement of goods, people and finance that were enshrined in the laws and practices of the member states.

In order to achieve a market truly without barriers, it was recognised that progress was needed towards co-operation or union in many areas: technology development and transfer; progress towards economic and monetary union; strengthing of economic and social cohesion; improvement of the environment and working conditions; a common approach to foreign policy.

It was also felt that measures were needed to make the Community work more efficiently and more democratically.

These objectives were incorporated into the Single European Act which was signed by the member states in February 1986 and came into force in July 1987. The Act amends and complements the Paris and Rome Treaties.

Between 1986 and 1990 it was the removal of barriers that received most attention in the UK. Only when the time came for planning the implementation of the other objectives of the Act did the debates over the Social Charter, sovereignty, and introduction of the ECU and subsequent abolition of the £, become major issues. In other countries debate over the implications was far less frenetic and certainly did not lead to events such as rifts in the Cabinet, nor was there such intense coverage of the Maastricht summit elsewhere.

EC MEMBERSHIP   Six members formed the original Community – Belgium, France, West Germany, Italy, Luxembourg and the Netherlands. In 1973 Denmark, Ireland and the UK joined. In 1981 Greece was added to the list, and in 1986 Portugal and Spain brought the number to 12.

Turkey and Morocco applied for membership in 1987. Cyprus and Malta have association agreements. Many of the EFTA (European Free Trade Association) countries are actively considering membership. Norway is likely to be the first to gain EC membership; Austria, Finland, Sweden and Switzerland will probably also be accepted. Eastern European countries would also like to be members, recognising the benefits of the common market. Hungary is best placed to receive a favourable response because it has been moving towards an enterprise culture and market economy for longer than the others.

The criteria for acceptance are mainly political and economic. Greece, Spain and Portugal were not accepted for several years because they were dictatorships. Turkey's application has not been accepted because its per capita income is only half of that of Portugal, the poorest of the existing member states. There is a limit to the extent to which the existing states can support a poor newcomer.

Old hostility and rivalry may also result in the veto of an application. Greece, for example, is quite likely to veto a Turkish application.

EC AIMS AND OBJECTIVES   The aims of the European Community, as set out in the Treaties and the Single European Act, are:
- to achieve an ever-closer relationship between the peoples of Europe;
- to improve the living and working conditions of its population;
- steady expansion, balanced trade and fair competition;
- a reduction in the deprivation that some areas suffer as compared with others;
- removal of restrictions on international trade;
- support to developing nations;
- the pooling of resources to preserve and strengthen peace and freedom.

To co-ordinate the actions that help to achieve these aims, and to manage the European Coal and Steel Community (ECSC), European Economic Community (EEC) and European Atomic Energy Community (EURATOM), there are five main institutions:

- European Commission;
- European Parliament;
- Council of Ministers;
- Court of Justice;
- Court of Auditors.

Decision-making in the Community

The European Commission is the EC's 'civil service'. It proposes Community legislation, supervises the day-to-day running of Community policies, administers EC funds, and ensures that member states comply with EC rules.

Figure 5.1 European Commission building, Brussels

Source: European Commission

The Parliament considers the Commission's proposals, first in committee, then in the whole house, and makes formal comments on them.

The Commission is not obliged to accept Parliament's comments, but it has to justify its actions if it doesn't. The Commission may make changes to its original proposals after receiving Parliament's comments. Revisions to the proposals must be reconsidered by Parliament.

Parliament can block legislation by withholding its opinion, or it can refuse to accept the EC budget, or – as a last resort – it can dismiss the whole Commission (but not individual members).

The Council of Ministers is the body that takes the decisions to adopt proposals. A council of ministers making decisions on agriculture policy is attended by the appropriate member of each country's government. Decisions on finance are taken by a council of finance ministers from the member countries. Thus, although councils to not always comprise the same people, they always have a specialist representative from each country. Each country has a number of votes related to the size of its population (for example the UK has ten votes while Denmark has only three).

The Court of Justice comprises 13 judges, at least 1 from each member country, and interprets and applies Community Law. The Court's judgments are binding on the member states and have primacy over national law.

The Court of Auditors is responsible for checking the soundness of management of the Community's finances.

TYPES OF COMMUNITY LEGISLATION

REGULATIONS

These have general application and apply to all member countries. They do not have to be confirmed by national parliaments to have binding legal effect. If there is a conflict between a regulation and an existing national law, the regulation prevails.

DIRECTIVES

Member countries are compelled to comply with directives within a stated period. The method of implementation is left to national governments.

DECISIONS

These are binding on specified member countries, companies, or individuals. Decisions involving financial obligations are enforceable in national courts.

RECOMMENDATIONS AND OPINIONS

These have no binding force, but merely state the view of the institutions that issue them.

THE COMMISSION

Commissioners are appointed by the member governments for four-year renewable terms, and are based in Brussels. There are 17 Commissioners, 2 each from France, Germany, Italy, Spain and the UK, and 1 each from Belgium, Denmark, Greece, Ireland, Luxembourg, the Netherlands and Portugal.

Commissioners are not national representatives and must act in the interests of the Community as a whole. Sir Leon Brittan QC, one of two UK Commissioners, was, on several occasions, at odds with the British

Government of Mrs Thatcher in the late 1980s, even though he had previously been one of her Cabinet Ministers.

One of the Commissioners is designated the President, and six as Vice-Presidents.

The Commission has 23 Directorate-Generals (DGs) such as agriculture, transport, finance and external relations and the Commissioners each take responsibility for 1 or more DGs. Sir Leon Brittan, for example, is the Commissioner for competition policy and also for financial institutions. Bruce Millan, the other UK Commissioner, is responsible for regional policy.

Activity 5.2   Prepare a list of the 23 DGs and name the Commissioner responsible for each. *See The European Commission and the Administration of the Community* obtainable free from the EC Publications Office.

Although the Commission is a 'civil service', compared with the British civil service, it is far smaller.

The European Commission charged with setting up vast amounts of new legislation, administering EC policies and monitoring compliance with the legislation, comprised fewer than 15 000 people in 1990. This included nearly 2200 translators and interpreters, needed because the Commission has to work in all of the EC's 9 official languages.

This is not the 'vast bureaucracy' that some parts of the media would have us believe it to be. In fact the total number of employees in all the institutions (Commission, Parliament, Court of Justice, etc.) is fewer than 23 000.

The Commission is very much a multinational organisation. Every EC country is well represented amongst its employees, the largest groups being Belgian (3500) and Italian (2700). Almost 10 000 of the Commission staff are based in Brussels, and a further 2300 work in Luxembourg.

Because it is relatively small, the Commission makes great use of external organisations for expert advice. Amongst these is the Economic and Social Committee, set up under the Treaty of Rome, which advises the Commission and the Council. It comprises 189 members who represent employers, trade unions, consumer and other interests. The UK has 24 members on this Committee.

THE EUROPEAN PARLIAMENT   The Parliament is a directly elected body of 518 members.

Activity 5.3   **1** What is the name and political party of your Member of the European Parliament?

2 What is the name of the constituency where you live, what areas does it contain, how big is the electorate, and what were the voting figures at the last European Election?

Parliament's activities are split between three locations: The administration is in Luxembourg; full public sessions of the Parliament are held for 1 week each month in Strasbourg; and the meetings of the 18 committees are held during 2 weeks of each month in Brussels.

REPRESENTATION IN THE PARLIAMENT

It is intended that each country should be represented by a number of Members of the European Parliament (MEPs) that is roughly proportional to its population. Figure 5.2 shows the number of Members for each country in the 1989 elections when 4 countries – France, Germany, Italy and the UK – each had 81 members. The unification of Germany in 1990 meant, however, that it was under-represented. A figure of about 98 MEPs is needed for Germany to have fair representation.

In the UK, England has 66 constituencies, Scotland has 8, and Wales has 4. The UK uses a majority-vote (sometimes called a 'first-past-the-post') system for its European elections, except in Northern Ireland. In Northern Ireland, instead of having three constituencies there is a single three-member

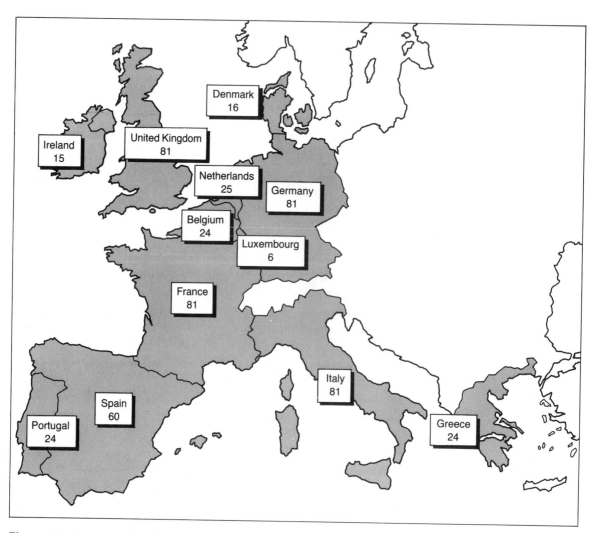

Figure 5.2 Representation in the European Parliament
Source: European Parliament UK office

constituency in which the MEPs are elected by proportional representation. The other EC countries use various methods of proportional representation.

Activity 5.4   Consider the figures given in Table 5.1 which shows the results of voting in the 1989 European elections in the UK. Had there been majority-voting in Northern Ireland, the two Unionist parties would have gained all three seats.

1 Investigate the reasons for the UK choosing to have proportional representation in Northern Ireland.

2 What would the effect have been on the number of seats that the political parties gained in the remainder of the UK if proportional representation had been used throughout the UK?

Table 5.1 UK voting in European elections

Remainder of the UK election results 1989

Party	Votes	Votes %	Seats	Seats %		
Conservative	5 224 037	34.16	32	41.03	Electorate	42 590 060
Labour	6 153 604	40.23	45	57.69	Valid votes	15 294 091
Green	2 292 705	14.99		.00	Turnout	35.91
Social and Liberal Democrats	986 292	6.45		.00		
Scottish Nationalist Party	406 686	2.66	1	1.28		
Plaid Cymru	115 062	.75		.00		
Social Democratic Party	75 886	.50		.00		
Others	39 971	.26		.00		
Total	15 294 243	100.00	78	100.00		

Northern Ireland election results 1989

Party	First Preference	Votes %	Seats	Seats %		
Democratic Unionist	160 110	29.94	1	33.33	Electorate	1 120 508
Social Democratic and Labour Party	136 335	25.49	1	33.33	Valid votes	534 482
Official Unionist	118 785	22.21	1	33.33	Turnout	47.70
Provisional Sinn Fein	48 914	9.15		.00		
Alliance	27 905	5.22		.00		
Others	42 762	8.00		.00		
Total	534 811	100.00	3	100.00		

Source: European Parliament, UK information office

POLITICS – EUROPEAN STYLE

MEPs sit in political groupings within Parliament, not in national groupings. Thus all socialists sit together, all Christian Democrats, and so on.

So that MEPs can follow and take part in debates in their own languages, proceedings are interpreted simultaneously into the nine official languages – Danish, Dutch, English, French, German, Greek, Italian, Spanish and Portuguese. This interpretation is also available in the public gallery.

British visitors to the Strasbourg chamber are amazed by its vastness and

Table 5.2 Political groupings in the European Parliament

Start of 1989–94

	Belgium	Denmark	France	Germany	Greece	Ireland	Italy	Luxembourg	Netherlands	Spain	Portugal	UK	Total
Socialists	8	4	22	31	9	1	14	2	8	27	8	46	180
European People's	7	2	6	32	10	4	27	3	10	16	3	1	121
Liberal Democratic & Reformist	4	3	13	4	–	2	3	1	4	6	9	–	49
European Democratic	–	2	–	–	–	–	–	–	–	–	–	32	34
Green	3	–	8	8	–	–	7	–	2	1	1	–	30
European United Left	–	1	–	–	1	–	22	–	–	4	–	–	28
European Democratic Alliance	–	–	13	–	1	6	–	–	–	–	–	–	20
Technical Group of Euro. Right	1	–	10	6	–	–	–	–	–	–	–	–	17
Left Unity	–	–	7	–	3	1	3	–	–	–	–	–	14
Rainbow	1	4	1	–	–	1	–	–	–	2	3	1	13
Non-attached	–	–	1	–	–	–	5	–	1	4	–	1	12
Total	24	16	81	81	24	15	81	6	25	60	24	81	518

End of 1984–89

	Belgium	Denmark	France	Germany	Greece	Ireland	Italy	Luxembourg	Netherlands	Spain	Portugal	UK	Total
Socialists	8	3	20	33	10	–	12	2	9	28	7	33	165
European People's	6	1	10	41	8	6	27	3	8	1	4	–	115
Liberal Democratic & Reformist	5	2	12	–	–	1	6	1	5	2	10	–	44
European Democratic	–	4	–	–	–	–	–	–	–	17	–	45	66
European Democratic Alliance	–	–	19	–	–	8	–	–	–	1	–	1	29
Group of Euro. Right	–	–	10	–	1	–	5	–	–	–	–	–	16
Rainbow	4	4	–	7	1	–	2	–	–	1	–	1	20
Communists & allies	–	2	10	–	4	–	26	–	2	1	3	–	48
Non-attached	1	–	–	–	–	–	3	–	1	9	–	1	15
Total	24	16	81	81	24	15	81	6	25	60	24	81	518

Start of 1984–89

	Belgium	Denmark	France	Germany	Greece	Ireland	Italy	Luxembourg	Netherlands	Spain	Portugal	UK	Total
Socialists	8	4	20	33	10	–	12	2	9	–	–	33	131
European People's	6	1	9	41	9	6	27	3	8	–	–	–	110
Liberals & Democrats	5	2	12	–	–	1	5	1	5	–	–	–	31
European Democratic	–	4	–	–	–	–	–	–	–	–	–	46	50
European Democratic Alliance	–	–	20	–	–	8	–	–	–	–	–	1	29
Group of Euro. Right	–	–	10	–	1	–	5	–	–	–	–	–	16
Rainbow	4	4	–	7	2	–	3	–	–	–	–	–	20
Communists & allies	–	1	10	–	2	–	26	–	2	–	–	–	41
Non-attached	1	–	–	–	–	–	3	–	1	–	–	1	6
Total	24	16	81	81	24	15	81	6	25	0	0	81	434

Source: European Parliament, UK Office

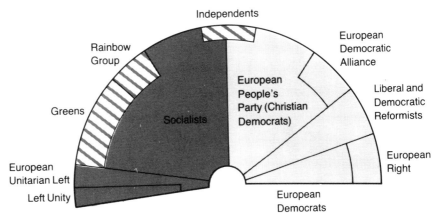

Figure 5.3 Political groups in the European Parliament
Source: European Parliament UK office

the orderliness of the debates. The noise and shouted insults that we hear so often in Westminster are rarely heard in this Chamber.

The need for interpretation detracts from the spontaneity of debate. Sarcasm and emphasis in the voice is usually lost in translation. Laughter comes in the middle of the next sentence if an MEP makes a joke.

There isn't much excitement at voting time either. Each member has buttons on his or her desk so that the result of a vote is known within seconds, and is displayed on a number of electronic display boards. Precautions are taken to prevent an MEP voting for one who is absent.

The Chamber is colourful, since all the documents have to be translated, and each language is in a different colour.

When the Council of Ministers meets to decide on new legislation it doesn't have to take any notice of Parliament's opinion. However, Parliament must have given a formal opinion before the Council is allowed to consider the proposal. This means that Parliament can influence the Council by withholding, or threatening to withhold, its formal opinion.

POLITICAL GROUPS
The MEPs in the 1989–94 Parliament represent nearly 80 different national political parties. Most have chosen to join one of the 10 political groups in the House although a few sit as Independents. Most groups contain MEPs from several countries.

Activity 5.5
Consider the figures given in Table 5.2 which show the membership of the political groupings during the 1984–89 and the 1989–94 sessions.

Investigate the political views of the various groups and decide whether the overall balance changed to the 'left' or to the 'right' during that period.

COMMITTEES
The European Parliament has 18 major committees.

The committees are concerned with detailed examination of and amendment to draft laws, and such issues as relations with non-member

Figure 5.4 European Parliamentary committees
Source: European Parliament UK office

countries, employment, women's rights, trade and consumer protection. Membership of each committee broadly reflects the strengths of the political groups in Parliament.

Commissioners and Commission officials frequently attend committee meetings to explain the Commission's attitude. Experts and representatives of specialist organisations are often called upon for advice and to give evidence.

Activity 5.6   Choose 1 committee and investigate its membership and activities.

COUNCIL OF MINISTERS   Council meetings are attended by the national ministers responsible for the areas of legislation to be decided on, agriculture, finance, industry, environment, social affairs, etc. Commission officials also attend and participate in discussions but do not have a vote.

The Foreign Affairs Council, composed of the national Foreign Ministers, co-ordinates the activities of the other councils and also deals with areas where special councils have not yet been set up – for example external trade.

Council meetings of Heads of State (EC Summits) are held twice each year to discuss broad areas of policy. The ordinary decision-making meetings are much more frequent – about 80 to 100 per year.

Council meetings are chaired by the Minister of the country holding the Presidency of the Council. This changes every six months, rotating in alphabetical order around the countries. The UK holds the Presidency in the last six months of 1992, the last six months of 1998, etc. (assuming no more countries join).

In some areas, mainly those concerned with the completion of the Single

European Market, the Council can adopt legislation on a qualified majority-vote. Each country has a number of votes (*see* Table 5.3). A qualified majority is 54 votes out of a total of 76. This means that even two large countries cannot block a decision.

In other areas, such as taxation, the free movement of people, and workers' rights, the Council must reach a unanimous decision. This means that even a single small country can block such decisions.

Table 5.3 Qualified majority voting in the Council of Ministers

France	10
Germany	10
Italy	10
UK	10
Spain	8
Belgium	5
Greece	5
Netherlands	5
Portugal	5
Denmark	3
Ireland	3
Luxembourg	2
Total	76

54 votes are needed to approve a Commission proposal

COURT OF JUSTICE

The 13 judges, at least 1 from each Community country, are appointed by agreement with the national governments for a renewable term of 6 years.

The Court's judgments are binding on each member country and have primacy over national law.

The Court's importance was demonstrated in 1981 by the success of two individuals, Mrs Worthington and Mrs Humphreys who brought a case to court against their employer, Lloyds Bank PLC, because it refused to give female employees under 25 the same pension rights as other workers. The Court decided that an employer's pension contributions were a part of a worker's remuneration and discrimination of any form in this area was forbidden by Community law. The judgment affected 85 000 employers employing more than 11 million people.

Even more significant was the Court's decision in June 1990 that the UK Merchant Shipping Act of 1988 must be suspended because it conflicted with the rights of Spanish fishermen which are guaranteed by EC law. This overrode the rule in English law that a temporary injunction cannot be granted against the Crown.

In 1989 the European Court of Justice dealt with 385 cases but the number of cases referred to it is rising rapidly as the volume of European Community law grows.

The legislative process

A draft proposal is prepared by one of the Commission's Directorate-Generals. It is then formally approved by the Commission and sent to the European Parliament, the Economic and Social Committee, national

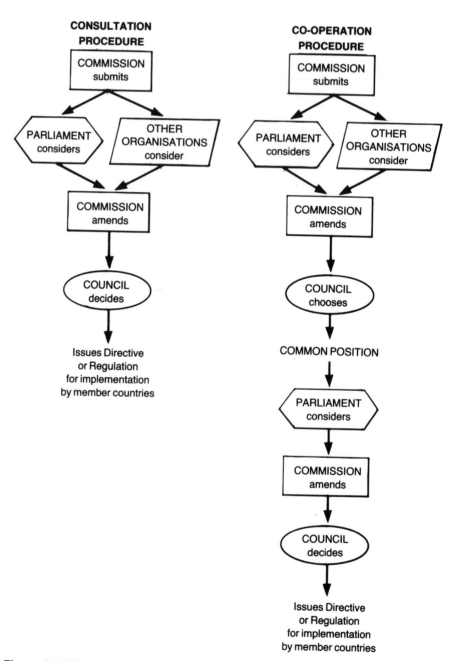

Figure 5.5 The legislative process
Source: European Parliament UK office

governments, and other bodies, for discussion. The Commission may take the comments from these bodies into account and issue a revised proposal.

A final draft is then given to the relevant Council of Ministers who take a decision whether or not to adopt the proposal and, if so, in what form (regulation, directive, etc.).

CO-OPERATION PROCEDURE

Up to the stage of being considered by the Council of Ministers the procedure is the same as above.

Then the Council, instead of formulating a directive or regulation, agrees a 'common position' which member country governments must then implement with legislation in their own countries, normally within one to two years.

In the UK the legal foundation for this is the European Communities Act 1972.

An example of legislation introduced in response to a common position is the Consumer Protection Act 1989. Common positions have sometimes been implemented under existing legislation.

In the UK, Community legislation is examined by Select Committees in the House of Commons and/or the House of Lords, and occasionally inside the Chambers.

THE DEMOCRATIC DEFICIT

The European Parliament neither drafts Community legislation, nor has the final say on whether a particular law is passed. The Commission drafts the law and the Council of Ministers decides which laws shall be put into effect.

The co-operation procedure gives the European Parliament and the Commission a chance to reconsider the proposal. After the common position has been established by the Council of Ministers, the European Parliament has a second opportunity to consider the proposal. The proposal is then returned to the Commission so that they too have an opportunity for amendment. Finally the Council makes a decision on the adoption of the proposal as a regulation or directive.

Thus each body involved in the legislative procedure has the chance to consider the others' opinions.

However, once the Council of Ministers' final decision has been made, neither the European Parliament nor national parliaments can do anything about it.

The decision-making process is democratic in the sense that the Ministers represent democratically elected governments. However, they represent the national governments, not the Community.

Understandably the majority of MEPs think the European Parliament should have more power and 79% want more power over the Council. Additionally, 92% want more power over the Commission.

Other suggestions have been made. National parliaments could be given more time to discuss legislation when it is still possible to influence council decisions; there could be a second chamber to the European Parliament;

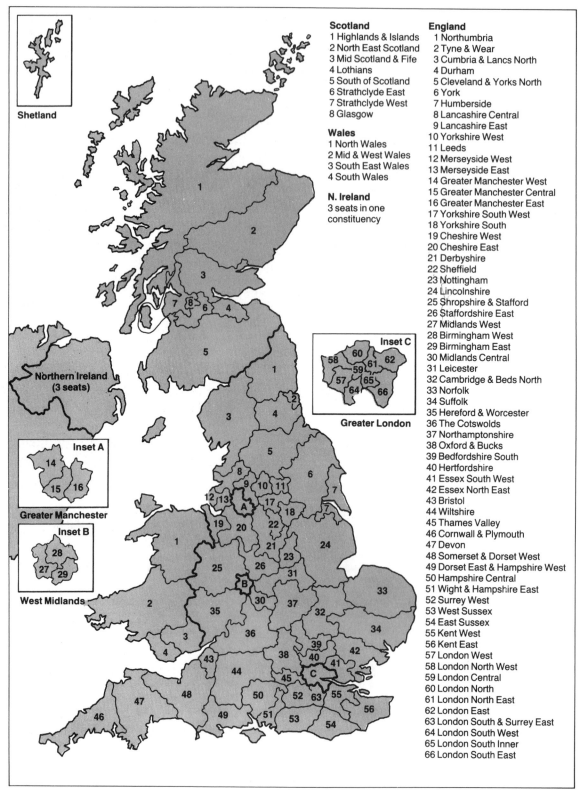

Scotland
1 Highlands & Islands
2 North East Scotland
3 Mid Scotland & Fife
4 Lothians
5 South of Scotland
6 Strathclyde East
7 Strathclyde West
8 Glasgow

Wales
1 North Wales
2 Mid & West Wales
3 South East Wales
4 South Wales

N. Ireland
3 seats in one
constituency

England
1 Northumbria
2 Tyne & Wear
3 Cumbria & Lancs North
4 Durham
5 Cleveland & Yorks North
6 York
7 Humberside
8 Lancashire Central
9 Lancashire East
10 Yorkshire West
11 Leeds
12 Merseyside West
13 Merseyside East
14 Greater Manchester West
15 Greater Manchester Central
16 Greater Manchester East
17 Yorkshire South West
18 Yorkshire South
19 Cheshire West
20 Cheshire East
21 Derbyshire
22 Sheffield
23 Nottingham
24 Lincolnshire
25 Shropshire & Stafford
26 Staffordshire East
27 Midlands West
28 Birmingham West
29 Birmingham East
30 Midlands Central
31 Leicester
32 Cambridge & Beds North
33 Norfolk
34 Suffolk
35 Hereford & Worcester
36 The Cotswolds
37 Northamptonshire
38 Oxford & Bucks
39 Bedfordshire South
40 Hertfordshire
41 Essex South West
42 Essex North East
43 Bristol
44 Wiltshire
45 Thames Valley
46 Cornwall & Plymouth
47 Devon
48 Somerset & Dorset West
49 Dorset East & Hampshire West
50 Hampshire Central
51 Wight & Hampshire East
52 Surrey West
53 West Sussex
54 East Sussex
55 Kent West
56 Kent East
57 London West
58 London North West
59 London Central
60 London North
61 London North East
62 London East
63 London South & Surrey East
64 London South West
65 London South Inner
66 London South East

Shetland

Northern Ireland
(3 seats)

Inset A
Greater Manchester

Inset B
West Midlands

Inset C
Greater London

Figure 5.6 UK European constituencies
Source: European Parliament UK office

there could be several representatives of national *parliaments* rather than single representatives of national *governments*.

The 1991 British government was opposed to any changes in the legislative powers of the European Parliament, arguing that democratic control over the Ministers is a concern of national parliaments, although it favoured tighter control over the Commission. The German government, however, supported proposals that would release some of the power from national governments, providing the European legislative process was more democratic.

The European Parliament is not without power, even though its power is limited in the law-making process. In 1979 and in 1984 it rejected the Community budget because it disagreed with the Council's spending priorities. Parliament also has the power to dismiss the whole of the commission by a vote of censure but this would be a very drastic step.

LOBBYING   In the UK anyone can arrange to visit 'the lobby' of the House of Commons 'to lobby' his or her MP. This could involve giving the MP some information that he/she might not otherwise have, or persuading the MP to support a particular view in the Chamber. Many MPs also have 'surgeries' in their constituency so that constituents can visit them there to lobby.

MEPs are also available for lobbying in much the same way. MEPs travel around Europe extensively to attend committees (in Brussels), to attend full Parliamentary sessions (in Strasbourg) and to meet constituents (in the home constituency).

Unlike the British civil service, the European Commission is also available for lobbying. Meetings with officials and even Commissioners are relatively easy to arrange. Because part of the Commission's role is to listen to experts and special interest groups, it is responsive in this way.

Lobbying can be two-way. It is possible to get information about future proposals from the Commission before they reach the formal stage of submission to the Parliament. Again this differs from the British civil service which has much of its activity covered by the Official Secrets Act.

Summary   1 The major EC institutions are the European Commission, the European Parliament, the Council of Ministers, the European Court of Justice, and the Court of Auditors.

2 The Commission puts forward proposals for the Parliament's consideration and comment. A Council of Ministers takes decisions on proposals.

3 There are 17 Commissioners, based in Brussels. The Commission employs about 15 000 people. It is split into 23 departments (called Directorates General), each responsible for an area of policy.

4 The European Parliament comprises 518 members (MEPs) who sit according to political, not national groupings. Parliament's administration

is in Luxembourg, its open meetings are in Strasbourg, and committees meet in Brussels.

5 One person represents each country at the Council of Ministers. The minister of the national government who attends is the one most appropriate to the business of the day. The Presidency of the Council changes from country to country, every six months. For some decisions a qualified majority is needed, for others the council must be unanimous.

6 The Court of Justice comprises 13 judges. It interprets Community law. Judgments are binding on individuals, organisations and governments and have primacy over national law.

Assignment 5   LEGISLATING FOR THE ENVIRONMENT

Background

Entrepreneurs who have been hiring out mountain bikes to tourists, for a breathtaking ride down the rugged hills of one of France's most beautiful national parks, have been stopped in their tracks by conservationists.

The ban follows a six-month enquiry into the state of the Mercantour National Park on the French-Italian border. Cyclists are blamed for ploughing up trails, uprooting important prairie grasses, breaking up paths and destroying the grazing grounds of the rare mountain goats and deer for which the region is famous.

Seventy-nine species of orchid which grow there were also under threat.

Riders caught face a fine of 450 francs.

Problems arising from mountain bikes have been encountered in the UK and elsewhere in Europe. While they allow people to get fresh air and exercise, and enjoy the countryside they are not completely 'environment friendly'. Even walkers have damaged the Pennine Way so that parts of it have been closed for repair.

Activity

Legislation is proposed to control the use of mountain bikes.

Describe the process that will be followed to arrive at the legislation and the institutions and people involved.

Decide who should be consulted in the discussion phase and find out what their views would be.

Take the role of a Commissioner for the relevant Directorate-General and formulate a proposal to put before the European Parliament.

Adopt roles as MEPs and discuss the proposal, returning it to the Commission for revision if necessary.

Consider the bill from the point of view of members of the Council of Ministers, and decide how the proposal would be implemented if it became EC policy.

6 Community policies

Objectives Investigate European Community's policies in the areas of agriculture, regional aid, social affairs, research and technology, European monetary union and foreign affairs.

The Community budget

Community spending reached about 48.8 billion ECU in 1990, approximately 1% of the EC total GDP.

The Community budget used to be financed by national contributions. It is now met by:

- customs duties and agricultural levies on imports from the rest of the world;
- a proportion of the VAT collected in the member countries; and
- a formula introduced in 1988 which is based on the GDP of the member countries.

Activity 6.1 Refer to Figure 6.1. From 1973 to 1989, which items of the Community budget increased most and which increased least (or decreased)? What are the reasons for this?

Note: *Regions* is the spending on regional policies, including the development of less-favoured regions. It aims to stimulate trade and provide the more industrialised regions with new markets for capital and consumer goods. *Social* policy spending includes promoting freedom of movement; vocational training; retraining of workers; dealing with problems of unemployment; promoting equal opportunities; worker protection and participation in the workplace; improving health and safety in the workplace; making special provisions for the elderly and disabled; and protecting workers, especially women and children, against exploitation.

Agriculture

WHY IS A POLICY NEEDED? In many member countries agriculture is changing from a traditional activity, to a modern economic sector having close links with suppliers and the processing and distribution industries.

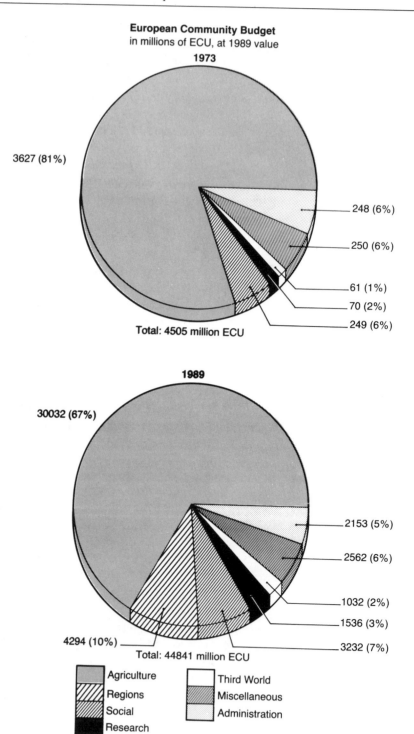

Figure 6.1 European Community Budget, 1973 and 1989
Source: Eurofile, European Commission

In 1960 agriculture employed 15.2 million people in the Community. By 1987 the number had dropped to 5.2 million, but the entry of Spain and Portugal increased it to about 10 million. There was a fall in the number of farms, but an increase in size and specialisation. Higher yields were achieved by the use of fertilisers, pesticides, high-quality seeds and feedstuffs.

These trends were most significant in the more prosperous countries. In the less prosperous ones, agriculture is still comparatively unsophisticated. For example, the average size of farms in the UK is 65 hectares while in Greece and Portugal it is less than 5 hectares.

Throughout the world governments find the need to intervene in agriculture, a sector of the economy that is politically sensitive, economically fragile, and difficult to manage.

The Common Agricultural Policy (CAP) aims to:

- ensure security of supply;
- achieve stable prices for farmers and consumers;
- protect the environment;
- make it easier for farmers and farmworkers in the various countries to adjust to new technology and changing patterns of demand;
- improve links between agriculture and the rest of industry.

Food is essential for survival. In Europe the CAP has ensured that adequate supplies are available without there being a dangerous dependency on countries outside the EC.

Despite technological and biological progress, agriculture is dependent on natural conditions such as soil and weather which can cause changes in the yield. Demand, on the other hand, remains fairly stable. Without a policy to regulate prices and markets there would be massive swings in prices.

Activity 6.2   **1** In the UK, the National Farmers Union, consumer organisations and environmentalists may have conflicting views on the Common Agricultural Policy. Why?

2 To what extent would the same arguments be valid in Germany, France or Greece?

In many areas modern farming is approaching ecological limits. Pollution of groundwater with nitrates and pesticides is very high, the number of wildlife species is shrinking and the appearance of the countryside is changing for the worse. A policy is needed which prevents farmers using unacceptable methods in their struggle for ever-greater yields.

In some areas there is no alternative to employment in agriculture. In regions handicapped by poor soil and harsh climate the CAP is essential in preventing depopulation and dereliction. Without it elderly farmers would be forced to remain on the land after finding their incomes were inadequate, until retirement, while younger people would move away from the area.

Activity 6.3   Forecasts of global warming suggest that the climate could change over the next few years. Investigate what the effects might be and identify the areas of Europe that are most susceptible.

WHAT IS THE CAP?   The EC encompasses a wide variety of agricultural areas, from the north German plains, over the Alps, to the coasts of southern Italy.

The CAP originates from Article 39 in the Treaty of Rome March 1957. The Stresa Conference of July 1958 produced first guidelines that could be properly described as practical policy. The Council of Ministers, meeting in December 1960, gave it legal force. The first organisation to control markets and supplies was for cereals in 1962. By 1970 87% of agricultural production was subject to EC rules and by 1986 this had risen to 91%.

The CAP offers prospects of new outlets but means keener competition. For consumers there is a wider and better choice of food. Specialisation and economies of scale offer *relatively* cheap prices.

The CAP ensures that there is free movement of agricultural products within the Community. It prohibits the charging of customs duties, grant subsidies or quotas that would distort competition.

'Community preference' means that priority is given to the sale of Community products, rather than products from the rest of the world. Since Community prices are higher than on the world market, the CAP protects the internal market against cheap imports and any excessive fluctuations in world prices.

The CAP ensures that costs are shared by all concerned. However, direct taxation and social security for farmers and farm workers remain national responsibilities.

CAP achieves its aims by *intervention* and *external protection*.

INTERVENTION   About 70% of products benefit from a support price which provides, under certain conditions, a guarantee of price and disposal.

The Community has established intervention agencies for products such as cereals, butter, skimmed-milk products, sugar and beef. When supplies are abundant these agencies buy in the surplus production to stabilise market prices. They are sold again once the market is back in balance internally or by means of exports to non-Community countries.

Originally, the intervention agencies bought products at a fixed price (the 'intervention price'). More recently the agencies have issued invitations to tender so that the buying-in price reflects the market situation. On the sugar market the full intervention price is paid for those quantities the Community needs to supply its own market. If farmers produce more, they themselves will have to shoulder the burden of disposal.

With pork, table wine and some types of fruit and vegetables the agencies may pay aid for private storage to take a proportion of the product off the market temporarily.

Generally speaking, the intervention prices are higher in the Community than on the world market. This ensures that domestic farmers sell to the internal market, protecting supplies. To prevent imports 'external protection' is needed.

Activity 6.4   Draw 2 flowcharts, 1 with CAP and the other without, to show what happens when there is:
- more demand;
- less demand;
- more suppliers;
- fewer suppliers;
- a better crop;
- a poor crop.

EXTERNAL
PROTECTION

About 21% of produce is protected by measures that prevent low-price imports from outside the Community.

Products that are not staple foods and can be produced more or less independently of the soil, such as eggs and poultry, quality wines, flowers and many types of fruit and vegetables, are protected by levies or customs duties.

The General Agreement on Tariffs and Trade (GATT) forces the Community to keep its import duties on a number of products at a constant level. The processing industries for these products – which include rape-seed, sunflower seed, cotton-seed and protein plants like peas and field beans – receive a subsidy if they use Community-grown products. This accounts for about 2.5% of agricultural products.

For about 0.5% of products (specialised products like hemp, flax, hops, silkworms and seeds) the producers receive flat-rate aid according to the hectarage or quantity produced.

Activity 6.5   Can we claim to have a 'free market economy' when there are subsidies and intervention in agriculture?

HOW DOES THE
CAP AFFECT
PRICES?

The EC population of over 320 million spend about 20% of their incomes on food. Changes in farm prices affect food prices in the shops.

When the CAP was first introduced it was felt to be desirable to protect the income of farmers, most of whom worked on small- or medium-sized family farms, because their incomes were less than in other occupations.

Direct financial aid could have been given but it was less expensive and less bureaucratic to allow higher prices.

However a guaranteed market and price encouraged producers to take advantage of every opportunity to increase output and thus food mountains came into existence.

Although the Community was slow to respond , eventually support prices were frozen or reduced and direct financial aid was introduced to limit the effect on farmers' incomes.

It would be difficult to completely revert to using world market prices. The quantities traded on the world market are often very small compared with the total production and sometimes reflect short term surpluses in the main producer countries. They fluctuate wildly and are sometimes below the full cost.

Farm-gate prices have risen more slowly than food prices and these in turn have lagged behind the overall cost of living. They have also risen more slowly than disposable income.

REFORMING THE CAP

Activity 6.6

1 The European Commission's CAP attempts to provide a stable supply that meets the demand for agricultural products. Identify the factors that caused it to go so disastrously wrong and resulted in 'food mountains' and 'wine lakes'.

2 How could a new policy remove the problems but still achieve the CAP's aims?

The aims of the CAP have not been challenged but conditions have changed from when it was first introduced and many of the policies are being reconsidered.

When the CAP was introduced much of the Community's food requirement was imported. However, per capita consumption reached a ceiling in the 1970s and population growth declined so that imports reduced and the Community became almost self-sufficient.

Indeed, supply began to exceed demand in sectors such as cereals, milk and beef. In the 1980s wheat production exceeded consumption by almost 30%, and there were surpluses of butter (34%), skimmed-milk powder (28%) and beef (10%). The world market also had an ample supply of these. Third World countries could only absorb a small part of the surpluses and only if the Community subsidised the prices.

In the mid-1980s stocks of feed grain stood at 200 million tonnes, about 2½ times the world trade volume.

World prices dropped to an all-time low in 1987. There was increasing tension between the producing nations as they competed to sell their products, particularly the European Community, USA, New Zealand, Canada and Australia. Export promotion and export refund schemes, like the one introduced by the US government in 1985, resulted in a 'subsidy war'. The chief victims were the developing countries whose export prospects were destroyed.

The CAP policy of intervention prices is not an effective way of protecting farmers and farm workers. This arises from the fact that there are massive differences in costs between regions. Farms in regions with good soil and climate, larger farms, and those with more technology are able to achieve lower unit costs. 'Problem farms' – those with the lowest productivity and in regions with difficult conditions – represent only a small proportion of total output. About 80% of production is in the hands of about 20% of the producers.

Thus, by the mid-1980s the original Common Agricultural policies were proving expensive and surpluses were accumulating. From 1985 there have been a number of changes to the policies.

Lower intervention prices, close to the world market price, have been implemented. These are less attractive and put the 'richer' farms under pressure but they are still viable. However, farms with poor natural conditions, those that are small, and those using less technology, have ceased to be viable. Support has been needed to avoid economic desolation in some regions and a concentration of production in others.

When deciding what to produce the farmer examines profitability. Conversion to another product may involve considerable expenditure for new machines, livestock housing, different production processes, and training so that the changes will often be postponed. With productivity growing by 1 to 2% per year there is sometimes a need for stronger incentives to change than a gradual cut-back in the intervention price.

The Community reached self-sufficiency in milk and milk products in 1974 and production continued to rise by about 2.6% while demand went up by only 0.6% annually. In 1984 a quota system was introduced. The quota is apportioned amongst the member countries who assign quotas to farms or dairies. There are penalties for exceeding the quota.

Another way of reducing production, used for cereals, some fruit and vegetables, and other products, is 'maximum guaranteed quantities'. When production exceeds the council-set MGQs, price and aids are automatically reduced.

These systems imitate the market mechanism so that any overproduction results in a drop in average returns for all producers.

Consumers are becoming more conscious of quality. Since high quality is often correlated with lower yields the introduction of different intervention prices for different qualities has had the effect of curbing total production and achieving better product quality.

Farmers who 'set aside' at least one fifth of their arable land for five years have been offered a premium. However, for this to remove the surpluses a tenth of the agricultural area would have to be set-aside immediately and a further 2% each year thereafter.

The Community also offers support for farmers to carry out 'extensification'. In areas where there is a surplus of at least 20% farmers qualify by reducing their production capacity or using less intensive practices. This latter method involves the reduced used of fertilisers and pesticides, fulfilling another Community aim.

Transitional aid is offered for farmers to move into new markets. Diversification into flowers and ornamental plants, medicinal plants, aromatic herbs, various kinds of berries and fruits, and plants helpful to the textile or chemical industry are all encouraged. Alternative uses of land for leisure, such as riding, also qualify.

An essential part of new policies is careful monitoring of agricultural production and Community expenditure so that the problems of the 1980s are not repeated.

The existing stocks were a problem. At the end of 1986 there were 1.3 million tonnes of unsaleable butter, 850 000 tonnes of skimmed milk powder and nearly 15 million tonnes of cereal. The cost of disposing of them was estimated at ECU 7 billion, about a third of the entire agricultural budget.

In 1987 a special disposal programme was started. Money was allocated for the programme. One million tonnes of butter was exported over two years, and some was sold off cheaply to consumers in the Community. By 1989 the butter mountain had disappeared. A similar approach has been adopted with the other mountains.

Activity 6.7   What prevented the EC eliminating all its surpluses by donating them to developing countries (especially those suffering famines) and what stopped some of the developing countries accepting the produce that was offered?

To safeguard farmers from hardship a number of methods were adopted. Small farmers were totally or partially exempted from levies and quotas. There was direct income aid. To avoid this artificially ensuring the long-term survival of inefficient farms it was made transitional – limited to five years. There was also an early retirement scheme.

CAP IN THE FUTURE   Future policies will target the less favoured regions.

The Commission anticipates that the population in rural areas close to large conurbations will increase as industries and services move to the periphery of the cities or into the surrounding countryside. Residential and leisure developments will compete with modern intensive farming for this space.

More remote areas will suffer from depopulation and ageing of the remaining population.

Encouragement will be given to the development of medium-sized communities, spread throughout the regions, rather than a few compact large developments. The development of businesses which revitalise rural regions, for example those involving research and science, will be supported.

Alternatives to food crops will be encouraged. The growing of timber, for example, has long-term benefits.

The Commission hopes that strict rules will be introduced to govern the application of manure and mineral fertilisers to prevent the leaching of nitrates and phosphates into the groundwater, and the limitation of pesticides. It also wants to introduce regulations that prevent unnecessary suffering in the production methods associated with animals.

There is a shift in demand for foodstuffs, away from staple foods such as bread and potatoes to fresh fruit, green vegetables, and expensive types of meat, because the public is becoming more health-conscious. This can be seen in the demand for 'natural' foods even where these are more highly priced.

There is also a demand for pre-cooked foods and greater variety, especially as people eat more food that is derived from other Community countries.

The CAP must further facilitate the movement of produce between member states.

Regional policy

There are large differences in the prosperity and levels of development in the various regions of the Community. The difference between the region with the highest income in the Community and the one with the lowest income is twice as great as the income difference in the USA. The difference between highest and lowest unemployment figures is three times as great.

There are several specific handicaps corresponding to these differences. Businesses considering setting up in an area want a good network of roads and railways, a good telephone system, and pleasant living conditions for its employees, including shops and housing.

Differences like these are harmful to the Community. Those in the less-favoured areas need to know that they are not doomed to suffer an ever-widening divergence. The prosperous areas are also often densely populated and in danger of ecological damage.

Three Community funds exist to deal with regional disparities:

- the European Regional Development Fund set up to reduce regional imbalances;
- the European Social Fund which supports vocational training, retraining of workers, and recruitment of young people;
- the Guidance Section of the European Agricultural Guidance and Guarantee Fund which supports schemes to improve conditions for agricultural production and marketing.

The targets for these funds are shown in Figure 6.2.

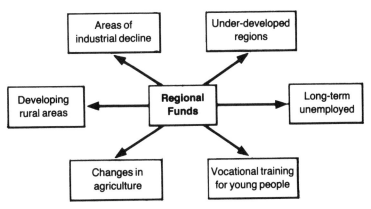

Figure 6.2 Applications of European Community regional funds

The problems encountered include:

- inadequate infrastructures such as transport, sewerage, water and power supplies, and telecommunications;

- weak or outdated production methods, or products that don't suit the current market;
- agriculture with the wrong products or poor technology; improvements must avoid overproduction and poorly thought-out modernisation;
- urban decay and rural depopulation which cause social and environmental problems as well as economic ones;
- unemployment which causes particular problems for young first-time job seekers and for workers with few or inappropriate qualifications.

Schemes supported by the funds are a partnership between the Community, national, regional and local organisations. They must arise from local initiatives so that there is sufficient motivation and appropriate actions. But the decision on funding must be taken at Community level.

Regions identified for the receipt of aid because they are deemed to be under-developed are Greece, Portugal, much of Spain, Southern Italy, Sicily, Corsica and Sardinia, Ireland, and Northern Ireland.

Those targetted as areas of industrial decline are scattered throughout the Community but the biggest concentrations are in the UK (Wales, Midlands, North and Southern Scotland) and Northern France.

Rural areas targetted for development are mainly in France and Northern Spain, together with Northern Scotland, Cumbria, Wales and the South-West of England.

Activity 6.8   Choose one region and suggest how you would apply the funds to achieve improvements.

Social policy

The Community Charter of Fundamental Social Rights for Workers (the 'Social Charter') was approved by the Strasbourg Heads of Government meeting in December 1989. At its meeting in Madrid the previous June, the Council of Ministers concluded that 'in the context of the establishment of the Single European Market, the same importance must be attached to the social aspects as to the economic aspects and therefore they must be developed in a balanced manner'. The Commission drew up a 45-point 'Action Programme' to give legislative form to those parts of the Social Charter where legislation was deemed to be essential.

There was only one dissenter at the Heads of Government summit in Strasbourg. Mrs Thatcher, then Prime Minister of the UK, described the Social Charter as 'more like a socialist charter' and 'full of unnecessary constraints and regulations'.

The Charter deals with:

- freedom of movement;
- employment and remuneration;
- improvement of living and working conditions;

- social protection;
- freedom of association and collective bargaining;
- vocational training;
- equal treatment for men and women;
- information, consultation and participation of workers;
- health protection and safety at the workplace;
- protection of children and adolescents;
- elderly persons;
- disabled persons.

In many of the Community countries these topics are covered by legislation. This is less the case in the UK.

Activity 6.9   Obtain a copy of the European file on the Common Charter of Fundamental Social Rights for Workers.

Study the 45 action points.

Identify those that you feel to be 'socialist' and any that you feel 'unnecessary constraints and regulations'.

Research and technology

Research and technology play an increasingly important and central role in modern society.

To get the best value for money in the development and use of technology the EC is aiming for technical standardisation and the opening up of public procurement. Public-sector departments account for 10% of EC spending, and a further 10% is spent by public-sector industries. Before the introduction of open procurement policies, public-sector organisations spent only 2% of their budgets on products and services provided by organisations outside their own country.

The EC's 'Framework programme' is a policy designed to target research into six key areas, as follows.

QUALITY OF LIFE   To improve the quality of life funds have been channelled into medical research (particularly cancer and AIDS), age-related health problems (senile dementia, cataracts, etc.), early detection programmes and medical technology. Because natural radiation accounts for 70% of the radiation to which the population is exposed (half arising from the radioactive gas radon which occurs naturally in rock) radiation protection is also being investigated.

The quality of the environment has a direct effect upon people's lives. Research is being carried out into soil protection, pollution pathways, measures to improve the quality of surface water (in rivers, lakes and the sea), processing of toxic and dangerous waste, dieback of forests (acid rain is now thought to be less significant in this), and the impact of human activities on climate systems.

INFORMATION TECHNOLOGY/ TELECOM- MUNICATIONS

ESPRIT was the first EC programme for research and development in information technology, beginning in the early 1980s. It has developed office systems, computer-integrated manufacture (robots, computer-aided design, etc.), and advanced information processing methods (such as voice recognition and synthesis).

The *RACE* programme is concerned with ensuring that telecommunication systems and services developed in Europe remain consistent.

DELTA is a programme concerned with the development of computer-aided education; *AIM* is funding development of biocomputing and medical computing; *DRIVE* is developing aids to road traffic flow (route guidance, navigation systems, vehicle-to-vehicle communications) and vehicle safety.

INDUSTRIAL TECHNOLOGY

The *BRITE* programme is concerned with new technologies, particularly in the motor industry, chemicals, textiles, aircraft, shipbuilding, machine tools, civil engineering, etc. These traditional industries are still of great economic importance.

EURAM helps in the development of sophisticated materials (metals, ceramics, etc.) that currently have to be imported under American or Japanese licence.

There are also developments to make measurement and analytical results more uniform throughout the Community.

BIOLOGICAL RESOURCES

Biotechnology includes areas such as genetics, microbiology, biophysics, bio-informatics, with applications in agriculture, the food industry, pharmaceuticals, medicine and environmental protection.

Europe had been suffering from fragmented research, with duplication and teams working in isolation. The Commission tries to minimise wasted effort by disseminating information on the various projects. It is sometimes hampered by the desire to be first (among researchers and national governments).

ENERGY

The 12 member states, along with Sweden and Switzerland, are carrying out research into nuclear fusion energy. This has the advantage that no radioactive waste is generated. Non-nuclear types of energy are also being investigated, including solar energy, wind power, geothermal power, energy from biomass, and new sources of solid fuels. Energy conservation is also being addressed.

Monetary policy

EUROPEAN CURRENCY UNIT (ECU)

The ECU came into existence in 1979 when the European Monetary System (EMS) was launched. Within the EMS arrangement, currencies are only allowed to fluctuate within narrow ranges around a central rate. The central rate is calculated on the basis of the ECU, a weighted average of all EC currencies.

The ECU is the sole unit of account in the EC. Its value is revised periodically to reflect the relative economic strength of each member state. It offers stability in terms of interest rates and exchange rates.

The ECU is used, not only as the basis for the divergence indicator of individual currencies, but also for measuring the creditor and debtor imbalance of the individual nations and as a means of settlement between the EMS's central banks.

The commercial banks were the first main users of the ECU outside the EC institutions. It is estimated that about 10 billion ECUs are dealt with every day in foreign exchange dealings between banks in member states. ECUs are increasingly being used as the unit for short- and long-term loans.

The ECU is used extensively by EC and many non-EC countries, including most major industrialised countries for business transactions. This means that firms can invoice in ECUs rather than a national currency.

Italy, France and Belgium are leading the way in the range and proportion of transactions in ECUs. Transactions in ECUs offer simplified cash management and lower costs for multinational businesses and fewer exchange risks (due to the ECU's predictability) in pricing, invoicing, payments and financing.

ECUs are not as yet used extensively by individuals. However, their use would have benefits for travellers to avoid the inconvenience of carrying numerous currencies and the cost of changing currency. ECU bank cards and travellers' cheques are accepted by all EC banks and some hotels. In France and Italy there are advantageous ECU life assurance policies.

Activity 6.10

Design coins and notes for the ECU.

You will need to consider size and shape, pictures and emblems, words, and values.

EXCHANGE RATE MECHANISM (ERM)

In October 1990 the UK joined the ERM, 11 years after it began operating, the tenth nation to join (Greece and Portugal being the others not in at that time).

The main reason was the prospect of greater exchange rate stability which meant that businesses could plan and invest with greater certainty.

ERM is also design to combat inflation. Sterling is pegged to the Deutschmark, a low inflation/low interest rate currency. The economic discipline of keeping sterling within 6% (later 2.25%) of the DM should help control rising prices.

Each currency has a central rate against the others set by the Central Bank governors and finance ministers. Eight of the currencies fluctuate within a band of 2.25% of their central value. The £ and the peseta can fluctuate by 6% on either side of their central value.

Currencies are kept within their bands by bank intervention. For example, if the franc falls to its lowest permitted value against the Deutschmark the French and German central banks buy francs and sell Deutschmarks to increase the value of the franc. Other European central banks may be asked to participate in the intervention. Central banks have access to unlimited short-term credit to finance such intervention.

Instead of intervention a country may use domestic monetary policy to keep its currency within the limits. For example, raising interest rates will strengthen the currency.

If intervention and monetary policy fail to keep the currency within its limits the government may agree to a realignment (i.e. revaluation or devaluation). This is a last resort and has been used only 12 times since 1979, the most recent being devaluation of the lira by 3.7% against the Deutschmark in 1990.

EUROPEAN MONETARY UNION

In June 1988 a committee under the chairmanship of President Delors made far-reaching proposals about measures to achieve the objective of economic and monetary union in the EC.

Monetary Union operates so that policies are managed jointly with a view to attaining common macro-economic objectives.

This means each country giving up some of its independence in the economic policies it follows. Just how much these policies are independent now is strongly debated but it is clear that there is some inter-dependence among European economies.

No one is prepared to say what constitutes 'full' Monetary Union.

However, some moves have been made towards monetary union. The Single European Act brings about a single market within which persons, goods, services and capital can move freely. There are measures aimed at achieving competition and a market economy and common policies for structural change and regional development. The European Monetary System operates to stabilise exchange rates and there is some co-ordination of economic policies.

As yet, there are no binding rules to govern national budgetary policies. Such rules would impose upper limits on budget deficits of individual member states, exclude access to direct central bank credit and limit the recourse to external borrowing from non-EC countries.

HOW FAR SHOULD WE GO?

Supporters of a single currency for the whole of the EC look to the USA as their model. The USA is a nation of over 240 million people, divided into 50 states. There are no barriers to trade between the states and they share just 1 currency.

As part of the Delors plan for European Monetary Union there would be a single European currency under the control of a European System of Central Banks (ESCB), operating across Europe rather like the Bank of England operates in the UK. Since it would determine a single interest rate for the whole of Europe as well as controlling the currency, its structure and accountability would be of critical importance and the subject of very strong debate.

In 1990, the UK proposed an alternative to a single currency – the 'hard' ECU. Essentially this is a thirteenth currency for which there would be notes and coins so that it could be used as an alternative to the national currencies, without immediately replacing them.

Activity 6.11   Consider the suggestion for a thirteenth currency – the 'hard' ECU – to be used as well as the existing national currencies. Separate exchange rates and interest rates could still exist.

Should this be the ultimate goal, or would you prefer to see a single currency with all this implies for economic policies?

Foreign affairs

The EC is large enough to be a real force in world affairs. However, it is much 'younger' than Japan and the USA and is still growing as more countries join the Community. It is understandable, therefore, that its primary concerns are to sort out the relationships between member countries and to establish Community organisations that democratically determine policy and deal with regional differences.

The Community's history as an economic grouping of countries has meant that the economy was the first area in which it took an international role. In the GATT (General Agreement on Tariffs and Trade) and in the North Atlantic Fisheries Organisation the EC (through the Commission) speaks on behalf of the member countries.

By 1986 imports to and exports from the EC represented about 9.6% of its GDP. This compares with 7.2% for the USA and 8.5% for Japan. The EC's share of world trade was 19% compared with the USA's 17% and Japan's 10%.

It negotiates, on behalf of the member countries, on customs procedures, franchises, import quotas, protection against unfair foreign competition, and export credits.

The Community has had agreements with the other European Free Trade Association (EFTA) countries (Switzerland, Austria, Sweden, Norway, Iceland and Finland) since 1973. Trade with the EFTA countries accounts for about 25% of EC trade.

International trade is currently the most important basis for the EC's external relations, but not the only one.

The EC has views on research, science and the environment. It also contributes to the development of the Third World.

Because member countries retain sovereign control over their foreign policies it has been difficult to develop a common policy and a single voice on topics such as defence and human rights.

Progress was made by consultation to reach a European foreign policy on human rights in South Africa (where again Mrs Thatcher of the UK was a dissenting voice), on the Palestinian problem, Afghanistan, Central America, disarmament and terrorism.

However, the Gulf War of 1990, and the attempt at deposing President Gorbachev in the USSR in August 1991, made it clear that a quick response was often needed.

There are frequent high-level talks with developed countries such as Canada, the USA, Japan, Australia and New Zealand, and with state-controlled countries like the People's Republic of China and Romania. The well-established links with Romania, Hungary and Comecon (an East European economic association) was one of the factors that assisted in democratisation and moves toward market economies in Eastern Europe.

Summary

1 The Community budget is about 1% of the total national budgets.

2 The Common Agricultural Policy (CAP) accounted for 67% in 1989, decreasing to 59% of the budget in 1990. It aims to ensure continuity of supply, stable prices, protection of the environment, and to facilitate technological change. It achieves this by intervention in the internal market and protection against external competition.

3 The Regional Policy accounted for 10% of the budget in 1989, rising to 12% in 1990. It encompasses the Regional Development Fund which is used to reduce regional imbalance, and the European Social Fund which is used to reduce unemployment, facilitate the movement of labour, and provide training schemes.

4 The Social Fund (7% in 1989, 9% in 1990) is used to improve living and working conditions, provide social protection, especially for children, the elderly, and the disabled, improve health and safety, and support equal opportunity policies.

5 The Research and Technology budget (3% in 1989, 4.7% in 1990) deals with information technology, telecommunications, industrial and bio-technology, energy, the environment, and transport.

6 The Community is working towards more widespread use of the European Currency Unit (ECU), a tight Exchange Rate Mechanism (ERM), and European monetary union (EMU).

7 Other areas where closer co-operation is sought are: overseas aid, foreign affairs, defence, the environment.

Assignment 6   **THE EUROPEAN COMMUNITY**

Background

'Britain is alone as the date is set for monetary union' (*The Times*, 29 October 1990).

'They know they cannot change the Treaty of Rome without British consent' (*The Times*, 29 October 1990).

'EC bid to break deadlock on farm subsidies' (*The Guardian*, 6 November 1990).

What is the process for formulating and implementing policies in the EC?

What subjects does the EC have policies on, and, briefly, what are those policies?

How are businesses affected by those policies?

Activity

Work individually.

Write a speech to be given to the local Chamber of Commerce.

You will need notes to assist you in delivering the speech. You will also need handouts and/or visual aids to enhance the presentation.

Be prepared to answer questions at the end of the speech.

7 Single European Market

Why have a single market?

The opening lines of the 1957 Treaty of Rome stated that:

> 'The Community shall have as its task, by establishing a common market and progressively approximating the economic policies of member states, to promote throughout the Community a harmonious development of economic activities, a continuous and balanced expansion, an increase in stability, an accelerated raising of the standard of living and closer relations between the states belonging to it'.

Despite the clear terms of the Treaty, during the period following its signing many barriers to the Single Market remained. These included barriers to the free movement of people, varying national technical specifications, health and safety standards and environmental regulations, differences in quality controls and taxation.

The recession of the 1970s tended to make member states focus on the protection of their national markets. There was increasing awareness that unless Europe could create a single market by bringing together its separate national markets it would lose ground to Japan and the USA.

Paolo Cecchini carried out a study of the likely effects of a single European market. He concluded that the economic gain to the Community, expressed in 1988 prices, would be about 200 billion ECU, or about 5% of the

Community's GDP. It would deflate consumer prices by about 6% and boost output, employment and living standards. The direct cost of frontier formalities, he estimated, was equivalent to adding 1.8% to prices, and making arrangements to accommodate the differing national technical regulations added another 2%. The considerable potential for economies of scale could reduce costs by between 1% and 7%.

What does a single market mean in practice? It means free movement of people, goods, services and capital. These are ambitious targets. In reading the following sections, ask yourself, to what extent they have been achieved.

THE FREE MOVEMENT OF PEOPLE

EC nationals and foreign tourists are not subject to checks at the frontiers between member states. There is good co-operation between the member states to control drug trafficking, terrorism and other crime.

Students are free to choose their university and study in any member country. Their degrees and diplomas are recognised throughout the Community.

Employees and the self-employed can reside in any member country of their choice for the purpose of employment and can remain there after termination of employment. There is no discrimination on the grounds of nationality so that employees can seek work and be employed on the same terms, and with the same career chances, as the nationals of that country.

Figure 7.1 European Community passport

FREE
MOVEMENT OF
GOODS

Goods can move freely through the Community without being delayed at internal frontiers. Producers have genuine access to a market of over 320 million consumers. The harmonisation of technical standards, production methods, and consumer protection prevent there being any barriers to trade.

Economies of scale ensure that research and development is cost effective and consumers have a wide range of better and cheaper products.

Health and safety of consumers and the public is safeguarded to an equally high level throughout the Community.

Individuals and businesses can choose where in the Community to be based, without hindrance.

FREE
MOVEMENT OF
SERVICES

Companies are able to offer their services throughout the Community and consumers are free to choose the best service at the best price.

Airlines have the freedom to operate frequently to whatever destinations they choose, producing competition that keeps fares low and improves service, but must maintain high safety standards. Road transport makes rational use of the vehicles available, at lowest cost and with minimum paperwork.

Co-operation in research and harmonisation of technical standards ensure that telecommunications are widely available and use the latest technology. European television offers the widest range of channels, programmes and services allowing people to demonstrate the tremendous range of cultures and creativity.

FREE
MOVEMENT OF
CAPITAL

People can travel throughout the Community using a currency of their choice without restriction, and ultimately, perhaps, there will be a single currency.

Individuals and companies can transfer funds freely in all the member states. Everyone is free to invest or save wherever he or she likes within the Community.

There is freedom of choice, from a Community-wide range of services, in the areas of banking, insurance, savings, mortgages, loans and leasing.

Activity 7.1

List the barriers that existed (or perhaps still exist) that affect you personally.

Hint: compare the freedoms in Europe with the restrictions when travelling to or dealing with elsewhere in the world.

The Single European Act

The Single European Act, which came into force on 1 July 1987, was aimed at removing the barriers to Europe becoming a single market.

The Act describes the internal market as 'an area without internal frontiers in which the free movement of goods, persons, services and capital is ensured'.

Unlike previous attempts to remove barriers, the SEA aimed to be completely comprehensive. It sought to create, step by step, an integrated and coherent framework. It didn't tackle just one economic area, it didn't favour any single European state, nor did it concentrate on minimal proposals that would be easily acceptable to all the states.

The result was, as Jacques Delors (President of the European Commission) said: 'In the first six months of 1988 the Community took more decisions than in the ten years from 1974 to 1984'.

The Act focused on why each barrier existed, and the consequences of removing it.

Take, for example, the internal frontiers. These frontiers maintained public security and controlled entry and exit of travellers, particularly illegal immigrants, criminals and terrorists. They ensured that the movement of goods and animals met with national health standards. They allowed VAT and excise duties to be collected.

Activity 7.2   **1** Has the removal of frontiers given the criminal, drug smuggler and terrorist the freedom to move without hindrance?

2 What measures would you take if you were in charge of crime prevention?

Removing barriers on the movement of just people cannot achieve the aim of a single market. It is also necessary to remove the restrictions on the movement of goods which arise from environmental control, health and safety standards, consumer protection, and technical differences. The reasons for the differences had to be examined, where possible eliminated, hence removing barriers to the movement of goods.

Less obvious were the restrictions on the freedom to provide services in different countries. International trade negotiations – notably the 'Uruguay Round' – had made less progress on liberalising services than they had on manufactured goods.

It was clear when the Single European Act was being formlated that it would take time for the barriers to be identified and analysed, and then dismantled by suitable legislation. A timescale was agreed – all barriers would be removed by midnight on 31 December 1992, making 1 January 1993 the truly effective date.

The completion of the internal market makes certain regions more attractive than others. Policies are needed to ensure that the less-advantaged areas receive help. The Single European Act is closely tied to regional and other EC policies, including employment, transport, agriculture and competition, some of which were discussed in the last chapter.

The Community's new rules also seek to prevent businesses fixing prices, making agreements on market shares, or setting quotas, all of which would interfere with fair competition. Governments are prevented from favouring particular firms in their own country by special grants or tax advantages.

The interests of each member state have to be weighed in the balance of the interests of the Community as a whole and each Community law has to be painstakingly translated into national laws.

A key feature that helps in implementing the Single European Act is the qualified majority voting by which legislation can be carried through the Council of Ministers. The need for a unanimous vote is retained for delicate issues such as indirect taxation (VAT and excise duties), fiscal provisions, the free movement of people, and the rights and interests of workers.

There is a great deal of inertia.

In order to study the Act in detail, it is useful to divide it into three categories:

1 removal of physical barriers;
2 removal of technical barriers;
3 removal of financial barriers.

A study of these is carried out in the sections that follow.

REMOVAL OF PHYSICAL BARRIERS

Frontier controls are not just a physical constraint but also an economic constraint, imposing a burden on industry flowing from formalities, delays and handling charges while goods are checked.

The removal of barriers is controversial at a time when there are major terrorist threats and the abuse of drugs is on the increase.

It is generally accepted that controls are needed to check upon people and goods entering and leaving the Community. At all the points of entry and departure (land, sea and air) there need to be checks. It is necessary, therefore to distinguish between internal and external movements to remove the unnecessary delays and costs.

Activity 7.3

If we remove the frontiers so that movement of people and goods is unrestricted within the EC, but retain the frontiers between EC and non-EC countries we still have to suffer the delays and bureaucracy when crossing, for example from Germany to Italy, through Switzerland.

What can be done about this?

PEOPLE

Travellers are stopped at frontiers for reasons of immigration and tax. Police and immigration officials screen travellers to check their passports or ID cards and, if necessary, to search them. It is also necessary to check whether travellers owe the tax on the goods they are carrying with them (note that it is 'tax'; 'customs duties' haven't existed since 1967 and 'customs' signs were removed from borders by 1 January 1988).

Although the movement of Community citizens is not hindered under the terms of the Single European Act, the movement of non–Community nations will still be monitored.

GOODS

There are 3 reasons why goods are checked: administrative, fiscal and health. These include collecting statistics, monitoring the import and export of restricted goods (weapons, high-technology products, etc.), enforcing trade quotas, collecting tax, controlling plant and animal diseases, keeping out banned products, and many more.

By 1988 the administrative checks had been moved away from internal frontiers. The introduction of a single administrative document on 1 January 1988 simplified the procedures. The second stage, to finish by the end of 1992, was to co-ordinate policies and develop common legislation so that the internal controls are made redundant.

Barriers to free trade also arise from enforcing different health and hygiene standards. The Community's objective was to raise standards in all member states to the highest levels. Checks at the source and destination, and spot-checks *en route* could then monitor standards as they do for any 'domestic' movement of goods.

Countries limit the import and export of goods as a means of controlling their economy and assisting domestic businesses. Tariffs and quotas are 2 ways of achieving the control. The Single European Market implies that there must be no tariffs or quotas on the movement of goods or services between EC countries.

TRANSPORT

Transport regulations concerned with the safety of road transport (the so-called 'construction and use' regulations) are concerned not only with the vehicles themselves, but also the training of drivers, working hours, etc.

When the Single European Act came into force there were quotas restricting the number of cross-frontier journeys that hauliers could make, and safety checks were often made on lorries at the frontiers. The removal of quotas, and the harmonisation of safety standard differences so that frontier checks were no longer needed, helped achieve a more open transport network.

REMOVAL OF TECHNICAL BARRIERS

HARMONISATION OF PRODUCTS

Prior to the completion of the Single European Market, British chocolate could not be sold as 'chocolate' in some member states because of differences in definition. German law prohibited the sale on its territory of beers brewed in other member states because additives in them contravened the German national purity laws. In Britain we would insist that a Frankfurter sausage included the word 'Frankfurter' in its name to distinguish it from our familiar British sausage.

Thus there were many restrictions, some of them apparently petty, which prevented the sale of the products manufactured in one member state in some of the others. In some cases it was the product that was unacceptable, in others it was the packaging, or a description that was misleading.

The difficulties arose because of different standards for safety, health, environment and consumer protection. Years have been spent on trying to reach agreement on technical minutiae.

The way of overcoming the problems was *harmonisation*. This involved adjusting national regulations to an agreed Community standard.

The public often see efforts towards harmonisation as bureaucratic interference from Brussels and the myth has developed that the Community is trying to create 'Europroducts'. Nothing could be further from the truth. There is a big difference between 'harmonisation' and 'standardisation'.

The aim is to ensure that there is a universally high standard of safety, health and hygiene, and descriptions that are understood by all the Community's peoples. Member states will no longer be able to keep out another state's competing products simply because they are slightly different from their own.

The Commission is concerned that consumers have the widest possible choice and that products meet acceptable standards in terms of consumer health and safety. On the other hand it wants producers to have the opportunity to market their products throughout the large European market, achieving economies of scale and reductions in product development costs, without restrictions upon competition.

In the area of food and drink, for example, it is now possible for the consumer to choose between yoghurts with or without fruit, pasta made from durum or soft wheat, and beer made entirely from natural ingredients or including artificial additives.

In some areas the Commission does aim for standardisation. For example in telecommunications and other similar high-technology areas where the equipment needs to interlink.

Activity 7.4 Water and air pollution know no boundaries. What can be done about clouds of toxic gas that float across frontiers, or polluted rivers that flow into EC countries?

EDUCATION AND PROFESSIONAL TRAINING

A prerequisite of getting many jobs is to be properly qualified. This involves acquiring knowledge and skills and getting a certificate to prove that you have them.

Differences in knowledge and skills form educational barriers to the free movement of people. As part of progress towards the SEM these need to be analysed and any true differences (usually related to the technology) separated from the *pseudo-differences* that arise from different descriptions of knowledge and skills. True differences can only be overcome by harmonisation of the qualifications and training. Pseudo-differences can be overcome by redefining the knowledge and skills in a commonly recognised way.

Education remains primarily a matter for national policy but if people are to have the ability to move between member states for jobs their education, training and qualifications need to be recognised and valued throughout the Community.

This is most obvious in the area of professional people. Progress was first achieved in the health sector. Doctors, nurses, dentists, veterinary surgeons and midwives have had their basic training harmonised and thus have the 'right of establishment' – in other words the right to practise in all EC countries. Progress has also been made in the agriculture, forestry and horticultural sectors, and in mining, electricity, gas, oil and water industries.

Individuals holding equivalent qualifications can practise their expertise in another state. Where there are significant differences in the qualifications there is a need for a period of 'supervised practice' before full rights to practise are given.

Because it is very difficult to make valid comparisons between the educational systems of member countries the principle of 'mutual recognition' is applied to the qualification rather than the training (university, non-university, on-the-job experience). There also has to be a mutual trust between the countries which says 'if they are qualified to practise in . . . then they must be good enough to practise it here'.

Activity 7.5   Professions like medicine, dentistry, veterinary surgery, nursing, architecture are usually mentioned as being free of restriction to practise within the EC, because they were the first to agree recognition of qualifications across the boundaries.

Choose some professions or trades that you are interested in and investigate whether the professional and trade organisations that offer qualifications and regulate practice have achieved the same level of recognition.

SERVICES   Management consultancy, banking and insurance, transport, information technology, bingo halls and laundrettes all fall within the realm of services.

In many ways a service can be likened to a product in that it is *produced* and *sold* by the supplier and *bought* and *consumed* by the customer.

The same service, in different countries, may be *genuinely* different (e.g. a mortgage may be offered under different terms, have different rules for payment, legal obligations, etc.) or it may be different only in the *packaging*, i.e. the way it is described.

Harmonisation seeks to eliminate pseudo-differences if they conceal the genuine differences in what services consist of. It also aims to 'level-up' the quality of service offered.

It is important to distinguish between *standardisation* which means 'making the same', and *harmonisation* which allows the supplier to compete fairly and the consumer to choose on the basis of reliable and consistent data.

In the area of financial services the Commission is concerned with the protection of investors, depositors and policy-holders. If people are to obtain financial services from anywhere within the Community there must be acceptable standards of financial security to which all banks and insurance companies conform. It also means that the information given in prospectuses must be unambiguous bearing in mind the different cultures and backgrounds of people in the various countries.

TRANSPORT   Transport was in the past, a highly regulated market with restrictions on competition. Measures have taken place to deregulate all methods of transport – road, rail, inland waterways, marine and air – but at the time of writing considerable protectionism still exists. For example, a cartel exists in most of the world that considerably reduces competition between airlines. This applies in Europe where almost all of the larger airlines are owned by national governments. Air fares are fixed by agreement between governments that effectively prevent services being offered more cheaply. Fares are higher than they need be. It is as expensive to fly by a scheduled flight from London to Athens as it is from London to New York.

NEW
TECHNOLOGY

The development of new technology, particularly in the areas of aerospace, computing and telecommunications, is very expensive. Agreements have in the past been arrived at between companies and between governments. The Commission is concerned to make these more widespread so that technology will advance at a rate that at least equals Japan and the USA.

At the end of 1986 the European television scene was transformed by the advent of Europe's first television satellites. As a result people with the necessary equipment gained an unprecedented volume of television programmes. An international audience requires programmes that are different from a local or national base.

Prior to this there had already been a spread of cable networks and satellites had been used extensively for communications.

No single state will be able to provide, at competitive rates, the amount of equipment and programmes required by these technological advances.

The Commission supports the free circulation of programmes throughout the Community. To back this up there has to be a legal and technological framework that doesn't have national barriers. National laws on advertising, sponsorship and the protection of young people need to be harmonised. The different standards for the transmission and reception of signals (PAL, SECAM, etc.) have to be replaced.

Activity 7.6

Plan the programme for a week's transmission of a new TV station to cover Europe. Remember that you will be dealing with people who speak different languages and have different cultures.

Begin by researching how the satellite stations deal with the difficulties, and how the early-morning ITV chooses its international topics.

BUSINESS
METHODS

Each country had its own legal framework covering the creation and regulation of businesses. In the UK, for example, there are *sole traders*, *partnerships*, and *limited companies*. An optional form of company structure is proposed and a harmonisation of company laws will be developed. Progress has also been made in harmonising the national accounting methods and laws. Other areas that have to be developed are company taxation and liquidation rules and cross–frontier mergers.

Each member country has its own methods of protection for intellectual rights and products. These include copyright, patents and trade marks. The proposal is that there should be a single registration system and a unified appeals procedure.

The development of computers has prompted the introduction of legislation, in the UK, to prevent unauthorised access to data, copying of software, etc. Biotechnology is another area where new developments in the industry create legal and ethical issues.

REMOVAL OF FINANCIAL BARRIERS

Whenever goods are moved from one country to another, they are elaborately documented at the border so that the authorities can collect the taxes – VAT and excise duty.

We ensure that tax accrues to the country where the goods are finally consumed. There is a system of remission on exports and imposition on imports, similar to the division into 'outputs' and 'inputs' when keeping records of VAT within a company.

Without checks at the frontier that goods are actually crossing the border it would be impossible to verify that claims for refund of VAT for exported goods were valid. It would be too easy for a trader to claim that goods had been exported, and hence were zero-rated, and then sell them on the home market and pocket the VAT collected. Alternatively they could sell at a reduced price, undercutting their competitors.

Without frontier controls there would also be a great temptation for private individuals and traders to simply go to low-tax countries, buy goods there, and take them home for their own use or onward sale off the record.

One way of removing the problem is to reduce the disparities between countries' tax levels to the point where there is no longer the incentive to 'cheat the system'. This does not mean having exactly the same rates, it does mean having differences at which there is no worthwhile gain. The USA is an example of where this applies. In the USA they found that differences of up to 6% between the sales taxes of adjoining states didn't appear to distort trade significantly.

The proposal within the EC is for a 2-rate system, a standard rate for most goods and services, and a reduced rate for necessities. Countries are free to fix their standard rate between 14 and 20% and the lower rate between 4 and 9%. With the main excise duties – on oil products, alcoholic drinks and tobacco products – the degree of harmonisation proposed is designed to ensure that even when added to VAT, the tax element in the price of the goods should not differ enough for that to be an incentive for cross-border shopping.

VAT is now a source of EC budget funds. Some countries are net exporters, while others have a net surplus of imports. This information may be derived by accumulating individual traders' VAT returns. The VAT collected to a central fund can then be reallocated to the individual countries appropriately.

COMPETITION – IS IT FAIR?

Legislation arising from the Single European Act is concerned with preventing anything interfering with 'fair competition'. Powers to achieve this were taken as long ago as 1962, although most transport was excluded for many years, and as late as 1991 international air services between the EC and external countries, and domestic air services within member states were still not covered.

The legislation seeks to prevent price fixing, agreeing to share a market between what would otherwise be competitors, 'ganging up' to discriminate against third parties and imposing territorial restrictions which partition the common market. However, it only applies to businesses of an appreciable size, or having a significant part of the market, and is specifically aimed at restrictions in international competition.

Some exemptions are allowed. Patents and the licensing of knowledge and expertise is permitted, and so is franchising, co-operative research and development, motor vehicle distribution, cargo liner activities, and small road and water transport undertakings.

Undertakings that have a dominant position in a market are prohibited from misusing their market power by predatory pricing, limiting production, markets or technical development, refusing to supply, or imposing discriminatory trading conditions.

The Community has the power to prohibit mergers between companies that would lead to or strengthen a dominant position, harming competition.

Governments sometimes give financial or other aid to companies in their country. The justification for such subsidies or other aid is examined by the Commission to decide whether the help they give to achieving Community objectives outweighs the loss of competition.

Governments, local authorities, schools, hospitals and other public agencies represent huge purchasing power in each of the Community countries. They often place orders for goods or services with local suppliers or arrange for work to be carried out by local contractors even when better qualified competitors in other member states might be interested in the contracts. The cost of such lack of competition was estimated at 20 billion ECU in 1989. Legislation has been implemented that makes it illegal for restrictions to be placed on tendering and placing of contracts.

The original definition of 'public bodies' is being widened to include organisations operating in the telecommunications, transport, drinking water and energy sectors, where public demand is capable of providing firms with a sufficiently large market to strengthen their world position, even if they are not public-sector organisations. This will, therefore, include many of the utilities privatised in the UK in recent years.

PROTECTING IDEAS

Society needs industrial, commercial and intellectual property to be protected, so as to encourage creative effort, innovation and investment. Much of this protection is provided by patents, trade marks and copyright. Traditionally these were national measures which varied from one country to another, and were only effective within the territory of the country concerned.

Those who wanted to have the benefit of a trade mark, for example, were obliged to take legal measures in every one of the countries in which guaranteed rights were wanted. The rights thus acquired, after multiple procedures, which were often long and costly, would vary from one country to another. In some cases access to a national market would not be possible because rights had already been assigned to a competitor.

The existence of different national legislation makes for protectionist barriers which interfere with free competition and the free movement of goods – basic principles of the Single European Market. The Court of Justice could prohibit the use of a patent or trade mark that is unfair in the sense of disguising illegal agreements between companies, national discrimination, or an attempt to restrict trade between member states. The European treaties do, however, allow import restrictions where these are justified by the need to protect industrial or commercial property rights. The task therefore was to eliminate or reduce the number of occasions where such restrictions could be justified.

The benefits of a unified Community system are:
- fuller, consistent protection;
- administrative simplification;
- the possibility of businesses operating policies better suited to the scale of the Community, free of national barriers;
- easier adaptation of the rules to cope with ever faster technological change, for example in biotechnology and computing; this adaptation could be done by states individually but that would mean doing the work 12 times with the risk of creating new disparities.

EUROPEAN PATENTS
A patent is an official registration which can be requested by the author of an industrial invention or discovery and which gives that author the exclusive right to use the invention for his or her own benefit for a specific period. The author can license a third party to exploit the discovery.

Two conventions have been drawn up for this purpose.

The Munich Convention (1973) came into force in the Community and other Western European countries in 1977 and can be used instead of or in parallel with a national patent. The European patent is relatively expensive but is less onerous and involves fewer procedures than obtaining three or four national patents. The number of applications has risen from 1500 per month in 1980 to over 4000 per month at present.

The Luxembourg Convention (1975) supplements the Munich Convention. Amongst its provisions is a restricton of the exclusive rights conferred by a European patent. If for example, a company holding a patent delays the marketing of a product 'in prejudice of the general interest' then a compulsory licensing system can be forced on it.

COMMUNITY TRADE MARKS
A trade mark is one of the most common ways of protecting a consumer product. There are several million trade marks in the Community and they have no time limit.

Put simply, a trade mark enables the holder to prevent another person or business using an identical or similar distinguishing sign where there would be the risk of confusion in the public mind.

The Community aims to reduce differences in national legislation and has introduced a Community trade mark system. This will provide for:
- a 10-year registration, renewable for another 10 years;

- refusal of registraton if the proposed trade mark is already held by another owner or is unlawful (for example likely to mislead the public);
- a procedure for settling legal disputes in the case of counterfeiting or contested validity.

COPYRIGHT   'Works of the intellect' are not subject to patent or trade mark but they do benefit from national and various international copyright conventions. However there are many gaps and disparities, particularly in publishing contracts and the duration of copyright protection. These are particularly troublesome in fields where the speed of technological progress calls for massive investment, for example the design and production of integrated circuits and computer programs, data banks, and development of new audio and audiovisual formats such as digital recording.

The Community aims to deal with the following.

- Piracy, or unauthorised reproduction for commercial purposes, of films, disks, cassettes, or computer programs.
- Private copying, which poses a real problem in the music sector, where digital recording, in theory, enables anyone to make a copy as good as a studio master recording. The proposal is to guarantee the rights of authors to remuneration, technical limitation of the possibility of reproduction, introduction of a levy on recording material or equipment, etc.
- Right of distribution. Compact discs are practically immune to wear. Television stations and cassette producers vie with cinemas to obtain new films, while the producer may have an interest in commercialising them by stages. The Commission envisages giving recognition to the right of authors to authorise rental of their work, or at least to obtain fair remuneration from the rental.

The Commission aims to protect the author's exclusive rights of reproduction, adaptation and distribution of computer programs and data banks for a period of 50 years. There is also provision for legal protection on the topography of semi-conductor products where the development of a sophisticated microchip can require an investment of 100 million ECU while it costs only 50 000 to 100 000 ECU to plagiarise an existing topography. Similar measures have already been taken in Japan and the USA.

Copyright is also a problem on television programmes because of the spread of television broadcasting across frontiers.

HOW DOES THE
SEM AFFECT
SMALL
BUSINESSES?

Translator: 'I started a by-return fax service for local businesses. Recently I tried marketing in Germany, by fax. This produced so much business that I have had to recruit more people to my business.'

Brewer: 'We joined forces with a larger brewery to export our speciality bottled beer to Italy. They handled the administration and shipping, we produced the beer.'

Manufacturer: 'I make industrial clothing and have recently lost several big customers to Italian competitors.'

Retailer: 'I've been exporting my toys and games, made in the Far East to our designs, for many years. Last year I exhibited at a trade fair in the Netherlands. A Dutch company is now taking a franchise from me.'

Solicitor: 'We were not getting our share of the growing business for European clients setting up in the UK. I now have a link with a Portuguese practice, making it easier to serve clients doing business in both Portugal and the UK.'

Local government contractor: 'I run the refuse disposal services for three local authorities and recently lost one contract to a French competitor.'

The Department of Trade and Industry mounted a campaign to make UK businesses aware of the Single European Act (SEA) and its likely effects.

Some organisations took notice and prepared themselves to take advantage of the opportunities the SEM offered, and to resist the threats from increased competition in the domestic market. Others ignored it.

It is useful to keep monitoring the effects. The DTI suggests that changes and scope for action could be categorised as:

- markets;
- products and services;
- business relationships;
- finance and people.

Activity 7.7   Choose a business in your locality and investigate how the SEM might be affecting it.

Task 1 Markets

Have they observed any changes in their customers' behaviour? Do they have any customers in the public sector? If so, are there firms from other countries trying to sell to them?

Has the company taken any action to find out what foreign competitors there are? If so, have they attempted to assess the strength of the competition, perhaps by buying samples of the competitors' products?

Does the company realise that transport costs are less because there are fewer frontier checks? Does this make the idea of exporting more attractive or make it easier to buy from foreign suppliers?

Is the company aware of any businesses trying to sell to the UK for whom they could act as agent, or with whom they could negotiate reciprocal trading agreements or a joint venture?

Task 2 Products and services

Because barriers have been removed it may not be necessary to have different versions of a product for different countries. On the other hand, common standards, certification and testing methods may mean they have to modify some of their products. Do either of these apply to their company?

Have they needed to offer a wider range of products or a different mix of services to cater for the wider market? Have they needed different sizes or dual labelling?

Is the protection of products and ideas (by patents, trademarks and copyright) still adequate?

Task 3 Business relationships

Has the business considered advertising or attending trade fairs in other countries?

Has it considered using agents, distributors, wholesalers or franchising?

Has it considered setting up a joint venture to overcome the barriers of language and customs, to enhance the product range, or to open up new markets?

Does it know how to find overseas partners (by advertising, talking to suppliers or customers who have foreign links, or by one of the specialist agencies)?

Task 4 Finance and people

Would the company know how to acquire finance for exporting and what grants are available for market research and for attending trade fairs and making promotional visits?

Does the company realise that other countries have different trading conditions, such as different periods of payment?

Does it know how to get credit guarantees?

Has it considered what staff training is needed to develop skills in market research, sales techniques, and export administration?

Note: Always check with your course tutor before contacting anyone outside the college, for study purposes.

Summary

1 The Single European Market (SEM) aims to facilitate harmonious expansion of the EC nations' economies, provide a stable market, and improve the living and working conditions of EC citizens.

2 The Single European Act (SEA) of 1987 committed the member nations to removing barriers to a SEM by the end of 1992.

3 Legislation arising from the SEA removes the physical, technical and financial barriers to the free movement of people, goods and services, and capital. It aims to create fair competition.

4 The SEA leads to harmonisation, not standardisation; to compatibility, not uniformity.

Assignment 7   **THE SINGLE MARKET**

Background

1992 is all about removing barriers

What does this mean for:

1 A local motor trader.
2 A manufacturer of domestic appliances such as washing machines.

3 A high street bank.
4 A supermarket.
5 A pharmacy.

Note: Do not contact any businesses without your tutor's approval.

Activities

Work individually.

Write five short formal reports, intended for the chief executives of these organisations, identifying the barriers that will be removed when the SEM is fully implemented, outlining the timetable for implementation, and explaining the particular different effects on each of the organisations.

Part Three
Living and working in Europe

8 Getting established in another European country

Objectives
1 Considering making a move to another European country? If so, this chapter will get you ready.
2 Making preparations to send appropriate personal belongings.
3 Obtaining documentation to drive in Europe and familiarise yourself with regulations.
4 Knowing how to get medical attention while travelling.
5 Arranging documentation to enter and stay in the country.
6 Finding temporary accommodation and subsequently rent or buy a property.
7 Choosing a form of transport that meets your needs and pocket.
8 Using post and telecommunication services competently in a variety of situations.
9 Comparing the cost of living in European countries, recognising the importance of buying habits and real net income as well as prices and wages.
10 Identifying food, personal and household products, and furnishings that are most readily available in the major EC countries.
11 Selecting appropriate places and times to shop.
12 Coping with immediate language needs when arriving to live and work in the country.
13 Identifying the level of language skills needed and prepare a learning programme to acquire them.
14 Being competent in selecting a restaurant, choosing from a menu, and making payment, in other EC countries.
15 Following acceptable patterns of behaviour in a variety of social situations.

Deciding to make a move

Those of you who are studying full time will soon be thinking about the options available to you at the end of the course. It may be that you want to continue in full-time education by proceeding to a higher level course. On the other hand you may be keen to get a job. An increasing number choose to take a 'year out' by travelling or working for a year before resuming studies. Participating in an exchange scheme is also popular.

For those of you who are on a part-time course, probably at the same time as working at a full-time job, the perspective is different. Although you may be studying to improve your career prospects you are not forced into a decision by the end of the course.

For all of you the choice is between staying in the locality where you currently live, or taking the more adventurous step of moving away. How far you move is less and less restricted by country borders. For those of us who live in EC countries the barriers to free movement are fast disappearing.

Whatever your motives for moving to a different country – better employment prospects, opportunities for jobs or courses that aren't available in the UK, learning the language, the climate – it is better if you are well prepared.

Preparations for moving

WHAT SHOULD I TAKE?
When you go to live and work in another European country you will need more than the clothes, packed in a suitcase, that you would take for a holiday.

If you have a car then you may be able to pack your belongings into it but if you are going to travel by rail, air or sea you will need to send some of your belongings in advance. Take with you just the items you need on the journey and for when you first arrive.

There are a number of shipping firms that will transport your belongings. The Post Office will deliver a package, of up to 30 kg, guaranteeing delivery in six to eight weeks.

A trunk is a good way of packing the clothes, etc. that you are able to send in advance. It holds a lot, is light and strong, and relatively cheap.

Personal belongings are not subject to any formalities. Customs officials have the right to check that you are not infringing the regulations such as smuggling goods in excess of the duty-free allowances or goods meant for sale. If you are travelling on business you may take your professional equipment with you but you must not sell it.

Activity 8.1
List the items you would need on the journey to your destination and immediately after arriving.

List the items that could be sent to be delivered up to four weeks after your arrival.

Investigate the cost of travel and shipping.

DRIVING IN EUROPE
If you drive a car in another EC country your UK driving licence is valid for up to three months, or for a year if you take residence in the country. Outside the EC you need an international driving licence.

Community driving licences have existed since 1986. They are valid in the same way as national licences but their designs have been harmonised, together with the conditions under which they are issued.

Third party insurance is required in all EC countries. An insurance 'green card' is recommended. You will not be asked to produce it at the frontier but it proves that you are insured against any damage you may cause while driving.

National symbols ('GB plates', etc.) are still required.

Since 1988 the 'Customs' signs at frontiers have gradually been replaced with signs showing the 12 gold stars in the shape of a circle with a blue background and the name of the country in the middle.

When driving between France, Germany, Belgium, Luxembourg and the Netherlands you can stick on your windscreen a green 8-cm disc which entitles you to cross the frontier without stopping, although only at reduced speed. You may only do this if you and all the passengers are EC nationals and you are complying with the regulations concerning personal belongings and duty-free allowances. Spot checks are sometimes carried out but use of the discs has reduced the queues that often used to form, especially during the summer.

Most EC ports and airports have separate customs and immigration channels for EC nationals to help simplify and speed up the checks.

Regulations concerning the movement of animals and plants from one country to another varies among the member states. Check with the country's embassy or consulate before you go.

Be sure you are familiar with the laws and regulations of the country you are driving in. *Priorité à droite* (vehicles joining a road from the right have priority over those already on it) is a particular problem for UK drivers in France, although it rarely affects you on a rural main road. With the exception of parking and speeding, UK drivers are generally law abiding. This is not true of some other countries' drivers some of whose actions may come as a shock to you. Be prepared for the unexpected. In Germany it is the speed of drivers of high-power cars that you need to beware of. They will expect you to move out of the way as they approach with headlights flashing, and if you don't move there is the distinct possibility of an accident. Paradoxically, whereas the British tend to turn a blind eye towards other people's anti-social behaviour, Germans will not hesitate to tell you when you are doing something that is considered socially unacceptable.

In most EC countries the traffic police are stricter than in the UK. On-the-spot fines have not reached the UK yet but we now have fixed-penalty fines as other countries have had for some time. Disqualification is a much more common occurrence in mainland Europe, and in France, for example, your licence can be taken away at the roadside. Driving under the influence of drink or drugs invites a prison sentence.

MEDICAL ATTENTION EN ROUTE   If you are outside the UK for less than three months in other EC countries then you are entitled to emergency medical, dental and hospital treatment and prescriptions (only hospital treatment if you are self-employed). You must have a form E111 which you can obtain from your local DSS office before you set off. If you don't have this form you may have to pay at the time of treatment and obtain a refund when you return to the UK.

THE FORMALITIES All you need to enter another EC country is an identity card or valid passport. People under the age of 18 need the written permission of their parents. A new-style passport was introduced in 1985. It is still a national passport but its design is harmonised so that the format and content is the same throughout the EC, simplifying and speeding up frontier formalities.

You can spend up to three months in another EC country as a 'tourist'. If you want to stay longer it must be for a specific reason. However, if you go there to take up a job, or to look for a job, there may be formalities to follow.

Taking up residence

GETTING PERMISSION TO STAY If you find a job in another EC country you are entitled to reside there and to be issued with a residence permit by the local authorities. The employment may be part-time but must not be so limited as to be purely marginal. The formalities can be straightforward or difficult, depending on the attitude of officials and their experience of dealing with the situation.

In France, for example, you must apply for a '*carte de séjour*' which entitles you to stay for over three months. You may apply for the *carte de séjour* at the local prefecture or town hall (*mairie*). You will need your passport, birth certificate, three passport photos, and a marriage certificate if appropriate. You must have an approved translation of the birth certificate and marriage certificate. This is best done before leaving the UK, by an approved translator. Your local French Consulate will advise you where one can be found. You must also provide evidence that you have bought, or are renting, accommodation. You will also need evidence of your employment, such as a contract of employment. If you are self-employed then you must have registered with the French Chamber of Commerce.

The entitlement to residence only applies after 1993 for Spanish and Portuguese nationals who find employment in another country, and foreigners who find employment in Spain or Portugal. Even before 1993 there is no restriction on Spaniards and Portuguese being self-employed elsewhere in the EC, or other nationals being self-employed in Spain or Portugal.

The decision to grant or refuse you a permit must be made within six months of your application but you can start your job before you get the permit.

Residence permits can be refused on the grounds of public health, public order or security. Except when the refusal is on grounds of national security it will be accompanied by the reasons and an appeal is possible.

Residence permits are valid throughout the issuing country. For temporary employment (3 to 12 months) they are valid for the period of employment. Where employment is permanent the permits are for at least five years. They are renewable after that and remain valid for one year after you leave the country.

A residence permit cannot be withdrawn on the grounds that you are temporarily incapable of work because of illness or accident, or because you have lost your job involuntarily. You must, however, ask the employment office at your place of residence to issue a certificate confirming that you have become involuntarily unemployed.

If you remain unemployed for more than 12 months, the validity of your residence permit may be shortened to less than 5 years.

If you are in possession of a residence permit its renewal cannot be refused on public health grounds, on the grounds of your financial situation or because your passport has expired. Criminal convictions for minor offences are not in themselves grounds for automatic expulsion.

Once you have found a job in another EC country you are entitled to have your family with you. Family means spouse (husband or wife), children (or grandchildren) under 21, children (or grandchildren) over 21 if they are dependent on you, parents or grandparents (and those of your spouse) if they are dependent on you. Other dependent relatives (including relatives by marriage) may be taken into account.

The spouse and other members of the family do not have to be nationals of an EC country to be entitled to rights of residence. You will all be entitled to the same rights and benefits, and the same obligations, as nationals of the country where you reside. Your family is not required to live with you permanently under the same roof. Provided they are dependent on relatives they are entitled to look for work and take up employment even if they are not nationals of an EC country.

Once you have taken up residence in the country you should register with the British Consulate closest to where you are living and working.

FINDING A PLACE TO LIVE

It is advisable to book initial accommodation in advance. The local tourist office, or your travel agent should be able to help. If this turns out to be unsuitable, or too expensive, you may wish to find new accommodation once you arrive.

Remember you will be staying permanently, not for a short time as you would on holiday or for a college term. You should think about renting a house or apartment, or even buying it.

Look first, before committing yourself to the accommodation. Inspect it and if you are not happy with it ask if there is an alternative. You might wish to avoid accommodation next to the main road, for example. Check whether the price for lodgings includes breakfast, etc. If the price is too high, ask if there is anything cheaper because you may have been shown the most expensive accommodation first.

If you have your own transport, check to see if there are any parking restrictions. If you don't have your own transport, make sure that you can get to and from your college or place of work easily.

As in the UK, local newspapers have advertisements for rented accommodation, houses for sale, etc. In France, for example, the local newspaper's 'annonces classées' (classified ads) usually has sections for 'appartements', 'maisons et villas', etc.

Once you are established in the college or place of work and have made friends, perhaps some of whom live locally, you may be able to get assistance with finding accommodation.

Activity 8.2

1 Determine how you would find accommodation when moving to a new part of the UK, i.e. local newspapers, telephone directories for estate agents.

2 Search out sources of information for your chosen area in the other country. Newspapers and telephone directories are available in main libraries. College libraries could arrange to have a limited range for this and other European studies activities. Foreign newspapers are readily available from shops in big towns and cities. Newspapers such as *The European* contain estate agents' advertisements and major UK estate agents have EC properties on their books.

3 With the aid of a dictionary, make a list of the words and abbreviations used in the advertisements, and their translations. *Hint*: choose advertisements in languages with which you are familiar.

RENTING ACCOMMODATION

In some ways renting accommodation is as complex as buying a property. This arises from the laws giving security to tenants which result in the owner vetting potential tenants very carefully and insisting on comprehensive tenancy agreements.

In much of Continental Europe – France, Germany, Belgium, the Netherlands – the desire to buy property is not as strong as in the UK. Property in these countries does not tend to appreciate in value as much as it has traditionally in the UK. Rented property isn't 'downmarket' as it tends to be in the UK. You can rent an apartment, a house (semi-detached houses are rare in mainland Europe) or even a French château (if you can afford it).

Apartments, in particular, are very readily available, and popular with the locals. You often find that the owner lives in one of half a dozen apartments in one building.

A landlord/landlady can ask for a deposit and you may be responsible for the electricity, gas if there is any (it is less common than in the UK), telephone, etc. You may also be responsible for your share of communal facilities if you rent an apartment. Bills for electricity, telephone and water tend to be bi-monthly rather than quarterly. In many parts of Europe *all* the utilities are metered.

Take care over the period of notice that is required. It may be as much as three months, and this could be a problem if you change jobs and need to go to live elsewhere.

You may be granted the rental for a fixed period. Check what rights you have to renew it, and what changes in rent can be made.

BUYING A
PROPERTY

If you intend to buy a property it is important to get independent professional advice. The procedure for buying will differ from that in the UK, and your rights and responsibilities as a property owner differ too. You will probably also have to arrange a mortgage.

Prices may be quite different from what you would expect for a similar property in the UK. Just as in Britain, prices differ from area to area.

In general, house prices in France are cheaper than the UK but close to Paris, in the commuter areas like the Seine valley, and in holiday areas, prices are comparable with the south-east of England. By contrast, rural Britanny is on a par with northern Scotland. In Spain and Italy the differences are even more marked with the highest prices occurring in the tourist areas. Germany tends to be expensive and for this reason a far greater proportion of German nationals live in rented accommodation than is usual in the UK.

In Spain estate agents are the norm for people wanting to sell their property. You should, therefore, get a list of agents in the area where you intend to live, from a magazine such as the *International Property Times* or from the local equivalent of the Yellow Pages. In France more people sell their properties privately so you should consider getting newspapers such as *Le Figaro*, *Le Monde* and *France Soir*.

Don't assume that getting finance to buy property will be the same as in the UK: it won't be. You will probably not be able to borrow more than 80% of the price (in the UK it is often as high as 95%) so you will have to find a larger proportion of the price yourself. Interest rates tend to be much lower than in the UK so repayments would be lower if it wasn't for the fact that the period of the loan is usually less (typically 15 years) and this returns them to the same sort of level as in the UK. However, your property will be paid for earlier!

Fixed interest-rate mortgages are much more common in Europe than they are in the UK. Mortgages tend to be repayment-type; the endowment-linked mortgage is almost unknown in France, for example.

The main hurdle to be overcome in getting a mortgage in a new country is convincing the lender that you are credit-worthy. You will need evidence of permission to reside in the country, of having a regular income (three months or more of payslips), and that you are paying tax legally.

Owning property communally is normal in many parts of Europe. In the UK it is confined to London and one or two other major cities. This presents special problems. The methods of dealing with the situation differs from country to country but can be illustrated by outlining the 'copropriété' system in France.

In the deeds of your apartment there will be an indication that you own a number of shares in the common areas of the property. At least two meetings per year will be held to discuss maintenance, etc. which you are compelled to attend by law. They are also a useful way of meeting your neighbours. Most *copropriétés* appoint a '*syndic*' to manage their affairs for them. He or she will arrange maintenance, insurance, payment of bills for communal services, etc. and collect the service charge and a management fee for doing the job.

Grants for the improvement of property are less easy to obtain in the other major European countries than they are in the UK, especially for a foreigner. Services such as building, plumbing, electrical and joinery work also tend to be more expensive than in the UK. You should be careful, therefore, about becoming the sole owner of a property that needs extensive repair.

Getting around

PUBLIC TRANSPORT Those people who work in UK cities will be familiar with bus services for commuting, and although there are problems – traffic congestion and fumes – they do provide a reasonable alternative to the car. If you live near cities such as London, Birmingham, Manchester, Glasgow, etc. you may also have experience of commuter rail services. These suffer from their own success. Demand is so high that they are often overcrowded and delays occur because the network is running so close to capacity.

Other major European cities have similar commuter services, and similar problems. Rome and Paris suffer particularly badly from congestion and have even worse parking problems than London. They also have less patient drivers, far quicker on the horn, and with a far higher accident rate.

The Underground is a vital asset to London, providing a way into and around the city centre without getting caught in the traffic jams. Underground railways are not confined to London. Paris, for example, has a famous underground railway – the Metro – and is not unique amongst Continental European cities.

A method of transport that is not common in the UK, but exists in several other European countries is the tram. Because they have priority over traffic where they share the highway, and sometimes have their own route through the towns, they are not so likely to be involved in traffic congestion.

Although it's not a form of public transport, there is another way of travelling to work, especially if you live not too far from your workplace – by bicycle.

In the UK cyclists are treated as eccentrics. There is an increasing number of them in cities, struggling against the motorist, who pretends they aren't there, and against the fumes. In some European countries they are seen for what they really are – friends of the environment. Many urban authorities provide separate cycleways for cyclists and drivers treat them with care and consideration.

If you have to travel to work in country areas then the UK is the place to be. It has a comprehensive rural bus service that, despite its apparent deficiencies, few other countries can match. Because distances between centres of population tend to be greater in many of the other countries than they are in the UK it is not economic to provide a frequent rural bus service. People are consequently much more dependent on their own transport.

For business travel in the UK you would probably consider the railway as an alternative to driving. Inter-city trains are generally on time, despite the reputation they gained some years ago. Long distance coach services provide an economical and reasonably fast alternative to rail travel.

Services in other countries are variable in this respect. Germany and France have outstanding inter-city rail services. The French TGV, for example, is much faster than the British high-speed train. Germany's trains have an outstanding reputation for quality and timekeeping.

With longer travelling distances air travel is a more feasible solution. Air fares tend to be much lower in other parts of Europe than in the UK.

BUYING A CAR   If you want to buy a car in another EC country you can buy it in whichever country you wish (probably where it is cheapest). You can register and insure it in the country where you purchase it. You can then use it and eventually drive it back to your own country.

Although your UK driving licence is acceptable in other EC countries while you are a visitor, the position may be different once you are granted a residence permit. One of the barriers to the free movement of people before the SEM, was the need to acquire a driving licence of the country in which you lived. A UK licence holder would not need to take a driving test but would have to produce a medical certificate of good health, and be able to prove they have good eyesight. Eventually the need for a different licence will be removed.

You must check that you have the necessary documentation to legally drive your car. As well as the registration document that proves ownership, you will need, in most countries, to tax it and to insure it. One feature of the French regulations is the requirement to display an insurance sticker on the windscreen.

Insurance can be very expensive in some European countries. Generally these are the ones with poor accident records, and where repairs are expensive. It is increasingly common for both drivers to complete a standard form at the scene of an accident and sign both copies to show that they agree on the circumstances of the mishap. This facilitates the insurance company's task, reduces costs, and speeds up the process of settling the claim.

If you decide to bring your car back to the UK permanently you will need the following documents:

- the invoice;
- technical documentation accompanying the vehicle (conformity certificate, registration papers, etc.);
- customs document;
- document confirming payment of or exemption from import duties.

Certain taxes, including VAT, are payable at the time of import.

You will need to register your imported car on a permanent basis in your own country. For a 'new' vehicle (i.e. which has never been registered previously) you need to obtain a certificate of conformity from the dealer you have bought it from or the manufacturer. They should not refuse to issue it, charge you excessively, or delay its issue. This certificate confirms that the vehicle is of an approved type for the country into which you are taking it.

Dealers must not refuse after-sales or warranty claims even though you have bought the vehicle in another EC country.

Activity 8.3   Choose a car or motor cycle that you could expect to afford after a short time in a job. Check whether it is available in the countries where you might work. If not, determine what equivalents there are.

Find out how much it would cost to buy it in that country and how much it would be in the UK. Remember to take into account the VAT and duties that you would have to pay when importing it into the UK to get a fair comparison.

Is it better to buy it there or in the UK?

Communications

POST   Each country has its own postal service. In some countries the post and telephones are run by the same organisation. In others, like the UK they are separate.

In most countries stamps can be bought in shops, as well as post offices, just as they now can in the UK.

Post offices in France are identified by the blue and white 'PTT' sign. Post boxes are yellow and can be found outside post offices and elsewhere, although they are not as common as in the UK. Germany's postal system is symbolised by a Bundespost emblem – a post horn. It is clearly seen on post offices and the yellow post boxes. Spain's post boxes are also yellow; be careful which boxes you post in, some marked '*extranjero*' are for foreign mail only. By contrast post boxes are red in Italy.

As well as the normal service (sometimes two-tier as in the UK) most countries have a 'datapost' or express service and facilities for recorded delivery and parcels.

TELEPHONE   There is some variation among pay-phones in various EC countries. In Germany, the yellow pay-phones are easy to spot and are used much as UK ones. Pay-phones are also yellow in Spain. With these you place coins in a chute on the telephone, lift the receiver and dial the number. As the coins in the chute are used, add more as necessary.

The Italian telephone system has a reputation for being unreliable. Pay-phones operate by tokens ('*gettoni*'). These can be obtained from post offices, tobacconists and bars. Some phone boxes have *gettoni* machines. Having lifted the receiver you insert several tokens and then dial the number. Cafés and bars almost invariably have pay-phones but charges may be high because they can set the rate themselves. An interesting feature of France is the presence of blue 'taxi phones' which can be used for local calls only.

FACSIMILE   An excellent alternative to sending a letter or making a telephone call is to send a fax message. Most businesses and an increasing number of individuals now have fax machines.

Think of it as sending a letter by phone-line. All you have to do is write your letter, dial the number of the recipient, feed the letter in, and it arrives at its destination! Because of the speed that the information is transmitted it is often cheaper than sending a letter or having a telephone conversation. And of course you can send pictures, maps, diagrams, etc. Some fax machines have a built-in answering-machine to take messages from callers when you aren't available to take a 'phone call.

MINITEL   An important service offered by the French PTT (post and telephone authority) is MINITEL.

This is a service that you can access via a computer terminal and the telephone system. In many ways it is like the UK's PRESTEL service.

In 1991 there were three and a half million users throughout France. The cost to rent a terminal was about £8.50 per month in March 1991 and connection charges were about 10 pence per minute.

As a subscriber you can use it to book rail and theatre tickets, to carry out transactions with your bank account and to obtain telephone numbers.

Opening a bank account

At an early stage in planning a move to another European country you should consider opening a bank account there. While it is simpler to have an account with a bank that is based in the country where you are living, credit cards, travellers cheques and Eurocheques make it possible to manage with only a UK bank account.

The exchange rate between currencies fluctuates and it is sometimes worthwhile changing your money some time before you travel to take advantage of favourable exchange rates. However, within the EC the currencies are now linked within the ERM (exchange rate mechanism) which restricts the amount that the exchange rates of the EC currencies can vary.

Travellers cheques can be in £, local currency or ECUs. The bank will charge a fee for providing these.

You may obtain Eurocheques from your bank, for a small fee, which can then be used in exactly the same way as normal cheques and written in the local currency.

Most major bank cards, cheque cards and credit cards are usable in EC countries. Transactions are in the local currency and will be shown in both the local currency and in £ when you receive your monthly statement.

Beware of writing cheques when you don't have funds to cover them. In the UK this will invite a letter or 'phone call from the bank manager; in some countries, such as France, it is a crime.

Activity 8.4   **1** Obtain, from your local bank, details of the travel services it offers.

2 Contact the bank to ask about the services it can offer you in the country where you will be living and working, and possibly give you details of banks in that country with which it is associated.

3 Remember that your needs as a resident will be very different from those of a tourist or short-stay business traveller.

Cost of living

A good rule is to adjust your habits to those of the locals as their tastes will be best catered for. This will make shopping convenient and economic.

In France prices are on average slightly higher than in the UK and for certain things they are much higher. The quality of goods, particularly food and clothes, tends to be rather better though. German food prices are considerably cheaper than the UK's.

Wages (before and after tax) need to be considered as well. If products were twice the UK price you would consider the country expensive if you were a tourist. However, if wages were three times those of the UK, you would be better off living and working there than you would be in the UK.

Switzerland is a good illustration of this. Staying in Switzerland as a tourist can be traumatic. The quality of goods is high but prices are too. As a resident, earning Swiss-level wages would make the prices seem more reasonable.

A survey for the *Sunday Times* in August 1991 revealed that the cost of a shopping basket containing plain flour, white sugar, sunflower margarine, frozen chips, rump steak, carrots, milk, coca-cola and pure orange juice, was highest in France (£15.19) with the UK (£14.76) second, Belgium (£13.71) third, and Germany (£9.81) lowest.

Table 8.1 Food prices in 1985 and 1991

	actual price in 1991	% increase	estimated price in 1985
France	15.19	18	12.87
UK	14.76	33	11.10
Belgium	13.71	9	12.58
Germany	9.81	10	8.92

The survey found that the same basket bought in the USA would cost only £8.25.

EC statistics reveal that in the last six years food prices have risen more quickly in the UK than in the other countries.

YOUNG PERSONS' PRIVILEGES

As a young person travelling in Europe you can take advantage of discount schemes and other privileges. The 'European Youth Card' entitles the holder to price reductions and easier access to cultural events throughout the EC.

The EC provides financial support to young people for the pursuit of artistic and cultural initiatives. It organises various events, such as a European piano competition, a European youth orchestra and also a competition for young script writers. It also supports schemes that involve young people in restoring monuments and protecting the environment.

SHOPPING

If you are living and working in a country you are likely to be buying food, household products, clothes, electrical goods, and perhaps furniture or carpets.

Food and personal needs are the sectors where you will find most differences, and these are picked out for special attention in the sections that follow.

Many clothes are now 'international' – you will be able to think of major brand names for quality jeans, trainers, sweaters, etc. The same names can be found in France, Italy, Germany, Spain, etc. but prices may differ from the UK. The styles of fashion clothes for women originate in the fashion houses of London, Paris and Milan and copies of the originals are widely bought by Western European women. You will find differences in the styles of business wear for men, but again there is more and more an 'international' style.

Electrical goods are mostly produced by multinational corporations, often Japanese-owned. The types of radio, hi-fi and computers available in the rest of Europe are similar to the models available in the UK and, unlike the USA, most European countries have voltage and phasing that are compatible with the UK so appliances that you have will work in other EC countries.

On the other hand, televisions, video recorders and video cameras are not compatible throughout Europe. The UK uses a system called PAL, and so do many other European countries. However, France and many countries in Eastern Europe use a system called SECAM (the USA, Canada and Japan use a third system called NSTC). This will present difficulties if you buy or take equipment from a country with one standard to another with a different standard. Although video tapes are the same (mainly VHS now), programmes recorded on them cannot be played back on equipment of the other standards. Equipment capable of playing back more than one system is coming onto the market, albeit at a premium price.

If and when you come to furnish your house or flat you will have the choice of buying locally or paying to transport your belongings from one country to another. There are differences in taste between European countries but a more significant factor is the climate. Curtains and carpets serve a very different function in southern Italy from that in northern Denmark.

OPENING HOURS

Many European shops open earlier than their counterparts in the UK, are closed longer at lunchtime, and stay open until later in the evening.

As in the UK, however, there is a tendency for shop opening hours to extend, and no doubt 24-hour 7-day shopping will soon be as common in Europe as it is in the USA. It is, of course, the large stores, supermarkets and hypermarkets that lead the way in this.

The equivalent of the British 'corner shop' is often open from early morning until late at night, offering convenience shopping to compensate for higher prices.

In the southern areas of Europe many shops open at 08.00 or even 07.00, have an extended lunchtime, typically 13.00 to 16.00, and then stay open until 18.00, 19.00 or later. In more northern parts lunchtime is usually one and a half to two hours.

As in the UK there is often a 'half day closing' which varies from area to area, and even from town to town. In France Monday is the day when many shops are closed and in Germany they close on Saturday afternoons. In the UK shops are beginning to open on Sunday. This is true of tourist areas in mainland Europe, but in general Sunday trading is less common than in the UK.

SHOPPING IN
FRANCE

Department stores such as *Monoprix* and *Prisunic* are found in most big towns, and goods in them are reasonably priced. As well as supermarkets France has a large number of hypermarkets with a comprehensive range of goods. The best-known big stores are *Rallye*, *Codec*, *Leclerc*, *Casino* and *Euromarche*.

Markets are more common in France than they are in the UK and are often held two or three times per week in larger towns. It is best to shop in them during the morning for fresh produce and craft products.

As well as wine and lager-type beer the French drink bottled water, far more than we do in the UK, although sales of it here are increasing rapidly.

France is renowned for its bread and bread-like products, the best known being croissants. These are available at the *boulangerie* (bakery), while the *patisserie* (cake shop) and *confiserie* (bonbon seller) provide sweet treats.

Meat is of a high quality, though beef and lamb tend to be relatively expensive. Pork and poultry are better buys. Seafood, especially shellfish, is plentiful in coastal areas.

A seemingly infinite variety of cheeses is available. Some are fairly expensive, but there is something to suit every palate, from mild to 'adventurous'. Butter is usually sold in unsalted or semi-salted form. Grocery stores are named *épicerie* and *magazine d'alimentation*.

Fresh fruit and vegetables vary in price and availability according to the region and the season. In the south, for example, peaches, melons, tomatoes, etc. are ridiculously cheap in season.

Some foods are hard to find, for example, baked beans, marmalade, tomato

Figure 8.1 French fare
Source: French Tourist Office, London

sauce, pickled onions and many other 'British' foods. However fancy goods available in the *boucherie*, *charcuterie* and *delicatessan* should provide ample compensation.

SHOPPING IN
GERMANY

Unlike France, Germany has few small food shops except for bakers, butchers, and cake and confectionery shops. Germans tend to do most of their shopping in supermarkets and the department stores found in larger towns.

Many towns have small markets, where, as in Belgium and the Netherlands, you will find stalls selling flowers.

Famous for their beer, the Germans also excel in sausages (wurst). Some of the more common varieties are bratwurst (pork sausage), leberwurst (liver sausage), knackwurst (saveloy), and bierwurst (beer sausage).

Smoked cheese and smoked meats are also specialities of Germany.

Just as France has its distinctive types of bread, so does Germany. Brotchen (rolls) and roggenbrot (rye bread) are both very popular, but you may find swartzbrot (black bread) an acquired taste. Germany is famous for its cakes and pastries, such as *Apfelstrudel* (apple strudel) and *Schwarzwalderkirschtorte* (Black Forest gateau).

SHOPPING IN ITALY   Because of the sun and heat, goods are not displayed in shop windows as often as they are in the UK, and blinds are often drawn. Shops with blinds down are not necessarily shut! Supermarkets are the easiest places to shop, but there are many small general food stores (called 'alimentari') and markets with a wide variety of products.

In Italian markets it is common to bargain with the stallholder, except for food or where there is a sign *prezzi fissi* (fixed prices). The price asked could be as much as twice what the stallholder expects to get. It is not unusual to receive sweets, matches, stamps, etc. instead of small change.

Fresh fruit, such as peaches, apricots, melons and figs, are plentiful. Near the coast, fish and seafood, notably tuna, fresh sardines and crayfish, are a good buy. Cheeses such as parmesan, mozzarella and gorgonzola are readily available. Meat is relatively expensive compared with cooked ham, pork, and sausage. Italy is famous for its pasta.

SHOPPING IN SPAIN   Supermarkets are the easiest and cheapest places for food shopping, although small general shops are well-stocked. There are bakers' shops, but very few specialist butchers or greengrocers. In larger towns you will find department stores such as *Galerias Preciados* which stock a wide variety of products.

Seafood is very plentiful, although not particularly cheap. Amongst the meats, pork is a good buy, and lamb is reasonable, but the quality of all meats is variable, and choice is limited. Cooked meats, especially ham, and cheeses are good alternatives.

Rolls are often more palatable than Spanish bread. Fresh milk is unobtainable in some areas.

Language

As a visitor to another country, in a tourist area, you would normally find people who could speak English and, for the short period of a holiday, you could 'get by' with little or no knowledge of the local language.

When you move from tourist areas you will find there are fewer people who can speak English. Although many people now learn a foreign language at school, and English is a common second language in many European countries, you will encounter people who have not had the opportunity, or chose not to, study English.

Learning the local language and using it at work will demonstrate motivation and weigh well in your career progression.

Speaking the local language with friends will help them feel at ease and help you integrate into their society. It is a courtesy to try to fit in with your hosts, in this way.

This book is not the place to teach you the languages of Europe. However, some suggestions are given to help you decide where to start and what is most important.

The immediate task will be to overcome the problems of the first few days. Don't be afraid of making mistakes or being laughed at. People will be sympathetic if they see you are making an effort, and the only way to improve is to practise.

A phrase book may be of use for basic requirements such as securing accommodation and finding your way around transport systems. Frequently the phrase you want isn't quite what is in the book. Carry a small dictionary so that you can look up words to complement the phrases.

Make every effort to pronounce the words correctly for that language. In French, for example, stress is put equally on every syllable, whereas in English we stress the first one or two and 'swallow' the last one.

German words may appear unfamiliar but if they are split up become recognisable. They often sound like the English word when spoken even though they look different when written.

A vocabulary of 50 to 100 words will probably be enough to get started. Begin with basics like 'yes', 'no', 'excuse me', 'can you help me', 'please', 'thank you'.

Learn prepositions such as 'on', 'under', 'near', 'far', 'left', 'right'. These spoken with a questioning tone may be enough to ask a question.

You can also make use of sign language as an aid to communication.

Activity 8.5

1 Consider the scenario below. Break the scenario into a number of 'scenes' – the journey to the city; from the centre to your accommodation; finding a restaurant; choosing, ordering and paying for the meal; etc.

2 What language skills (listening, speaking, reading) will you need to deal with these situations?

3 Determine what questions you might want to ask, what answers you might receive and what you might need to read.

4 Divide into groups according to knowledge of particular European languages.

5 Carry out role plays for the various scenes.

Scenario

You arrive by air and on leaving the airport need to find the bus to take you to the centre of the city. From there you need a bus, underground train, tram or taxi to where you have booked to stay for the first few days.

Having unpacked your suitcase you want to go out to find somewhere to eat.

Next day you need to make your way to work, announce yourself, and understand the initial explanation of the job. At lunchtime you want to get to know your fellow workers. After work you find your way back to your lodgings.

You then go out again to buy various things that you need from the shops.

Later you want to keep up to date with world events by reading a newspaper, listening to the radio, or watching television. Alternatively you want to go out to a café or to the cinema.

When the weekend comes you want to explore the area. You may want to go to a disco, watch some sport, or join a club so that you can participate.

Soon you want to find a more permanent place to stay. You need to find what property is for rent or for sale and negotiate for it. It may need curtains, carpets and furniture. You may want to have the rest of your belongings shipped from home.

LANGUAGE COURSES

The important points about learning a language when living and working in a country are that:

- you are going to be there for a reasonable length of time
- many of the people you are associating with speak the language that you are learning.

Both these factors mean that you are 'immersed' in the language and will learn it more quickly and more colloquially than you would as a tourist or student in a class at home.

There are many language courses offered by local colleges and private organisations, and you can buy audio tapes and books to help you learn before you leave the UK.

Choose carefully. You want to learn how to use the language in everyday life and in a business context. That can be quite different from what is taught on courses for potential tourists.

Once you get to a country you may find it more difficult to find a course to learn the local language – the residents can already speak it! However many universities do have courses for foreigners, just as in the UK we have TEFL (Teaching English as a Foreign Language).

Eating out

In most other European countries eating out in bars, cafés and restaurants is much more common than in the UK. In many cities, for example, it is usual for people to travel from home to close to where they work, and then call into a café for breakfast. In the evening, too, they may eat before they travel home. If you are to make a habit of eating out you need to get the right dietary balance and work within a budget.

Fast-food restaurants do exist, and there are ethnic eating places in most big cities.

However, eating habits generally retain characteristics that make each country distinct.

As to finding suitable places to eat, recommendatoins from friends or colleagues are very useful. Otherwise, here are a few useful guidelines.

- In plush surroundings you will be paying for the decor as well as the food. A less impressive place builts its reputation on the standard of its cuisine and value for money.
- It is a good sign if the restaurant is frequented by locals.
- Avoid restaurants where the menu or prices are not displayed; they tend to be expensive.

- Compare the menus of several restaurants before choosing one.
- If a restaurant is popular you may need to book, especially on a public holiday or Sunday.

EATING IN FRANCE

'Croissants', bread or buns are the usual accompaniments for coffee at breakfast time.

Lunch is usually available between 12.00 and 13.30 and dinner between 19.00 and 20.30.

In restaurants, it is usually cheaper to select the three- or four-course set menus than the *à la carte* one. Most restaurants offer several menus at different prices according to the content and number of courses. At lunchtime you may find a *menu ouvrier* (working man's menu).

A service charge is often included (*service compris*) and occasionally the menu may also be *vin compris* (wine included). If the service charge is not included be prepared to give a tip of 10 to 15% if the service has been satisfactory.

Unlimited quantities of bread are often provided to acompany the meal, but not usually with butter.

As in UK restaurants the 'dish of the day' is normally a sound choice, described as '*spécialité de la maison*' or '*plat du jour*'. A variety of raw vegetables (*crudités*) is a common and pleasant starter.

The French prefer beef or lamb to be cooked rather less than is usual in the UK. *Bien cuit* (well-done) is usually what in the UK would be described as 'medium'.

Some restaurants serve a simple salad with the main meal. The French normally eat it after finishing the course. In some parts of France you will retain the same plate for the whole meal, and wiping it with your bread is acceptable. Another practice you may encounter is that of receiving and eating each item of the course separately. Until you are used to it you may find it strange to have the meat, then the salad, then the french fries.

This is not the place to discuss the specialities of the regions but *crêpes* (thin pancakes), served with savoury fillings, or flavoured with a liqueur, are a delight. In Provence the range of fruit is enormous – melons, apricots, figs, peaches, cherries, etc. are grown locally and are far fresher than those we eat in the UK.

Wine is the normal beverage to accompany a French meal. The key phrases are *vin de table* (cheap but usually palatable wine), *vin de pays* (the local wine), *une carafe* (a litre) or *une demi carafe* (half a litre), *cuvée de la maison* (a wine selected by the chef for the restaurant's patrons).

The French are not particular about the type of wine they drink with everyday meals but red is usual. For a special meal, however, they may be more selective – white with fish, red with meat, etc. Bottled water is widely drunk in France, both natural and sparkling. Coffee is not normally included in the set menu price, check *l'addition* (the bill) at the end of the meal.

UNDERSTANDING
A FRENCH MENU

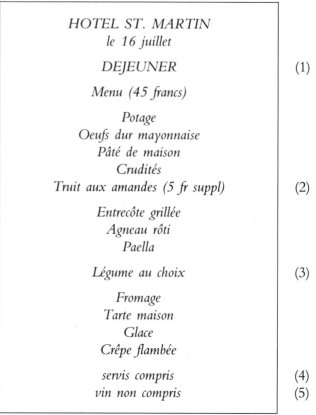

> ## HOTEL ST. MARTIN
> *le 16 juillet*
>
> ### DEJEUNER   (1)
>
> *Menu (45 francs)*
>
> *Potage*
> *Oeufs dur mayonnaise*
> *Pâté de maison*
> *Crudités*
> *Truit aux amandes (5 fr suppl)*   (2)
>
> *Entrecôte grillée*
> *Agneau rôti*
> *Paella*
>
> *Légume au choix*   (3)
>
> *Fromage*
> *Tarte maison*
> *Glace*
> *Crêpe flambée*
>
> *servis compris*   (4)
> *vin non compris*   (5)

Notes:

(1) *dejeuner*=lunchtime meal; *diner*=evening meal
(2) five franc supplement for this choice
(3) choice of vegetables
(4) service included in the price
(5) wine not included in the price

KNOW YOUR
DRINKS

The atmosphere in French bars and cafés is totally different to that of a British pub. Cafés are open all day and closing time may be midnight or even later. In a French café you are normally served at your table by a waiter, and you normally pay as you leave. A service charge may be included, if not it is normal to give a *pourboire* (a tip) if the service has been acceptable.

Most bars and cafés serve beer 'on tap' (*sous pression*); *un demi* is a quarter litre. If you ask for *une bière* you will normally receive a quarter-litre bottle.

The aniseed-based spirit called '*pastis*' is probably the most popular aperitif in France. There are several brands including Ricard and Pernod. The French way of drinking it is 1 part of pastis with 4–5 parts water, and ice.

Many of France's liqueurs are well-known in the UK – Bénédictine, Chartreuse, Cointreau, Grand Marnier, Crème de Menthe, Crème de Cassis, etc.

The basic hallmark of wine quality is the wording *appellation controlée* on the label. *Vin de pays* on a label indicates a reasonably good local wine, which is often excellent value.

The Bordeaux area is famous for its red wines (clarets), including Médoc and St Émilion. However its white Graves, Sauternes and Barsac are also excellent.

Burgundy (Bourgogne) is also an area noted for its red wines. Beaujolais is the best known but there are also Côte de Beaune, and Côte de Nuit. Chablis, the relatively expensive white wine also comes from this region.

Côtes du Rhone and Languedoc-Roussilon produce a large amount of wine, mainly in the *vin de table* and *vin de pays* categories.

Alsace, close to the German border, produces mainly white wines, of excellent quality.

Genuine champagne comes only from the region round Reims but sparkling wine at lower cost is produced in many regions, the best probably being those of Saumur and Vouvray in the Loire.

EATING OUT IN GERMANY

For traditional German cooking in authentic surroundings the best place is probably the *Gasthof* (inn). Restaurants tend to be more expensive and international.

There may be set menus at lunchtime but in the evening *à la carte* is usual. Unlike the French, the Germans tend to make lunch their main meal of the day.

The Germans often don't bother with a first course, but dishes like soup with noodles, eggs or dumplings can be found. For the main course, veal and pork are the most popular meats.

The Germans drink more beer than any other country in Europe. The main choice is between *hell* (lager type) and *dunkel* (sweeter and with more malt). 'Export' is stronger, and the strongest is *bock*. Local beer is served on draught in measures of *ein kleines* (a glass), *ein grosses* (half a litre) or *ein mass* (a litre).

The Black Forest is famous for its *schnapps* (fruit spirits). *Apfelsaft* (apple juice) and *Traubensaft* (grape juice) are popular.

Coffee is often consumed with cream cakes in the morning or afternoon.

Germany produces arguably the world's best white wines. The better known come from the Mosel and Rhine valleys.

There are three main classifications of wine in Germany: *Tafelwein* is a table wine from any EC country; *deutscher Tafelwein* is table wine from Germany; *Qualitatswein* is wine approved by a tasting panel who may award a *Prädikat* (commendation). If there is only one name on the label it will be the name of the village, if there are two the second will be the name of the vineyard. There may also be the type of grape – riesling, sylvaner, etc. As in France, the more specific the geographic location indicated on the label, the better the wine is likely to be.

EATING OUT IN ITALY

A *pizzeria* in Italy will not only sell pizzas, though that will be its speciality, nor will a *rosticceria* serve only roasts. The *trattoria* usually serves specifically Italian dishes, while the *ristorante* may be more cosmopolitan and expensive.

Lunch is normally taken between 12.00 and 14.00 and the evening meal from about 19.00 to 21.30. Service is almost always added to the bill and a cover charge which includes the cost of bread is sometimes included too. The price of a meat dish may be marked '*all etto*' which means the price is per 100 grams.

Pasta comes in a wide variety of forms – lasagne, cannelloni, ravioli, tagliatelle, etc. The other well-known dish is pizza, of course; try the *quattro stagionei* with its variety of toppings. Veal is the most common meat, as an escalope or in a stew.

Italian ice cream, '*gelati*' is famous and may be served in many forms.

The Italians offer a variety of coffees too. '*Espresso*' is in a small cup, black and very strong. *Caffè latte* is made with milk, and *cappuccino* is white and frothy, with a chocolate topping.

Italy produces a large amount of wine, some of it costing less than bottled water. The DOC system is similar to the French '*appellation controlée*'. The red wines you are most likely to recognise are Chianti, Valpolicella and Barolo. Soave (dry), Frascati, and Marsala (sweet) are the well-known white wines and you probably know of Asti Spumante, a sparkling wine.

EATING OUT IN SPAIN

The first course in a Spanish meal will probably be soup, either the delicate *consomme al Jerez* or the chilled soup made of tomatoes, onion, green peppers and garlic called *gazpacho*. Other courses may include fish or seafood served plain or in a spicy or garlic sauce and meat which may be grilled or stewed with peppers and tomatoes. An alternative is *paella* – saffron-flavoured rice with a variety of added ingredients that could include meat, poultry, vegetables and seafood. Vegetables and salad are usually served separately.

If you visit a Spanish bar you may well find small portions of food served on saucers for you to eat with your drink. These *tapas* may be appetisers but you can also order them as a meal.

Wine is very cheap in Spain. There are no outstanding labels but Rioja is probably the best table wine. Spain is famous for its sherry; *fino* is a very pale dry sherry which when it is aged to become darker and fuller is *amontillado*. *Oloroso* is heavier and richer.

Making friends and socialising

Apart from language, there are other cultural aspects to take up such as knowing how to dress and behave at work, and what to expect with regard to making friends and socialising with colleagues.

We are all aware of the stereotypes of various nationalities, but the fact is that each comunity, business, group of people and individual has their own particular attitudes, characteristics, and acceptable patterns of behaviour.

The best advice is to:

- *check in advance* about those things that lend themselves to this approach – dress, ways of addressing your peers and superiors, etc;
- *observe* how your colleagues and acquaintances behave towards each other, what they do at lunchtime, whether they meet together after work or leave promptly, etc;
- *ask* someone who is independent of a situation for *advice* about whether to take a gift if you are invited to a colleague's house for a meal, whether chocolates, flowers or wine are acceptable, etc.

Unless there is a uniform or special safety clothes you will be faced with deciding how formal your clothes should be for work and what is appropriate for various social occasions. The degree of formality at work will probably depend more on the type of business than the country.

My research suggests that the Belgians, French and Italians tend to be formal, the Dutch and Danes informal, and the Greeks, Spanish and Portuguese vary their business clothes according to the season.

How you should address people also needs to be established. You may find it possible to address people by their first names once you know them, but that may only apply to your peers and your superiors may still have to be given titles such as the equivalent of 'Mr', 'Mrs' or 'Miss'. In the UK we have learned to avoid the difficulty of 'Mrs' or 'Miss' by the use of 'Ms' in correspondence, and it is even creeping into speech. In other European countries it is still important to distinguish between '*madame*' and '*madamoiselle*', between '*señora*' and '*señorita*', etc.

In English there is no equivalent of the more formal *vous* and the less formal *tu* (in French) but in many countries, including France, Italy and Spain the distinction between the more formal and the informal is expected and raises eyebrows (at least) if used wrongly.

Shaking hands when one meets for the first time is usual in the UK, and is becoming more common at subsequent meetings, particularly among professional people. There is also a trend toward shaking hands again when you part, a more established custom in other European countries. The best advice is to observe the actions of others and be prepared to follow their lead. Certainly this is recommended where more familiar forms of greeting are possible, such as kissing or touching cheeks.

Business lunches appear to be quite common in France, where the serious discussion takes place over coffee so as not to interfere with the enjoyment of the meal, whereas in the UK the conversation is likely to go on throughout the meal. By contrast in the Netherlands business conversations may be conducted over a coffee, but you will probably find a meal on expenses is more rare.

In the UK, it is normal for people to come straight into work from home, but to meet together in a pub immediately after work for a while. The French and Belgians are more likely to meet in a café for coffee or breakfast but depart promptly.

It is said that humour is a very national thing. Whereas the British are full of 'foreigner' jokes the Belgians are more likely to make fun of Belgian characteristics. However, the kind of pride that the French have in their country makes it unlikely that they would wish to make fun of their own national characteristics although they would be content with jokes made at the expense of an individual. The Germans would rarely target the government in their humour but for the Greeks it is one of the favourites.

It is an old saying that 'politics, sex and religion' are subjects to be avoided in conversation and that the British talk about nothing but the weather. I am sure that neither is entirely true but you need to be careful in choosing topics. As a newcomer you will find that you can introduce almost any topic as long as you do it in the form of a question to indicate you are seeking facts. Beware though if you are in the company of several people whose views may differ. I once made the mistake of asking which were the best wines when with a group of French people. They were in agreement on red, but the discussion became quite heated over white wine.

Status may be an issue in some countries and industries. It may be important to demonstrate your rank by the car you drive, the size of your office, where you take your holidays in Germany because a competitive and ambitious society respects people who have achieved success and demonstrating it is socially acceptable. In a more egalitarian society such as Denmark it would not earn respect, even though the high standard of living could support such material symbols of success. In Belgium take-home pay would probably be a more respected indicator of success than titles, office, or other perks.

If you are invited to someone's house make sure you know whether it is for a meal, for a snack, or for drinks or coffee. Finding out may tax your skills of communication, and so will the need to discover what style of dress is appropriate.

You may feel that the occasion warrants you taking a small gift for the host and hostess. Chocolates, flowers or wine would be quite normal in the UK. In Spain, however, it is not the custom to take gifts. The Italian attraction for stylish things suggests that something out of the ordinary, though not necessarily expensive, would be appropriate. In Belgium flowers, but not drinks are acceptable. In France and the Netherlands flowers or chocolates, but not wine, are common gifts, but in Germany wine *is* acceptable, although flowers are the most frequently given.

No one would take offence if you were to send a brief, courteous thank-you note to say how much you enjoyed a pleasant evening.

Activity 8.6 As part of an exchange with a European college, organise the entertainment of a 'business associate'.

Summary 1 Living and working in another country is different from taking a holiday.

2 Formalities have to be dealt with for driving, residence, permission to work, medical care, tax and social security payment.

3 The biggest hurdles to be overcome when getting established are language, accommodation, transport, and work.

4 The newcomer needs to be aware of different practices for communication, dealing with emergencies, and banking.

5 The newcomer needs to adapt his/her shopping habits to the different cost of living, shop opening hours, and national product differences.

6 Eating out, making friends and socialising, business etiquette and protocols require the newcomer to develop new skills.

Assignment 8   **CHOOSING YOUR HOME AND WORKPLACE**

1 Draw up a table of the advantages and disadvantages of living in a European country, other than the UK, or France (since it is given here as an example). For France the list might look like this:

In favour
- employment situation is favourable;
- rates of pay are as good as or better than the UK;
- some industries are very advanced and successful;
- lower property prices than the UK;
- lower costs for many basics, e.g. food;
- good weather in some regions;
- interesting country and culture

Against
- language may be problem as a knowledge of French essential;
- the French are not always receptive to foreign employees;
- locals can initially be suspicious of foreigners;
- some regions are very remote and rather backward;
- higher costs for some items, e.g. electricity and telephones;
- French culture and lifestyle are at odds with UK way of life, in many respects.

2 Use the lists as the basis of a justification for:
a remaining in the UK; or
b moving to that other EC country temporarily; or
c moving permanently to that other EC country.

9 Employment issues

Objectives
1 Know where to look to find out about job vacancies, and how to be prepared so as to perform well in the selection process.
2 Recognise that many European countries have recruitment procedures that differ from those of the UK.
3 Be aware of the opportunities offered by exchange and young worker schemes, and how to participate in study and vocational training in other parts of Europe.
4 Understand the conditions of employment likely to be offered, and the protection afforded to employees by EC legislation.
5 Recognise the need to register for tax and social security purposes, and deal with tax returns and payments.
6 Appreciate the different contribution rates and entitlement for unemployment, sickness and other social security benefits.
7 Identify the advantages and disadvantages of studying in various EC countries and plan your continuing education, on the basis of the information you acquire.

The right to work

As a national of one of the EC countries you have a right to spend up to three months looking for a job in another member country. You need a passport or valid identity card but not a visa.

You have a right to accept a job that is on offer in any of the EC countries (prior to 1993 this does not apply to Spain or Portugal).

If you are unemployed and would like to look for employment in another EC country you can receive the unemployment benefits to which you would be entitled in your home country for a maximum of three months provided that:

- you have been looking for work in your own country for at least four weeks;
- you are registered with the unemployment exchange in the country in which are you are looking for a job;
- you have in your possession a form E303 which is available from the institution that normally pays your unemployment benefits in the country in which you are insured.

In order to be eligible for sickness benefits in the Community country where you are seeking employment you must, before leaving your own country, obtain a form E119. If you need treatment you must present this form to the sickness insurance institution in the country where you are seeking employment. As long as you are incapacitated from work you will be subject to medical checks by the institution in the place where you are staying.

If you are eligible for cash sickness benefits these will be paid in the country where you are living, by the institution with which you were insured before departure.

There is one major exception to the freedoms you have to seek work in other countries. Many public service organisations have rules that allow them to employ only nationals of their country for some jobs. This could apply to such organisations as the army, police force, tax authority and the courts.

Activity 9.1

1 List the ways in which you could find out what jobs are on offer in the UK.

2 Choose one other European country and investigate whether the same or similar sources of information are available there. Try to find out whether they have any methods of job hunting that we do not have.

Finding a job

Employment exchanges throughout the EC can help you to locate jobs, using the 'Sedoc network'. This system allows unemployment offices to exchange information on jobs throughout the EC. Some UK employment agencies specialise in advertising overseas jobs and in finding appointments for clients. However, these will probably be areas where there is a shortage in a specific skill and tend to be the Middle East rather than Europe. However, if you speak two or more languages well the agencies are likely to be very interested in you.

If your chosen career has a professional association the professional journal is likely to have overseas job advertisements. Some occupations, such as marketing, media, catering and computing are better served in international advertisements than others, such as law and banking. In this way, you can look for a job before you leave the UK.

Increasingly the better quality newspapers have days when they concentrate on European affairs and include a modest amount of job advertising. You would find more coverage of less senior posts in the national and local newspapers of your target country.

French and German employment agencies are prevented by law from dealing in full-time appointments, and can deal only in temporary jobs. This might suit your needs in the initial period of moving to your target country. They can be located through the country's equivalent of the Yellow Pages.

TEMPORARY WORK

A growing number of young people go abroad to work as *au pairs*, spending about a year working with a family. This is an effective way of learning the language and lifestyle of another country. Three countries, France, Italy and Denmark currently operate a scheme that provides a special form of protection. Under this scheme work is available to people between 17 and 30 who are in good health. A written agreement with the family you are to stay with is issued before you arrive there, and this must be deposited with the authorities in that country. The agreement specifies the conditions under which you will share the life of the host family, and the period of notice which each must give (unless there is serious misconduct on either side).

Conditions set down in the agreement may include the following.

The host family provides board and lodging and where possible a separate room. You must be allowed adequate time to attend language and other courses – at least one full free day per week, and at least one Sunday per month. You will receive pocket money, the amount of which must be stipulated in the agreement together with the intervals at which it will be paid.

The governments participating in the scheme guarantee that you will be coverd by social security in the event of illness, maternity or accident. When au pairing in non-participant countries the host family must take out an insurance policy to cover these things at their cost.

EXCHANGE PROGRAMMES

Work exchange schemes are also ways of getting a 'taster' of working overseas.

There are several exchange programmes, designed for people between the ages of 18 and 28, who are already in employment or about to enter it, and who have basic vocational training or first-hand work experience. These 'Young Worker' exchanges can be as short as 3 to 13 weeks or longer (4 to 16 months). The European Commission gives financial aid to institutions entrusted with the task of running the scheme.

The 'Youth for Europe' programme is aimed at giving young people an opportunity to find out more about the economic social and cultural life of EC countries. This scheme is available to people between 15 and 25 and is organised through various youth organisations.

Activity 9.2

1 Exchange schemes and taking time off to visit other countries seems attractive.

2 Consider how long you would want to spend on such a scheme and how it would fit in with or interfere with your education and career.

3 Should you do it at the end of full-time education, before you take up employment, or should you interrupt your studies to do it? What are the advantages and disadvantages of each strategy?

RECRUITMENT

Many UK companies have been recruiting from other countries for a long time. Often this has simply been due to shortages of suitably qualified people in specific disciplines. For example, hospitals in the West Midlands have recruited doctors from Germany, the Netherlands and Italy; schools in the South-East have recruited teachers from Germany, the Netherlands and Denmark.

However, increasingly it is because they have a policy of 'Europeanisation'. Cross-border mergers, acquisitions and joint ventures have made it necessary for businesses to set up operations in other countries and they are recruiting local staff to manage and operate them. They are also recruiting staff from the area of their new operations to work in established offices to provide local knowledge and links with the area.

When applying for a job you will follow the normal recruitment procedure for that organisation. There are no special or different procedures because you are 'a foreigner'. Remember, however, that the procedures in other EC countries may be different from the UK procedures. For most jobs you will be expected to have adequate skill in the local language.

There are different procedures and practices for recruitment throughout Europe. Few personnel managers in the UK, for example, would consult employee representatives before appointing a new member of staff. In Germany this is a statutory requirement.

The personnel manager needs to find where there are potential sources of labour. In Greece for example, there is a shortage of finance and personnel staff and also skilled white-collar workers. Is it realised that there is a pool of highly-educated graduates from UK and US universities who would be interested in working for international companies. The average graduating age in the UK is 21. In many European countries, where education is longer and military service is compulsory, students graduate later.

At the other end of the employment age scale, it is forbidden to have an upper age limit for a job in France. In the UK 'age discrimination' is legal even though discrimination on grounds of gender, ethnic origin, etc. are not permitted.

Matching job seekers with employers varies from country to country. In Italy, for example, newspapers regularly include columns of personal information on new graduates, classified according to the type of job they are seeking. Employers can then contact them directly.

In France, the Minitel information system (similar to Prestel) is used regularly by 30% of households. This can be used to access more details of jobs advertised in newspapers. The system is interactive and it permits the employer to carry out a pre-selection test prior to issuing the details.

In Greece the most commonly used system of recruitment is personal introduction. In Germany the state-run employment placement system covers all grades of employee – executive, white-collar, blue-collar. In Italy private employment agencies can only 'advise' potential employers about candidates because all recruitment is state-controlled.

Interviews are the most commonly used method of selection throughout Europe. In some countries, such as France and Germany, it is not permitted to ask questions on some personal matters that are normal in UK interviews. Previous salary, for example, is considered irrelevant to the candidate's suitability for a job. Other methods of selection are used, including aptitude tests, personality tests and even hand-writing analysis (in Belgium, France and Italy).

Once employed, there are differences in the rights and responsibilities of employees. In France, for example, all employees are required to have a medical check at the time of their appointment, and again each year. Refusal to undergo the examination is grounds for dismissal. In several countries, notably Germany, an employee has the right to see all the information in their personnel file and to add their own comments if they wish.

RECOGNITION OF QUALIFICATIONS

One of the first things that a potential employer looks at is your qualifications. This can be a barrier for you when you apply for a job in another country because employers will probably know very little about UK qualifications.

Up to now recognition and acceptance of qualifications gained in another country have been established only for some professions, such as doctors, pharmacists, dentists, nurses, midwives, veterinary surgeons, architects and lawyers.

A general system for the recognition of higher education diplomas which are awarded following training lasting at least three years has applied since 1991. The system covers such occupations as surveyors, accountants, physiotherapists, psychologists, opticians, etc.

The establishment of National Vocational Qualifications (NVQs) in the UK is helping to get inter-country recognition of qualifications. Qualifications offered by BTEC, RSA, and City and Guilds are all becoming linked with Competences associated with NVQ levels (BTEC National, for example is mainly level 3 or 4). This system offers a unified standard which can be compared with vocational awards in other countries.

There is some recognition of the fact that BTEC National and A-levels are of a slightly lower standard than the French baccalaureate but there is still a lot to be done before most qualifications have acceptance in other EC countries.

Activity 9.3

1 Many of you will have Records of Achievement from school or college. Otherwise, ask your tutor to get you one.

2 Make sure it is up to date, with all your qualifications entered and certificates filed.

3 Be sure that your non-academic attainments are entered and authenticated.

4 When applying for a job and, more particularly, when going for an interview have translations made of the relevant items. If you do this yourself, have it checked by someone very competent in the language.

Your rights as a worker

The principle of equal treatment applies to employed and to self-employed EC nationals. You should not be treated less well than nationals of another EC country in terms of salary, working conditions, living conditions such as housing or social benefits, education or vocational training.

There are regulations covering the place of business, provision of services and setting up of businesses that affect the self-employed.

You may not be dismissed from your job on grounds that would not also apply equally to nationals of the country. If a problem arises you have the same statutory protection as they do. This may mean the right to reinstatement or compensation if you are unfairly dismissed. Remember though, your rights are those defined by the rules of the country where you work, not the rules that apply in the UK.

One exception to this is military service. At the present time we do not have compulsory military service in the UK. If we did then you would be liable for service even if you worked elsewhere in the EC, just as a Greek working in the UK would have to return to Greece to do military service.

You are entitled to embark on vocational training on the same terms as nationals. You cannot be required to pay fees or charges other than those required of nationals.

You have the same rights and obligations as nationals of the country where you live and work in terms of home ownership, borrowing money, and entering into contracts. Thus you can build or renovate a house with the help of grants, housing loans with reduced rates, etc. or receive housing benefits. You also have to pay the same local taxes as nationals. Your spouse and family would have the same rights as you.

Social benefits vary from country to country. In one country, for example, a service may be provided free, while in another you receive cash with which to buy it. The scope of the benefits also varies, particularly in the level of help that is given to special groups such as the disabled.

You may join a trade union and have the right to vote and hold office in the union, except where it is a position governed by public law or management of a body governed by public law.

At the time of writing, only Denmark, Ireland and the Netherlands have granted voting rights to non-nationals for local elections. However the Commission has proposed that:

- nationals who have been resident in another country for a certain period of time will be able to vote in that country, but will not be compelled to do so, and may instead retain eligibility to vote in their own country;
- nationals may also stand for election in countries other than their own, provided they have resided in the country for a certain period of time;
- countries where there is a very high proportion of nationals from other states (such as Luxembourg) will have a longer time in which to implement the proposals.

EQUAL RIGHTS FOR MEN AND WOMEN

Women tend to be concentrated in certain sectors of employment, often those requiring fewest skills. They are the most vulnerable group as regards unemployment. They suffer from discrimination in two areas: occupational equality and equality of opportunity in society.

As a woman, within the EC you are entitled to equal pay for work of equal value. 'Pay' refers to basic wage and all other benefits, in cash or kind, directly or indirectly. You are also entitled to participation in vocational training, equal opportunities for promotion and equal working conditions.

EC directives seek to ensure that men and women have equality in all areas covered by social security laws, banning discrimination in contributions and benefits in the areas of:

- sickness and invalidity;
- accidents at work and occupational diseases;
- old age and retirement;
- unemployment.

Special directives address equality in self-employment and agricultural work.

WORKER PROTECTION

A number of Community 'Action Programmes' have resulted in improved protection for workers against illness and accidents at work. The protection includes standards for safety markings, identification of dangerous physical, chemical and biological hazards (asbestos, lead, noise, etc). There is agreement on the provision of preventative, protective and emergency services, on the training and information that should be available on health and hygiene, and on workers' consultation and participation in improving the workplace.

A directive relating to collective redundancies compels the employer to give notice of at least 30 days.

In the event of a company being taken over, the new employer cannot unilaterally change or cancel employment contracts or the arrangements for employer-employee relations. There is also a safeguard for employees who have retired and receive company pensions.

If you are employed in an EC country other than your own and are made redundant through no fault of your own, you do not lose your rights. You must ask the employment office where you are resident for a ceritificate testifying that you have lost your job. If the insurance payments you have made in the various EC countries you have worked in are sufficient, you will be eligible for unemployment benefit.

In 1991 the European Commission tried to introduce, as part of the Social Charter, regulations that limited the working week to 48 hours, and prevented Sunday working except in special circumstances. The UK is almost unique in not already having laws covering these two areas and the government, supported by employers' associations, battled against its introduction. In practice throughout most of Europe the legislation is already tougher than the EC proposals. In France, for example, the legal limit is 39 hours and workers are entitled to 5 weeks' paid holiday plus 11 public holidays.

Most countries interpret the legislation as protection for the employee and work over that limit and on Sundays does take place with the agreement of employer and employee. In other words, it prevents the employer *imposing* conditions beyond the legal limits.

PUBLIC HOLIDAYS AND HOLIDAY ENTITLEMENT

Although no single country has more than 15 public holidays during the year, there are over 40 weekdays during the year when businesses in one or more of the EC countries are 'out of action' because of public holidays.

Some of the holidays are familiar to us in the UK – Easter, Christmas and New Year. Other days with religious significance are widely observed.

Most countries have a national day, celebrating independence, the constitution, the Queen's birthday, etc. Most countries have a holiday on 'Labour day' – 1 May. Several have public holidays linked with the two World Wars – Armistice day or VE day (France) or Repentance day (Germany).

Table 9.1 European public holidays

Date	Day	Austria	Belgium	Denmark	France	Germany	Greece	Netherlands	Ireland	Italy	Luxembourg	Portugal	Spain
1 Jan	New Year	✔	✔	✔	✔	✔	✔	✔	✔	✔	✔	✔	✔
6 Jan	Epiphany	✔				✔	✔			✔			✔
16 Feb	Shrove Tuesday											✔	
17 Mar	St Patrick's day								✔				
19 Mar	St Joseph's day												✔
varies	Maundy Thursday			✔									✔
varies	Good Friday			✔		✔		✔	✔			✔	✔
25 Mar	Independence day						✔						
varies	Easter Monday	✔	✔	✔	✔	✔	✔	✔	✔	✔	✔		✔
21 Apr	Great Prayer day			✔									
25 Apr	Liberation day									✔		✔	
30 Apr	Queen's birthday							✔					
1 May	Labour day	✔	✔		✔	✔	✔			✔	✔	✔	✔
varies	Ascension Day	✔	✔	✔	✔	✔		✔			✔		✔
8 May	VE day				✔								
varies	Whit Monday	✔	✔	✔	✔	✔		✔			✔		
25 May	Corpus Christi	✔				✔						✔	✔
5 Jun	Constitution day			✔									
10 Jun	National day											✔	
17 Jun	Day of unity					✔							
23 Jun	National day										✔		

continued overleaf

Date	Day	Austria	Belgium	Denmark	France	Germany	Greece	Netherlands	Ireland	Italy	Luxembourg	Portugal	Spain
14 Jul	National day				✓								
21 Jul	Independence day		✓										
25 Jul	St James' day												✓
15 Aug	Assumption day	✓	✓		✓	✓	✓			✓	✓	✓	✓
5 Oct	Republic day											✓	
12 Oct	National day												✓
26 Oct	National day	✓											
26 Oct	St Dimitrius' day						✓						
28 Oct	Ochi day						✓						
1 Nov	All Saints' day	✓	✓		✓	✓				✓	✓	✓	✓
2 Nov	All Souls' day										✓		
6 Dec	Constitution day												✓
8 Dec	Immaculate Conception	✓								✓		✓	
11 Nov	Armistice day		✓		✓								
22 Nov	Repentance day					✓							
1 Dec	Independence day											✓	
24 Dec	Christmas			✓									
25 Dec	Christmas	✓	✓	✓	✓	✓	✓	✓		✓	✓	✓	✓
26 Dec	Christmas	✓		✓				✓	✓	✓	✓	✓	
31 Dec	New Year's Eve			✓									
Variable date									1	3		2	

Table 9.1 continued

As in the UK, particular industries have their own pattern of holidays. EC statistics reveal that most European employees have four or five weeks of holiday in addition to the public holidays. The French have more, six or seven weeks is normal, but remember that their working day tends to be longer.

An observer hovering high over the centre of Europe would be able to determine the most common holiday times for each of the nations by the number of convoys of cars bearing 'F', 'B', 'NL', 'I', etc criss-crossing the Continent on particular dates.

Danes lead the rush because they tend to take three of their five weeks of annual holiday at the start of the school holidays which last from June to early August. Like the Belgians, they don't usually take any of their annual holidays around the Christmas, New Year or Easter public holidays so offices are fully staffed except for a day or two at these times.

Next to head for the holiday areas are the Belgians whose school holidays are in July and August. They prefer to split the holidays, usually taking two weeks at a time.

The French and Dutch like to take at least a week of the holidays in the winter, for winter sports. The French still have enough left to take four or five weeks in summer, and during the school holdiays from mid-July to early-September the industrial cities are virtually deserted.

August is the main holiday period for the Portuguese and Italians too, with many people on holiday for a four-week period. The Irish also prefer to have a single long holiday. The Germans have their three to four weeks in July or August. A feature of the Italian holiday is the 'extended' family, with grandparents, aunts and uncles, as well as parents and children, going on holiday together.

Taxation

When you transfer your residence from one EC country to another your personal effects are exempt from taxes when imported into the destination country provided they have been acquired inclusive of tax, and have been in use for at least three months (six months for a car or motor cycle). You may need the bills to prove this.

You may also furnish a secondary residence, shipping effects other than transport from another EC country, without being liable for tax.

Motor cycles, cars, caravans and boats may be taken with you without liability for import taxes when you transfer residence from one EC country to another but they must conform to the safety standards of the country and you must transfer your driving licence from the original to the new country. The procedure for the transfer of licence must be followed even if you have a Community Driving Licence instead of a national one.

Various systems apply to value-added tax. Although one of the SEM's aims is to harmonise VAT rates, it will be some time before this has been fully achieved because of the degree of difference and the effect it would have on the economies if they were harmonised suddenly. In 1991, for example the UK zero-rated 'essentials' such as food and had a single rate of 17.5% for everything else. At the same time France had VAT at 5.5% on food, travel, etc., 18.6% on most goods and services, and a top rate of 28% on electrical appliances, tobacco, jewellery, etc.

The situation with income tax is much more difficult. Again it is an aim of the SEM to harmonise income tax but, like VAT, this is also a major income for national governments and so changes would have a profound effect upon their economies. EC pressure to harmonise rates is also seen by some countries as an attempt to remove the 'sovereignty' of national governments, i.e. remove the power to act independently. While differences remain, taxation complicates the task of moving to another country to live and work.

Income tax is already a complex system in a single country because of the allowances and tax bands, and the methods of assessment and payment, especially if you have unearned as well as earned income. If you own assets in more than one country, such as property or shares, then you will probably need the professional help of a specialist in trans-national tax to avoid paying more than you need to.

There isn't space in this book to cover the tax systems for every country. The following is a review of the tax system of the country most commonly visited – France.

In 1991 40% of the French government's tax income came from VAT (*taxe sur la valeur ajoutée – TVA*) and 20% from income tax. The standard rate of tax on earned income, after allowances for dependent children etc., was slightly lower in France than in the UK, in 1991 (22.5% compared with 22% for a worker on £10 000 p.a.). At higher level of earnings the French paid more.

If you don't intend to become a *permanent* resident in France, or you expect to spend more than six months of the year in the UK you will need expert advice because you will be liable for tax in both countries.

You must register with the *inspecteur des impots* as soon as you get a job or begin a business. You will be sent an income tax return to complete. Tax is not deducted by PAYE as it is in the UK and you will normally make your first payment in the September following your first year there.

Tax returns must be returned by the end of February each year. Tax is paid on the preceding year's income, usually in three instalments – February, May and September. Alternatively you may ask to pay in ten instalments, monthly from January to October.

As in the UK, there are allowances for dependent children, and tax on bank interest is normally deducted at source. French allowances are quite generous so that the average person pays less than in most other European countries.

Social security

The industrially advanced countries of Europe all have well-developed social security systems. These provide for medical insurance, unemployment benefit, sick pay, retirement pension, death grant, maternity benefit, housing benefit for low income families, family allowance and industrial accident insurance.

Both the employer and the employee make contributions which are based on the employee's wage. Usually it is a percentage of the gross pay. In some countries it is quite high. In France, for example, it amounts to about 15% of income, compared with about 10% in the UK.

Unlike the UK, where benefits are generally a flat rate, many EC countries pay a percentage of the claimant's former salary, subject to a minimum and maximum. For example, in France unemployment pay is 40% of last salary, and sick pay is 50% of salary.

As in the UK, the pension that derives from social security contributions is usually considered inadequate and employees usually belong to a superannuation or pension scheme arranged either by the employer, the trade union, or the employee's professional association.

MEDICAL CARE   When you are working in another EC country you are treated in the same way as a national of that country as regards social security. If you have not been insured long enough in a country then any periods of insurance in another EC country will be taken into account.

If you work close to a frontier and live across the border in another EC state then you enjoy the benefits of the country in which you reside, even though you are not an official resident. You must obtain a form E106 from the social security office with which you are registered in the country where you work and forward a copy of it to a social security office in the country where you reside. Form E106 covers medical care, the purchase of drugs on which you can get a refund, hospital treatment and childbirth.

Note that an E106 is valid only for a limited period, and you must extend its validity as necessary.

The British DSS has a branch, based in Newcastle, that specialises in providing details of social security, health care and pension rights in the EC.

Once you become a resident of another European country you lose your right to use the British NHS free of charge, unless you return to the UK permanently. You will still be given emergency treatment following an accident but routine treatment would have to be paid for and reclaimed from the social security in your country of residence.

Although most practitioners will give you immediate treatment in the event of an accident, it is advisable to register with a doctor, dentist and optician when you take up residence. Perhaps surprisingly, relatively few practitioners speak English so it is as well to search for one that does. Describing symptoms and treatment is difficult unless you are exceptionally competent in a foreign language.

As in the UK many European health services don't cover all the charges. In the UK, for example, you have to pay for check-ups at the dentist and optician, and for a medical check that supports a life insurance policy or job application. You also have to pay part of the cost of prescriptions. The situation is similar in most other European countries. What is different in some is that you have to pay the full amount at the time of treatment, and then reclaim the proportion to which you are entitled from the social services.

Activity 9.4   Obtain leaflets from various countries so that you can compare the social security benefits that are enjoyed in those countries, and compare them with those offered in the UK.

Continuing your studies

You will face three main barriers if you wish to continue your studies in another European country:

- finance;
- getting your existing qualifications accepted as entry qualifications;
- coping with studies in a foreign language.

The ERASMUS programme is aimed at enabling students to follow part of their studies in another Community country. It covers all subjects and the entire range of university studies. It is based on an inter–university network of exchange agreements. Students have their tuition fees and travel expenses paid. They sometimes also receive financial help for language courses and with living expenses, if the country they are studying in has a higher cost of living than their own.

The COMETT programme is aimed at trainees, including new graduates, persons in active employment, and training officers. It assists co–operation between universities and businesses in training for new technologies.

If you are a student in an EC country then you should be eligible to join a vocational course in another EC country and pay the same fees as nationals of that country. To gain acceptance onto the course you may need to get the diploma you have already obtained in your own country recognised as an entry qualification. This can be a problem due to the fact that the educational systems of the member countries vary greatly. Other problems you may encounter may be the restriction on the number of places on the course, communication delays, payment of fees and accommodation. All these problems are much the same as when joining courses in your own country but are magnified by the differences in the procedures, language, etc.

The best advice on overcoming these problems is to apply early.

As a student in another EC country you are not guaranteed residence because you will not be undertaking 'economic activity'. However, you can usually be permitted to reside in another European country, provided you have adequate financial resources.

EDUCATION STRUCTURE

In the UK and Ireland, higher academic education is broadly at two levels; the first level (bachelors degree) of three years followed by the higher level (masters degree). The best-known vocational qualifications are BTEC Higher National Diploma courses, and the professional bodies have their own specialist examinations. Most people begin their higher education courses at the age of 18 or 19.

Elsewhere in Europe it is more common to find that degrees approximate more to our masters degree, that the period of study is four to six years or more, and that students start later. Their studies may be interrupted by military service but they can usually defer that to the end of their course and undertake it before starting work.

At the time of writing, UK higher education courses are based in universities, polytechnics or institutes of higher education but these are soon to be merged into a unified structure. The British class system may be the basis for some people's belief that universities are more 'academic' and somehow superior to polytechnics, which tend to be newer and 'technical'. These beliefs are not borne out in fact and they are not held to in other EC countries.

However, in many parts of Europe there is a functional distinction between academic universities and technical universities. The academic universities deliver 'pure' subjects such as languages and science and are particularly appropriate for those wishing to progress into research or teaching. The technical universities deliver 'applied' subjects such as engineering, business studies, law, etc.

There are also non-university higher education colleges that provide technician and vocational education such as the IUT (*Institutes Universitaires de Technologie*) in France, Higher Vocational Schools in the Netherlands, and *Fachhochschulen* in Germany. Here the courses tend to be shorter and lead to different awards. The level of the qualifications is as high as a degree, but covers a more limited scope.

Education systems are by no means standard throughout the EC. Moreover, in Spain, and in Germany, the education system has a strong regional bias.

ACCESS   While higher education establishments are usually happy to see applications from foreign students they are unwilling to pay the students expenses to attend interviews, and foreign students usually cause them extra work because of language and entry qualification differences, and once they are there, accommodation and financial problems.

Access to courses may be based on the student's existing qualifications, or there might be an entrance examination, or access might be completely open.

In Belgium, for example, a 'legal' degree (nothing to do with law but tending to be 'academic') will have a nationally laid-down structure, syllabus and entrance qualification which will preclude foreign students. A 'scientific' degree (in subjects such as engineering, psychology, social science or art history) has more open access. Many universities are introducing 'technical' degrees in subjects that would previously have only been offered via a 'legal' degree to offer wider access.

Because of the demand for some courses, such as engineering, Belgian universities have competitive entrance examinations to select the students for these subjects. The French *Grandes Écoles* also have their own competitive entrance examinations.

Germany has a completely open access policy for higher education. Any German student who has gained his or her *Arbitur* (school leaving certificate) can enrol at a university to study a subject of his or her choice. This leads to classes being overcrowded.

Greek students are allocated to universities according to the marks they get in their exams; they cannot choose which they want to go to, nor can the universities choose or reject them.

Drop-out rates vary from country to country, but even more from subject to subject and university to university. It is particularly high in French universities, but low in the *Grandes Ecoles*, probably because of the high entrance requirements.

Assessment on degree courses is still primarily by examination, although coursework and projects are taking on increasing importance. German degree courses, for example, are assessed by projects and oral means, as well as written exams, and most have a *practicum* (practical experience) component.

FOREIGN STUDENTS
Belgium has a high proportion of foreign students, particularly French-speaking ones, partly because there are very many non-Belgians working in Belgium. Another attraction is the low fees. Germany also has a high proportion of foreign students.

At the other extreme, there are few foreign students in Danish, Portuguese and Greek universities because of the language difficulties. Nor are there many in Spanish or Dutch universities.

FINISHING DATES
Finishing dates are by no means universal.

Belgian courses usually finish between June and September. Students then often do their 15 months' military service so employers expect to get most of their recruits during September to December.

Spanish courses finish in June. After 18 months' military service students tend to hit the job market in January to May.

French students normally do 12 months' military service or about 16 months' voluntary service after graduation, and leave their job hunting late, applying from Easter onwards. September to October is the main recruitment period for employers.

The Portuguese usually finish their examinations in July so they reach the job market in February to July, after their military service.

Danish students often don't graduate until they are in their early 30s, having employment for much of their time as students. Losing their student status when they graduate and having to repay their student loans when they graduate is a disincentive to complete their studies. Exams are twice per year so there is no clear recruitment season for employers.

The Italians too tend to intersperse their studies with periods of work. Study grants of about nine months (*Borse di studio*) and four months (*Stage*) facilitate this for Italian nationals.

Recruitment by Dutch and German employers tends to be continuous throughout the year.

PLACEMENT SERVICES
Some universities have their own placement service to assist students in their job hunting.

Danish universities are not closely involved in placement, but the trade unions play a major part in this activity.

The Federal Employment Service is the only agency allowed to provide a placement service in Germany. It has special officers to deal with foreign applicants.

There are no placement services at all in Portuguese, Greek or Dutch universities.

There are well-developed external agencies to assist French university students to find jobs. Minitel (computer-linked information system similar to Prestel in the UK) is an excellent source of information on courses and jobs in France.

EMPLOYMENT PROSPECTS
Students in other European countries are generally involved in a wider range of activities than in UK higher education, and potential employers are interested in extra-curricula activities as well as educational qualifications.

There is a strong feeling among mainland European employers that the subject of the student's degree should be relevant to his or her career aims.

An increasing trend, particularly strong in Portugal, is for employers to take on graduates for a trial period of about six months before offering them permanent posts.

If the hurdles can be overcome, overseas study is an attractive proposition and overseas work experience or vacation work can be a stepping stone to permanent work in the country. An alternative route would be to study in the UK and take work with the UK branch of a non-UK organisation as a means of increasing your 'Euro-awareness' and enhancing your opportunity to transfer to another country.

Activity 9.5
1 Select three colleges in a country of your choice and obtain a prospectus from each.

2 Compare the colleges and list the advantages and disadvantages of each as a place to study your subject, and as a step into a career.

Summary
1 Citizens of the EC have the right to compete for and take jobs in other EC countries on equal terms with nationals of that country.

2 The job seeker will find that different methods of locating job vacancies are needed for each country. There are national differences in the methods of selection and recruitment.

3 There is no Europe-wide recognition or comparability of qualifications, except in certain of the professions, but there is a commitment to establishing transferability of qualifications as part of progress to the SEM.

4 Temporary work and exchange schemes provide a good way of sampling different working conditions and practices.

5 Although all EC citizens have the same worker protection, equal opportunity, social benefit and unemployment rights as a national of the country in which he/she lives and works, there are, and will continue

to be, differences in salaries, tax and social security contributions, medical care, working hours and holidays.

Assignment 9   **LIVING AND WORKING IN EUROPE**

Joining a course or business organisation elsewhere in Europe may be very different from doing the same thing in the UK. However, all will go much more smoothly if you are well prepared.

1 Choose a course or career that you are interested in. Make contact with a person studying or working in your chosen field, in another European country. Obtain from him or her the answers to questions that you have about pursuing that choice in their country.

2 Divide into groups and compare notes on your findings. Be prepared to answer any questions that the others might have.

3 Carry out the exercise again, this time using your questions to write down the answers you would give if someone in another country had sent them to you. Attempt to make a useful response. Compare your response with others in the group.

Part Four
Doing business in Europe

10 European business scene

Objectives **Objectives** For a selection of major European countries:
1 outline the types of business organisational structures and the nature of industrial relations;
2 identify the factors that influence the chances of promotion and how they differ between countries.

It is dangerous to draw conclusions which generalise about the people or businesses of a whole nation. If you were to generalise about Britain there would be very many people and organisations which didn't conform to the profile. The comments given below on some of the countries of Europe should be read with that caveat clearly in mind. However, there are differences between the people, lifestyles and business methods among the various European nations which are worth noting.

A study of the UK's history shows that regional differences were very pronounced in the early stages of the industrial revolution, but as communications have improved, these differences have lessened. It will be interesting to see if the same kind of harmonisation occurs in Europe as the various countries work together more and communicate better.

Business environments

FRANCE France is a large country with a low population density and distinct regions. *See* p. 53. People have strong regional loyalties and are reluctant to move, except to Paris. Paris is very definitely the 'hub' of France in every way. A Parisian who is transferred to one of the regions feels exiled.

Western France has an *Atlantic* tradition with long navigable rivers and maritime trade. Eastern France is *Continental* in nature with industry based on coal and minerals with the Rhine as a major route for imports and exports. The south is predominantly *Mediterranean* with all that implies in terms of culture, agriculture and tourism.

Politically France is very centralised. There is no hint of federalism, unlike Germany. The education system demonstrates this very well – the national curriculum and examination system allow for virtually no regional differences. Centralism may be traced back to the *Code Napoléon* which aimed to cover every eventuality by a framework of rules.

France has a much more homogeneous set of values than many smaller countries. There is a strong sense of pride in national projects such as Concorde and the Channel Tunnel. The government is directly and indirectly involved in industry and commerce and in some sectors the division between public and private businesses is not clear. There is much protectionism, for example in agriculture.

Although individuals are keen to outwit the government in the area of taxation, and government is often considered to be excessively politically motivated, nevertheless there is a respect for its integrity. Civil servants are well respected and highly paid.

Foreign-owned multinationals represent about 80% of the business machine industry, 70% of oil, and 60% of the agricultural machinery industry. Foreign investment is, however, closely controlled and monitored by the government.

French government and businesses have a good record of long-term planning. Nuclear power and high-speed trains are typical of the investment that has been made over many years through several changes in government.

There are two types of business – the SA (*Société Anonyme*) and the SARL (*Société à Responsabilité Limitée*). SARLs are usually small, with a maximum of 50 shareholders to whom the management is accountable. An SA can have one of two forms of management.

1 A board of directors made up of elected shareholders (*le Conseil d'Administration*) headed by *le Président* who chairs the board and acts as chief executive. There are normally between three and 12 *administrateurs* (directors). This is the more common structure.

2 A two-tier system with a supervisory board (*le Conseil de Surveillance*) and a management board (*le Directoire*) of two to seven directors appointed by the supervisory board. The management board, headed by the PDG (*Président Directeur Général*), runs the company.

Any business that employs more than 50 people must have a works committee (*comité d'enterprise*) which is entitled to send two representatives to meetings of the administrative or supervisory boards (but not to management boards). They do not have voting rights.

Business organisations tend to be centralised and arising from this they have strongly vertical hierarchies, clear-cut divisions and central planning, and they are elitist and legalistic. There tend to be more layers of middle management than in a Dutch or German company. The formal structure is, therefore, not responsive to the need for change. Informal relationships tend to become established to deal with the realities of everyday business life.

The PDG of a French business usually has a high degree of technical competence and gives more attention to detail than equivalents in other European countries. He or she is usually decisive. Subordinates will often criticise or show scepticism but they usually have a respect for authority based on competence rather than status.

Although performance appraisals are increasingly used in businesses there is still a tendency to link them with personal criticism, since collective decision-making, and hence collective responsibility is less common than in some countries. It may be that this arises from the competitive nature of schools and ambition to rise within the hierarchy of business. Relationships in teams formed to undertake a project tend to be formal rather than easy-going and friendly.

It is usual to have a detailed agenda for business meetings. Those attending will usually have prepared carefully and make their contribution at the appropriate time. Thus the meeting is a means of clarifying the situation and making one's position clear. Where a person of authority is present it is the occasions on which decisions are announced.

Business communications are on two levels, reflecting the nature of the business organisation itself. There is a formal, written level, in which the report is much used, and great importance is attached to clear but concise French, well constructed and correct. There is also the informal level which depends on a network of personal relationships.

Education and qualifications play an important role in careers and promotion. Technical qualifications such as engineering have a high status, as do law and finance. Sales and marketing were, until recently, less esteemed. Women have made considerable progress in the management of retail and service industries, especially law, finance and personnel but they are less numerous in senior positions in industry, especially outside Paris. It is noticeable that many of the senior positions in management are filled by people from 'old money' families.

France is the UK's third largest customer, accounting for about 10% of its exports. Originally the main exports were petroleum-related goods but manufactured goods and the service sector have now shown massive growth.

The French market for consumer goods is very similar to that in the UK. Demand for gardening and DIY goods is expanding and good quality British food and drink products are increasingly popular. The giftware, china, jewellery and stationery markets are also growing. Golf is the fastest growing sport in France but UK manufacturers face keen competition from Japan and the USA.

Amongst capital goods, demand for health care, security and pollution control equipment is significant.

Activity 10.1   In what ways does the organisational structure and management of a SARL differ from a small British limited liability company?

GERMANY   The unification of Germany in 1990 has produced a confusing scene in that country.

The Federal Republic (West Germany) was probably the richest of the European countries with a strong enterprise economy. By contrast, the German Democratic Republic (East Germany) was a Communist, centrally controlled economy in which wages and productivity were low, there was considerable overmanning in factories, the infrastructure was in decline, the quality of goods was poor, and most consumer goods were scarce. However, prices were low, especially for essentials like housing, transport, clothes and food and there was virtually no unemployment.

At the time of unification the people of the East looked forward to more freedom in a democratic state, higher wages, and improvements in their living conditions. What they did not realise was that higher wages would be accompanied by a higher cost of living, that they would no longer be guaranteed a job, and that some of their fellow citizens would be ruthless in exploiting the entrepreneurial opportunities.

The people in West Germany soon realised that the cost of unification was high. Massive funds were needed to improve the run-down infrastructure of the East and this demanded higher taxes. Industrialists could use the pool of 'cheap labour' from the East for unskilled work, to the detriment of wages and employment levels in the Western sector.

It will be several years before the turmoil arising from the unification dies down. It is clear, however, that the model of West Germany will be the one that emerges, not that of East Germany.

It is perhaps fortunate that Germany is a federal country in which the Landers (regions) have considerable autonomy. Frankfurt, for example, is the centre of banking and finance; Hamburg is a trading city; Munich is home of the sunrise industries (and of the arts); Dusseldorf, Dortmund and Essen lie in the area famous for heavy industry.

Germany has the largest automobile industry in Europe, with BMW in Munich; Daimler-Benz, Mercedes and Porsche in Stuttgart; Volkswagen in Wolfsburg; Ford and General Motors in Cologne.

Unlike France, where there is a spider's web of road and rail links centred on Paris, Germany has a network of transport and communcation links.

The Germans take business seriously. Many countries look to Germany as the producer of good quality products, and Germans are conscious of this and take pride in their products, their production methods, and their management methods.

The German government has a shareholding in many key businesses and there is public ownership of many of the services. There are also national and regional schemes to provide subsidies to industry, which result in high taxation.

German industry is extensively regulated by legislation and government guidelines. These are viewed as supportive and helpful and rather than trying to evade them, businesses are more likely to look at ways of enhancing and improving the framework.

Complementing this control over the economy there are organisations to encourage competition and prevent monopolies taking control of any market sector. There is an assumption that a merger will be harmful to competition and companies must prove that this is not the case before the merger is permitted. This tends to reduce the number of takeovers and makes it difficult for a foreign business to acquire a German company as a way into the market.

As in many countries, the banks have a powerful influence on commerce and industry. The Bundesbank is the key bank, with great influence over the financial markets. The biggest three of the others, nationally – Deutsche, Dresdner and Commerzbank – offer a wider range of services than would be normal in many countires where there are often separate banks specialising in investment, stockbroking, merchant banking, etc.

The relatively small number of takeovers and the strength of financial support to businesses by banks and government make it possible to plan strategically and make long-term investments that a less stable and certain environment would prevent.

Although Germany is well known for its large conglomerates there are also a lot of family-owned and medium-sized companies. In these, particularly, there is a concern for employee welfare which leads to the provision of facilities that are quite remarkable. Unions in Germany are organised by industry, not by skill so that a multiplicity of unions representing the workers of one organisation is unheard of. The unions have the highest membership amongst workers in mining, steelmaking and engineering.

There is extensive legislation protecting workers' rights and welfare. These are balanced by restrictions on the freedom of unions. This contrasts with the UK where there is relatively little legislation in this area and employers and unions jealously guard their 'freedom' to act without restriction. In practice the legislative framework means that strikes are rare, a last resort which follows arbitration and consultation procedures. Even then the strikes are usually short and are used to demonstrate strength of feeling rather than as a weapon to cause major damage to the employer.

There are two types of limited liability companies. An AG (*Aktiengesellschaft*) is a public limited company while a GmbH (*Gesellschaft mit beschränkter Haftung*) is a private company. Organisations with more than 500 employees have a supervisory board (*Aufsichtsrat*) consisting of up to 20 people which appoints the management board (*Vorstand*). The directors (*Vortstandsmitglieder*) who form the management board have to be re-appointed every four years. People who are employed as senior managers, but aren't on the management board, have a title which might lead British people to believe they were members of the board of directors – *Directoren*.

In smaller companies there is no supervisory board and the directors (*Geschäftsfuhrer*) are appointed directly by shareholders.

Employees in any company with more than five employees have a right to form a works council (*Betriebsrat*). Its elected representatives may consider the company's economic, personnel and social policies and have to be consulted on decisions affecting employment. A company with over 100 employees must set up an economic committee (*Wirschaftsausschuss*) comprising management and employee representatives to discuss sales, production and financial matters. It has no authority over the management's decision-making powers.

In a company with over 1000 employees one third of the supervisory board is elected by employees, and two-thirds is elected by shareholders. If there are more than 2000 employees then employees and shareholders elect half each. In the latter case there must be a personnel director (*Arbeitsdirektor*) on the management board.

Germans respect authority that is derived from status and competence. They tend to be most comfortable when functions have been thoroughly investigated and suitable procedures drawn up. Cutting corners is not popular. The result is that, when the unexpected occurs, people look for a method of dealing with it that is already defined. Improvisation is seen as a failure to plan properly, rather than as a useful skill. Planning and decision-making usually include consideration of contingency plans. Once plans are made and accepted subordinates will follow the instructions faithfully; conversely management is expected to give clear guidance and leadership.

Despite the presence of worker representatives on company boards, the opportunities for participation in setting targets and feedback on performance are sometimes seen as inadequate, and relationships between superior and subordinate perceived to be too formal.

It is easier for a person to rise from a humble start to a senior position in a German company than it would be in a French one. There are no equivalents to the prestigious *Grande Écoles*. Engineers have a high status, unlike many countries where marketing or finance have top spot. There is a highly developed apprenticeship system, and higher education is mainly vocational. It is worth noting that, as in most societies, it is as important to 'know the right people' as well as being technically competent.

Promotion tends to come by developing one's own technical knowledge or experience. Job security is highly valued. Many Germans like to stay in their own region. People believe that they should work hard and be rewarded eventually by promotion. Increased salary is not as great an incentive as in many countries and Germany has the lowest range of earnings of any European country.

GREECE

Greek industry is traditionally family-run. Those businesses which have grown into large organisations, are often closely associated with the banks, particularly the National Bank of Greece. When the socialist party gained power, 30 of the largest companies were nationalised and many of the senior managers were replaced by government appointees. The state now controls 70% of economic activity either directly or by having financial control. Amongst the smaller businesses there was a record number of bankruptcies at the end of the 1980s.

Shipping is a major industry, so is tourism. Greece is visited by 8 million tourists each year and foreign businesses have invested heavily in the Greek tourist industry. It is perhaps surprising that a nation which trades with the rest of the world and is host to so many foreign visitors still focuses around the family and village life.

The Ministry of Labour controls the pay structure. Industrial relations lack a formal structure and are confrontational, with a strong political element. Companies use a combination of bonuses and other fringe benefits to motivate and retain their staff. Many Greeks have two jobs, one of which may be their own business.

There are two basic business organisation types in Greece. The AE (*Anonymi Eteria*) is a private company, similar to the French SA, while the EPE (*Eterio Periorismenis Efthinis*) is a public company. An AE board must have at least three directors, elected by the shareholders. The chief executive of an AE is usually designated General Manager while in an EPE he or she is the Managing Director although a business may have both.

An independent and entrepreneurial attitude is common amongst Greeks and this is seen in their ingenuity in trying to receive money from government bodies rather than paying for something themselves. It is also demonstrated by employees who give the impression that an organisation exists solely for the benefit of the individuals in it. Communication and co-operation between parts of a business are often more a feature of personal relationships than of the business organisational structure.

As in many countries, there is a trend towards 'American style' management with new techniques and attitudes. The banks are keen to promote management discipline, implemented often through tighter financial control. They also favour a longer timescale in business planning, whereas traditionally, businesses tended to be opportunistic and reactive.

Business meetings tend to be informal, without an agenda or minutes, with participation often in the form of strongly put opinions. Face-to-face meetings are preferred to telephone conversations.

Loyalty and trust are very important and promotion will often be based on this rather than qualifications, or even expertise. Personal influence, political affiliation, and family associations are important in career development. Women are well represented in the professions, politics and business management although career women are often still treated with suspicion.

In the four years up to 1989, the UK's trade with Greece increased by 300%. Amongst capital goods, iron and steel products, road vehicles, electrical machinery and appliances are in demand.

Despite the lowest per capita GDP in the EC, the Greek market for consumer goods is quite sophisticated. Price and quality are usually of equal importance, but designer label clothes are very much in demand, irrespective of price. Demand for imported food, beverages and clothing is increasing but the UK has failed to take a share of this, except in whisky which saw a 64% increase in sales to Greece for 1988–89.

The DTI believes that the major opportunities for exports to Greece are in foodstuffs; agri-business and food processing, telecommunications; aerospace and airports; financial services; and consultancy. The retail sector is dominated by small family-run outlets and multiple branches are rare except in the largest chains of supermarkts and government stores. There are only six genuine supermarket chains and most of these are concentrated in greater Athens and Salonica. Of the five main department stores only one has a branch outside Athens.

Activity 10.2

1 As a sales manager for a medium-sized British food producer, how do you rate your chances of selling in Greece?

2 How would you set about selling your company's products there?

NETHERLANDS

Imports and exports account for 60% of the GNP. The Netherlands is the world's largest exporter of poultry, dairy products, house plants and flowers. The Dutch import large quantities of fertiliser and feedstuffs to support their agriculture industry.

The Dutch own half the trucks that transport goods around Europe. They have a history of shipping and trading, and once had extensive colonies. As you would expect in a trading nation, the banks have a strong influence on the business world.

Their economy is closely linked with Germany's because, being at the mouth of the Rhine they provide the port by which a large amount of Germany's exports leave and imports arrive. From the Netherlands it is possible to reach all of Europe's major economic centres within one day's surface travel.

The best-known Dutch companies are the multinationals Philips, Unilever and Royal Dutch Shell. These three, together with DSM, which mines and processes brown coal, and Akzo, employ 25% of the labour force. However, there are very many small- and medium-sized privately-owned companies.

In the past the state was involved in industry by large holdings in Fokker and DAF, but has recently taken a policy of privatisation. Foreign investment in the Netherlands is assisted by government incentives.

The Netherlands has a comprehensive social welfare system but this places a great strain on the economy because of the high level of public spending it involves. Personal and corporate tax levels are high, resulting in a high degree of tax avoidance and a black economy, particularly in the building trade.

There is a high national minimum wage, increasing entry of women into the labour market, and sluggish investment in industry. Although there is high unemployment, there are many vacancies in the lower paid job sector.

Employers are represented by the Protestant-Catholic NCW and the non-denominational VNO. They work closely together. There are three main union groups, representing about 40% of industry in total: the Protestant CNV, the Catholic NKV and the Liberal NW. Employers and unions meet at a Joint Industrial Labour Council. Both are also represented on the Social and Economic Council along with government representatives and independent consultants.

There has been a move away from central negotiation of wage rates towards more local deals. Industrial disputes and strikes are more common than a few years ago, but still rare because industrial relations are based mainly on negotiation rather than confrontation. Companies that employ more than 35 people must set up a works council (*Ondernemingsraad*) which receives financial information from the company and is consulted on investment and personnel matters.

The two most common sorts of company are: NV (*Naamloze Vennootschap*) which is a public limited company, and BV (*Beslotejn Vennootschap*) which is a private limited company. Both have a management board led by a managing director. A large company – defined by the amount of capital and number of employees (i.e., over 100 people) – must have a supervisory board of at least three people.

The management board, works council and three shareholders nominate candidates for the supervisory board (*Commissarissen*). The members of the supervisory board cannot be employed by the company. They approve company policy, appoint the management board and finalise the annual accounts. The supervisory board has many of the powers that shareholders have in British and North American companies. For example, decisions on mergers lie with the supervisory board, not the shareholders.

Dutch companies tend to have clear procedures which are respected and adhered to. Relationships between all levels is open and tolerant. There is a preference for spoken rather than written communication.

Business meetings are held frequently and follow an agenda despite an informality of manner. Everyone is expected to make clear, informed contributions with the aim of achieving a consensus.

The importance of making a profit is well understood, even in the lower levels of an organisation. Business plans tend to be cautious, favouring step-by-step development.

The Dutch take a long-term view on things, including their own careers. Education and qualifications are important factors in promotion. A sense of company loyalty is reinforced by pension structures, and pay agreements are highly standardised so that there is little financial incentive to move jobs. Individual performance-related pay is against the collective ethos.

Most senior executives have been educated at the Universities of Delft (engineering), Rotterdam (economics) or Leiden (law and the humanities). There is an aristocracy which is seen most clearly in the appointments in banks and the diplomatic service. There are apprenticeship schemes for manual workers similar to the German model, with further on-the-job training.

Even by 1990, there were few women in managerial roles. Women only began to come into the labour market in the 1970s and now account for about 30% of the workforce. Married women still tend to give up work when they have children.

Activity 10.3   How do union membership and industrial relations in the Netherlands differ from the UK?

SPAIN   Spain underwent two major changes as it prepared to join the EC. It reduced its preoccupation with its old colonies and Africa and focused instead on Europe resulting in business activities having a higher profile. It also threw off its legacy of Francoism and began to take a greater interest in democratic politics. Since the first referendum in 1976 there have been over 40 polls but there has been remarkable stability and continuity in government, with the extreme left and extreme right having only fringe influence.

There is still, however, a wide diversity of regional interests – notably among the Basques, Catalans and Galicians and strong pressure for separatism. The result is suspicion, even hostility, towards government and officialdom.

Government has a strong influence in industry, directly and through the state holding company *Instituto Nacional de Industria* (INI). The state airline, Iberia, and three traditional industries, iron and steel, shipbuilding and textiles are all effectively government-run.

In general, private business is dominated by family-run and foreign-owned organisations. These foreign companies are the principal source of technological, financial and management expertise. The stock exchange's influence is recent; previously the banks were the sole source of finance for the private sector. The accounting profession is in the process of forming a body to define and regulate standards. Company accounts are far less comprehensive than is required in the UK.

There are two types of company, the SA (*Sociedad Anonima*) and the SRL (*Sociedad de Responsabilidad Limitada*). A minimum of three shareholders is needed to form an SA and there are no limits on capitalisation. An SRL cannot have more than 50 shareholders and its capitalisation must not exceed 50 million pesetas.

An SRL company may have one or more directors and does not need to have auditors unless it is listed on the stock exchange or is a bank. An SA may have a single director or a board of at least three directors.

Traditional Spanish companies have a clear chain of command, and are separated into departments to assist in management control, rather than to assist specialisation. Many older companies are bureaucratic and authoritarian in their management. Data collection to assist with decision-making is not highly regarded and systematic procedures are seen as a fall-back rather than something to be regularly used. Improvisation in the face of crisis and emergency is admired.

Very few of the current decision-making generation speak any language other than their own so any sales literature promoting UK products must be in Spanish.

Rapid growth in economic activity has resulted in a serious shortage of skilled managers. A number of business schools are being set up, some of them privately run, and many managers are trained abroad, notably in France. Women have not made significant progress in reaching senior management positions yet. Until this growth took place, job security was an important consideration. People are still reluctant to move to another location for promotion because the family remains an important social aspect of Spanish life, and a secure base. However, there is now a shortage of skills, particularly in cities like Madrid and Barcelona, and this means that moving from job to job is possible, providing a faster promotion route than remaining in one company. Regional accents are still an impediment to progression in some career areas, where background is still the most significant factor.

1992 remains a special year in Spain, with the Olympic games in Barcelona, Expo 92 in Seville, Madrid's nomination as the European City of Culture, and the end of the seven-year transitional period towards full membership of the EC.

As tariff barriers declined in the run-up to full membership, demand for imported consumer goods increased, including clothing, toys and cars. Local businesses in all sectors have suffered from foreign competition and it has been realised that Spanish management and productivity have to improve. Many UK firms have formed partnerships with Spanish ones to acquire local marketing knowledge and distribution channels. However, the UK has lost ground to Germany, France and Italy with a share of imports to Spain that declined from 7.7% in 1985 to 6.5% in 1991.

Activity 10.4
1 If you were taking up a post as a junior manager with a company in Spain, what differences would you expect to find from a similar job in the UK?

2 How would you adapt to the situation?

Summary
1 Other European countries have more than one type of business structure, just as in the UK, where there is a private limited company and a PLC. Associated with each are rules about such things as capitalisation and composition of the board of directors and management.

2 Countries such as Germany and the Netherlands have legislation that gives employees greater respresentation in company policy-making than in the UK.

3 Each country has its own customs regarding relationships between managers and subordinates and among colleagues. Differences are lessening, however as an 'international' business culture develops, particularly among younger managers.

Assignment 10 **ORGANISATIONAL CULTURE**

Background

As a management trainee in the personnel department of a large UK manufacturing company, you have undertaken a number of tasks related to the works committee which has representatives from management and the employees.

Among the topics that it has discussed over the last four meetings are health and safety, employee performance appraisal, working hours and holidays, pay and productivity, quality issues, and plans by a Japanese competitor to set up a factory close to your own

You are shortly to transfer to an equivalent job in the offices of a company that has just been taken over by your own. This company is in another European country (you may choose which one).

Tasks

1 Outline the differences you expect to find in the way this company deals with the issues that are discussed at works committee meetings in the UK.

2 How do you think your career progression would differ if you stayed in the new company? In what way do you think your attitudes and behaviour would have to change for you to gain promotion?

3 What tensions do you expect to arise if the UK parent company tries to impose its approach to industrial relations upon the European subsidiary?

11 Buying and selling in Europe

Objectives
1 Identify the reasons for exporting.
2 Outline the stages in internationalism.
3 Distinguish between the various ways of operating in another European country and the opportunities for doing so.
4 Describe the market infrastructure that produces a potentially 'hot' country and methods of finding marketing opportunities.
5 Select suitable market entry strategies for various situations.
6 Derive a marketing mix that is suitable for a given export market.
7 Recognise the conditions that lead to a business becoming involved in importing and the skills needed to successfully negotiate a business deal with a foreign supplier.

Exporting

An organisation that wants to sell its products or services in another country faces a more complex task than when it is selling in its own country.

The distances between the organisation's headquarters, its base in the target country, and the customers in the target country are generally much greater so there are logistics problems. It takes more time for goods and documentation to pass between the locations, and the additional distances make the trade more susceptible to disruption.

The business methods of the target country are likely to be different to those of the home country so that there may be mismatches in documentation, methods of payment, procedures for arranging delivery, differences in quality checking and certification, and so on.

The culture and fashions of the target country are likely to be different from those of the home country which means that market research carried out at home will not be valid for the target country. This means that products developed for the home market, and pricing and promotion strategies, may need adaptation for an export market.

Exporting often involves handling different currencies, so care must be taken to avoid losses due to adverse currency fluctuations.

Activity 11.1
The added complexity of exporting outlined above has been described very much in terms of selling a product. In what way would the export of a service be more complex than offering it in the home country?

Given the additional complexities of exporting, vis-à-vis trading on the home market, why do so many businesses undertake it?

MOTIVES FOR EXPORTING

PRODUCT LIFE CYCLE

Every product or service has a life cycle. This extends from its birth (when it is invented or discovered) through to its death (when it is finally discontinued). This life cycle may be very short, as for a hit record, or very long (e.g. a type of sailing boat).

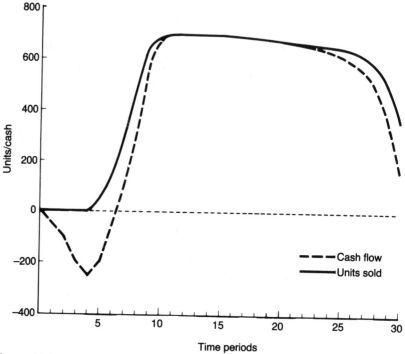

Figure 11.1 Product life cycle

Notes:

Periods 1–5 Research and development spending increases and towards the launch date (period 5) there is massive spending on promotion.

Periods 6–10 Sales of the product increase as the public becomes more aware of it. There is still a heavy financial commitment to promotion and there is some spending on product modifications so that income doesn't fully reflect the volume of sales.

Periods 11–15 The product has reached maximum market penetration. There is no competition.

Periods 16–20 Despite fighting off direct competitors successfully there is an erosion of market share as new products and changes in fashion and technology offer alternatives.

Periods 21–25 Sales volume is maintained by price cutting and special offers. Income declines faster than volume.

Periods 26–30 The product goes into a terminal phase. It is only a matter of time before the product is discontinued. It may be given a reprieve if competitors leave the market so that your product achieves a bigger market share and less competition allows you to stabilise prices.

Before a product can be sold it has to progress from the conceptual stage (where the inventor outlines their ideas), through research and development to a prototype and then to the point where volume manufacture can be started. Market research needs to be carried out thoroughly to identify the level of risk and to avoid committing funds to a product that is unlikely to sell well. In the later part of the development stage test marketing be carried out to discover how accurate the market research had been.

The launch of a new product can involve a major promotion campaign, with advertising, introductory offers, etc. The aim is to establish as big a market as possible in the minimum time. In this 'youthful' stage in the product's life there will be no competition and although it is important to get the right price, the product will not be very price sensitive.

As the product moves towards maturity it may be possible to find cheaper ways of manufacturing it. Producing in volume could also offer economies of scale and production costs should fall. However, a successful product will attact competition and it may be necessary to reduce the price to stay competitive and retain market share.

As the market for a product declines, because fashions or technology have moved on, or because there are alternative or better products, there may still be market opportunities. The main manufacturers may discontinue the product because they are interested only in high-volume production. A small, specialist manufacturer may be able to tap the remaining market, perhaps even at a higher price. There may also be a market for spare parts long after the product itself is obsolete.

Launching the product in another country where it is not already available may open up a market that is free of competition. It is important to remember, though, that the product may need adaptation for the new market.

A company specialising in 'declining' products may find an opportunity to make and sell a product that is obsolete in a country because no one manufactures it, but for which there is still a market. Many models of motor cars fit into the category of 'obsolete' products for which there is still a market.

The Morris Minor (the 'moggie') and the Volkswagen Beetle are popular models although normal production of them ceased long ago. The Citroën 2CV, a design nearly 50 years old, has a following that can only be described as a 'cult' and will probably result in small-scale manufacture by a 'niche' organisation.

COMPETITION   A successful product attracts competition.

An expanding market can accommodate additional players because the newcomers take a 'slice of the action' while the original companies are able to maintain their sales volume, or even continue to increase it.

In a static or declining market competition can have a very damaging effect on an existing manufacturer. In order to maintain market share it may be necessary to cut the price. In some situations the newcomer has an advantage. It does not have to make the large investment in research and development, and there isn't the risk of developing a product and then finding that there is no market for it. The newcomer may also be able to benefit from improvements in technology which means that it can buy and install machines that are cheaper, more reliable or faster than those of the original producer. On the other hand there are situations where the established company has the advantage with a loyal customer base and a well-known brand name.

If competition gets too tough the choices are to withdraw from the market, or to find new ones. An expanding overseas market may be attractive and encourage a company to export.

EXCESS CAPACITY UTILISATION

For a variety of reasons, a company may find that it has the capacity to produce more than it can sell.

An overseas market may be an attractive way of utilising the spare capacity, even if the price that can be obtained for the product is less than in the home country, and there are significant distribution costs.

Activity 11.3

ABC Ltd has the capacity to produce 20 000 units of its Super K product, but it can only sell 15 000 units in the UK at the optimum selling price of £16 per unit. Fixed costs are £120 000 and the variable cost to produce 1 unit of Super K is £4, so the total cost of Super K at this level of production is £12 per unit.

ABC Ltd could sell 5000 units in Spain but the best price would be the equivalent of £8 per unit.

Should ABC Ltd sell to Spain?

If the cost to transport and distribute 5000 units in Spain was £10 000 would it still be profitable to sell there?

GEOGRAPHIC DIVERSIFICATION

A country's economy often experiences periods of boom and periods of depression. Some products are more susceptible to changes in demand as the economic situation changes.

A company may choose to export to one or more countries to spread its risk. It is assuming that the market in one country will remain buoyant when it is depressed in another, and it is certainly true that depression often affects different countries at different times and to a greater or lesser extent.

COMMERCIAL FEASIBILITY

For some products it is only economic to manufacture in large quantities, for example when the unit value of the product is very small. The nature of the production process (such as with steel, chemicals, etc.) may be such that production needs to be continuous.

In both these situations it may be that the home market isn't large enough to support the introduction of the product and a business may look to a wider market to make the investment commercially feasible.

OPERATING OUTSIDE THE HOME MARKET

There are four ways by which a company may operate outside its home country:

- direct exporting;
- indirect exporting;
- carrying out production abroad;
- through a joint venture.

DIRECT EXPORTING

Direct exporting involves selling products in another country by means of an international sales force or through an agent or distributor.

A *freight forwarder* transports goods to the customer, but is not involved in the task of selling and collecting payment.

An *agent* acts on the exporter's behalf and holds inventory. Agents sell goods and carry out administration in connection with the sales. Although they store goods they do not make payments until goods are sold to a customer.

By contrast, a *distributor* purchases stock from the exporter and is then responsible for selling it and collecting payment. The exporter has no further interest in the goods once the distributor has bought them. Many distributors ask for exclusivity, i.e. they are the only distributors for that product in the region or even the country.

Another possibility is to set up a *consortium marketing group* through which consortium members jointly sell products in another country.

INDIRECT EXPORTING

A company undertakes indirect exporting when it does not have dealings in the country to which it is exporting. One way of doing this is by selling through an *export house* which handles all the transportation, documentation and foreign currencies dealings for export.

'*Piggybacking*' is a means of exporting by using the distribution channels of another company in a related (but not directly competitive) field. For example, a car parts manufacturer may 'piggyback' by using the distributors of a large motor car company.

MOVING PRODUCTION ABROAD

Licensing a patented manufacturing process allows a company to derive income from a product although it is made and sold by a completely separate organisation.

A company may choose to manufacture the components of their product in their own country and ship them as kits to be assembled and sold in the target market.

Otherwise, there is the option to become involved in a *joint venture* of which there are two types. One is based on an agreement whereby the partner in the export territory makes and sells a product and the partners share the profits according to some agreed formula. The other type takes this a step further whereby the joint-venture partners own a company that manufactures and sells the products.

Furthermore, a company may choose to have a wholly owned *subsidiary* in another country, manufacturing as well as selling their products.

FRANCHISING   If the company has a product or service with an internationally-known brand name or logo it may consider *franchising* it. The franchisee pays a fee for the privilege of using it. This may also involve providing management expertise to help the franchisee be successful.

If a company has particular expertise in a technology or management technique it may enter into a *management contract* with an overseas operator. Under the terms of the agreement the company receives a fee from the operator for providing training and up-to-date information in the specialist field.

Activity 11.4   If you were operating a successful clothing business in the UK and were looking to expand internationally, what type of operation would you consider if you were:

1 hoping to sell your existing products there.

2 hoping to buy-in new designs.

STAGES IN INTER-NATIONALISM   Almost all businesses begin on a small scale. They become familiar with the home market and establish a basic system for selling and distributing their products. At this stage most feel that they are not capable of dealing with the additional risk and complexity of exporting. Even if they grow they tend to keep to the market and products that they are familiar with.

At this stage, they are likely to refuse an enquiry from a potential customer from overseas. However, a very attractive enquiry, perhaps coupled with a setback in the home market may prompt them to consider supplying an overseas customer, and subsequently fulfil unsolicited orders from further customers.

This often leads on to the company actively exploring the feasibility of exporting.

The initial step is likely to be an experimental move into the market in another country. The chosen market is likely to be geographically close to the home country but it is equally important that the export territory should have similar business methods and a population with similar tastes and culture, to the home country. Such a market could be described as 'psychologically close'.

A cautious approach is to enter into only one or two countries and consolidate until becoming an experienced exporter to those countries.

The company may then become truly international by establishing sales offices in the export territories, and even considering production there.

MARKET INFRA-STRUCTURE   It is important to investigate the social and political aspects of export markets.

SOCIAL ENVIRONMENT   Nationalities have different attitudes to:

| age | birth | bringing up children |
| art | body language | cleanliness |

community	folklore and	music
cooking	mythology	names
courtship	games	numeracy
criminality	gender and sex	population
death, funerals and	gifts	property rights
mourning	government	religion
decoration – home	greetings	science and technology
decoration – personal	hairstyles	sports
divinity	hospitality	status
division of labour	humour	superstition and luck
dreams	hygiene	surgery and medicine
eating	inheritance	taboos
education	language	trade
ethics	law	visiting
etiquette	marriage	weather
family groups	modesty	working together

Nationalities vary in their attitudes to the acquisition of goods and services. It is much more difficult to sell household goods in a market where the population tends not to place great importance on the home, than in one where household acquisitions convey status.

Different nationalities also have different attitudes towards colours, design, and brand names.

Words which are 'foreign' to the country where the product is sold may appear more 'exotic' than the equivalent 'domestic' word and may therefore give an 'excitement' that helps sales. On the other hand, some products need a 'homely' image so that a domestic word is preferable.

Dark colours are often less popular in warm, sunny countries where they might appear too drab, but in a colder climate a bright colour would be 'jazzy'.

Education is also a social factor to be considered in assessing an export market. Sophisticated products and advertising could appeal to a well-educated target group but a simpler, basic message may be more effective otherwise.

The high awareness of environmental matters in Western Europe dictates that companies must emphasise the 'environmentally friendly' aspects of their products and processes.

Similarly, the role of women in society is seen differently among various European countries.

Activity 11.5   1 Choose an advertisement that appears on UK television, or in UK newspapers or magazines, for a product made elsewhere in Europe.

2 Identify the features that could stay the same in other countries, and those which you think are 'special' to the UK.

3 You or your fellow students may have been lucky enough to see the advert in another country, if so make a comparison between them.

POLITICAL AND
LEGAL BARRIERS

The countries of Western Europe all have free market economies in which a new organisation, offering competition to existing businesses is not hindered by the government. Within the EC group of countries it would be illegal to put barriers in the way of an organisation entering the market, unless it threatened competition by its market dominance, or affected the national security by its involvement in defence products.

Countries outside the EC may be less happy about a foreign competitor.

For example, Eastern Europe has a heritage of central control, in which a planned economy exists rather than an enterprise society. Although many of the countries are moving towards a free market there are problems, including a shortage of 'hard' currency, which make it difficult for a foreign company to penetrate the market. The poor quality of many of their own goods, makes EC products especially attractive. However, the prevalence of low prices and low wages in these countries, makes it difficult for the population to accept the higher prices and afford to buy.

Governments are understandably cautious of an outsider that might further damage a fragile economic infrastructure. For this reason, they may erect barriers to prevent or limit imports into their country.

The barriers may be financial or non-financial.

Import duties and tariffs are the clearest examples of financial barriers. Tariffs cause the price of an imported product to be higher, making it less competitive. Monetary controls, limiting the amount of currency that can leave the country, and exchange rate controls, place a restriction on what can be paid for and hence what can be bought from outside the country.

Quotas are another way of controlling imports. By imposing a maximum quantity that can be imported, and assigning portions of the quota to particular countries or companies, governments can exercise direct control over imports.

Imports can be restricted by having onerous administrative or technical regulations. Health and safety checks are amongst the most common of these. If a sample from every batch of a product that enters the country has to be tested then this introduces a delay and additional costs (that have to be passed on to the customer or absorbed by the importers giving reduced profit).

By restricting the channels of import to a few ports or airports, or by keeping the number of customs staff down, a government can produce a bottleneck that delays the movement of goods, and limits the amount that reaches the market in any given period.

Many non-EC countries of Europe belong to EFTA (European Free Trade Association) which aims to reduce or eliminate such barriers.

A government may encourage discrimination against imports. Particularly in a patriotic country this can be very effective.

You may remember the 'buy British' campaigns of a few years ago that encouraged the consumer to choose products made in the UK in preference to foreign-made ones.

Finally a government may have anti-dumping regulations. Dumping was experienced in the UK when countries with heavily subsidised coal and steel industries attempted to sell some of their surplus production to Britain. Because of the subsidies the price of the coal and steel was artificially low and the domestic industries (with lower levels of state support) couldn't match the prices.

Activity 11.6   What UK industries would benefit from protection against foreign competition or dumping? Are there any exports that might be damaged by retaliatory action?

IDENTIFYING INTERNATIONAL MARKETING OPPORTUNITIES   As part of the process of deciding which countries to target for export activities, businesses often categorise them by their 'temperature'. A 'hot' country is attractive. A 'cold' country is one that presents considerable difficulties to successful exporting.

A table can be constructed giving a score to the factors that affect the market potential of the countries being considered. *See* Table 11.1. The country with the best score is the most favourable market.

Table 11.1

	'Hot' Country	'Cold' Country
Political stability	High	Low
Market opportunity	High	Low
Economic development	High	Low
Cultural unity	High	Low
Legal barriers	Low	High
Physiographic barriers	Low	High
Geo-cultural barriers, etc.	Low	High

MARKET ENTRY STRATEGY DECISIONS   Having selected the target market, a potential exporter needs to decide on the entry strategy. Put extremely, this is a choice between making the export market a central feature of the company's activities and investing heavily in it, or treating exports as a desirable but peripheral addition to the company's existing market base and committing only a modest proportion of the company's funds to it.

The speed of market entry that is required will govern the method adopted. The possibilities include hiring an agent, employing a sales team, franchising the products, entering into a joint venture, establishing an office and warehouse for distribution, or even setting up a factory to produce in a foreign country.

It is relatively easy to appoint an agent. The agent, being already established in the country and having existing customers, can offer a quick entry into the market. This is also a flexible approach because, having no permanent commitment to buildings, plant and staff, it is relatively easy to pull out if the venture is not successful, or to switch to other products. It is important, however, to carefully negotiate contracts with agents.

The interests of the exporter may differ from those of the agent. The agent may be concerned simply with maximising profit in the short term, while the exporting company will be concerned with establishing a reputation and getting their brand names well known in the market, which are longer-term objectives.

The final decision will depend on the exporter's long-term profit objectives.

Activity 11.7   What entry strategy would you adopt if you wanted to introduce Guinness into the drinks market in Greece (refer to *The European*, 9 August 1991, to see how it was done in Spain)?

PROBLEMS FOR SMALL EXPORTERS   It is particularly difficult for a small company to become established in exporting.

If a company is used only to trading in the domestic market and lacks exposure to other cultures, it may find it difficult to select export markets and identify customers abroad.

A small business lacks the ability to commit management time and general resources to embark on an export venture. In particular, it will be restricted by its available cash flow. It may, for example, encounter problems in extending the credit terms usually expected – often two to three months in Europe. Therefore, a major priority will be investigating ways of financing exports.

A single bad debt, or loss or damage to goods in transit for one order, can be more significant to the finances of a small company. Ways of reducing such exposure will need to be found.

The paperwork and management of export operations, and the cost of supervising a sales force, are all bigger overheads for a small business.

Furthermore, different safety and quality standards may involve a small company in expensive modifications.

A long-term perspective may be needed when assessing payback, and small companies tend to have shorter planning horizons.

Activity 11.8   If you were employed by a small company manufacturing a range of central heating pumps which you wanted to launch onto the Belgian market, what entry strategy would you choose? Why?

PRODUCT POLICY   Having established the market entry strategy and the method of operation in export markets the potential exporter focuses attention on the products.

The product offered on the domestic market may need modification for export, perhaps several modifications for different markets.

It may be that a different level of quality is required for the export market. As we have seen earlier, Germans, for example, expect a very high level of quality in the products they purchase. It is not unknown to have two levels of acceptability for products as they come off the production line – a high standard for export, and a lower one for domestic sales.

Entering an export market is a good time to think about brand names.

A company may have a variety of products on the domestic market, all well established but without a common brand name that shows the customer that they are from the 'same stable'. A well-chosen, distinctive brand name could establish the company's image in the new market so that as more products are introduced to that market the reputation of the company goes before them.

The packaging used for products in the domestic market may need re-vamping for exports. This may involve having a different quantity in the pack, stronger packaging to allow for the extra distance the product will travel, a different style of packing to be attractive to the different consumer. Colour and labelling have to be considered in conjunction with the social preferences of the target population. *See* pp. 176–177.

It may be necessary for a company to take out patents and register trademarks in the countries to which they will be exporting. However, if the broadening of customer base gives products a much higher profile attracting attention from a wider audience they may attract counterfeiters. Clothing, watches, electronic products, car parts, etc. are susceptible to counterfeiting which can be very damaging to the original manufacturer.

Most businesses are concerned not with making a single sale but with establishing a relationship with a customer that results in that customer making repeat purchases of the same and other products. Good quality and good after-sales service are important factors in establishing this relationship.

Setting up an after-sales network is particularly difficult and expensive when products are sold across a wider geographical area. This is often an aspect that is neglected in the initial enthusiasm to begin exporting, with disastrous consequences. How a company deals with after-sales service will depend on the nature of the product. A product that is small and technologically complex might be best handled by having it returned to the home base. This approach would not be suitable for a large product unless the customer could dismantle it and return the faulty component. If it is necessary to have a local servicing facility it will be a case of weighing the benefit of economy that is offered by having an agency to do the work, against the benefits of guaranteed quality, better motivation, and direct control that a local branch of the principal company would give.

Activity 11.9   Describe what adaptations you might have to make to the central heating pumps, mentioned in the previous Activity, to make the product suitable for the Belgian market.

PRICING   Pricing is perhaps the most critical and difficult strategy to determine for a new export market.

When considering a new export market one needs to ask 'are the customers ready for it?' Marketing and selling a product that is already recognised and for which there is existing demand is a totally different proposition to dealing with a product that the target population has never heard of.

Although competition may well be linked with market maturity, the extensive coverage of the European media may mean that the potential customers are aware of a product even before it is available to them.

The extent to which the consumer is sensitive to pricing is likely to depend on whether the product is seen as a 'luxury' or a 'necessity'. This will vary according to culture and particularly according to the standard of living.

So far we have looked at market-based pricing strategies. It is also necessary to consider costs.

Exporting will involve additional overheads. Transport to the export market of a product made in the UK will be more costly than delivery within the UK. Distribution will be more expensive if the target market is more widely spread but it is conceivable that it could be more compact so that once the goods have reached the warehouse they can be distributed to retailers or customers more cheaply than in the UK.

Similarly, it should not be assumed that the cost of a sales force will be the same as in the UK. A large, sparse, sales territory will involve more travel time, and more expense.

Therefore, product costs for exports need to be calculated completely separately from the domestic costing.

LOGISTICS DECISIONS

How a product should be sent to the export customers depends on what is being sent, to where and how quickly, whether there is an intention to make regular deliveries, and so on.

The modes of transport available include rail, road, sea, air and any combination of these. It may involve a company using its own transport or using a carrier who regularly delivers to the customer's location, or asking a carrier to make a special delivery.

For a small package it is practical, fast and economical to use datapost, air mail or a courier service, such as Federal Express. For larger packages there is fierce competition between the carriers that operate internationally.

Activity 11.10 Investigate the international delivery services offered by one of the major carriers.

Air freight is generally faster than road or rail over long distances, but is more expensive, especially for heavy products, and there are restrictions on what airlines will carry – no explosives, toxic chemicals, etc. However, for perishable goods there may be no feasible alternative to air freight.

The chief argument against rail freight is the delay in assembly at source, and the further delay while the cargo is unloaded at the destination rail terminal. The same argument applies to transporting by ship or barge. However, there are several advantages of rail and sea freight. They are capable of carrying large and heavy loads; they are not held up by heavy traffic; there is less risk of accident; they are more likely to arrive on time; and they create less pollution.

Any delivery that involves more than one method of transport will tend to incur delays so there has to be some allowance for this in the schedules.

When freighting goods long distances, it is more economic to gather small consignments into one large load at a collection point and then transport it to a distribution point from which separate customer deliveries are made.

It may be that the goods do not all arrive at the collection point at the same time so storage facilities are needed. Similarly at the distribution point warehousing may be necessary until local deliveries can be arranged. Most freight forwarding companies have sited their main depots at places that have good local road networks and access points to long-haul transport routes (air, sea, rail or motorway).

Activity 11.11

1 Identify one place in the south of Britain and one in the north that have good feeder and long-haul communications and so are suitable to be freight forwarding 'nodes'.

2 Identify freight forwarding nodes in France, Spain and Greece.

The introduction of containerisation has simplified the transportation of goods. Individual organisations pack their products into containers which are international standard sizes. The containers are then delivered, usually by road, to freight forwarding nodes for the long-haul journey in batches – train loads or ship loads – to the distribution node.

Standardisation in size, shape and weight has made it possible for trucks, railway wagons, ships and cargo planes to be designed to accommodate them. You will probably be familiar with the sight of a train full of containers on special flat wagons, or ships stacked high with containers. Handling equipment such as cranes have been developed to lift the container easily from the deck of a ship to the back of a lorry or to a railway wagon.

Containers protect the goods from the weather, from handling damage, and from theft. A container that has been checked and sealed at source is acceptable to customs and excise without the need for a check at each frontier.

Activity 11.12   Investigate the standard size and weight limits of containers.

PROMOTION   Promoting products in an export market is where understanding of customers and consumers is put to the test. If product and price are right then it is going to be easier to sell the product. However, it is still necessary for a company to attract potential customers and convince them to buy that company's product, rather than a competitor's.

A popular method of promoting products initially is attendance at exhibitions. The Department of Trade and Industry (DTI) gives advice and practical help in finding and attending appropriate trade and retail shows. (*See* p. 184).

Advertising is best handled by an advertising agency that is familiar with the target country, and has experience in the kind of market that a company wishes to enter. Advertising can be an expensive waste of money unless the message is carefully thought out and delivered in the right place at the right time. The factors to be considered are media availability in the target country and constraints on advertising, as well as the social environment.

Advertising in Europe is monitored by national bodies like the UK's Advertising Standards Authority which has a strong influence but no legislative power over advertisers. There is also legislation in each country which protects 'public decency' and vulnerable groups.

When planning an advertising campaign care must be taken to conform to product restrictions, ensure that advertising claims can be substantiated and balance information with emotional appeal.

Table 11.2 Marketing data

Media spending (% by category)	Belgium	Denmark	France	Germany	Greece	Ireland	Italy	Netherlands	Portugal	Spain	UK
Newspapers	24	32	24	28	14	34	22	34	26	33	61
Magazines	33	15	26	43	24	9	19.2	11		17	
Television	16	–	21	16	50	37	49.5	5	54	32	32
Radio	2	–	10	7	6	12	3.6	1	13	13	2
Cinema	1	1	2	–	–	–	0.3	–	2	0.5	1
Outdoor	15	2	17	5	6	8	5.4	4	5	4.5	4
Other media	9	50	–	1	–	–	–	45	–	–	–

Getting advertising right in another country is very difficult unless you really understand the different cultures, and even within a country there can be considerable variation in attitudes. Benetton's 'new baby' advert in the UK in September 1991 produced a storm of protest that it was 'offensive' while many people felt it was innocuous although not perhaps very relevant to the company's products.

GOVERNMENT SUPPORT OF INTERNATIONAL TRADE

The Department of Trade and Industry (DTI) provides help and advice to firms wishing to enter, or already operating in, export markets by means of its 'Export Initiative'.

It provides export information to help firms prepare marketing plans and set up exporting and distribution operations. It also helps businesses set up a presence in the market through a range of promotional activities.

The Export Market Information Centre has a database on over 150 000 overseas businesses, nearly 100 000 articles, cuttings and reports on markets and products, and details of DTI-supported trade fairs and exhibitions.

The DTI publishes a range of country profiles, economic reports and research information on specific market sectors, and hints to exporters.

It has information on selling opportunities, such as foreign buyers looking for suppliers, agents who wish to represent British companies, and companies inviting tenders for projects.

The DTI-supported trade fairs offer opportunities for UK companies to promote their goods, at subsidised rates for space, stands and travel. They also assist in overcoming language difficulties.

Trade missions, sponsored by trade associations and chambers of commerce give opportunities for businesses to travel with 10 to 20 other exporters in the same market sector to make contact with agents and customers. The DTI provides financial support for a number of visits.

The Export Credits Guarantee Department (ECGD) helps individual companies to minimise financial risk by offering insurance and financial guarantees.

Insurance may be taken out against the possibility of insolvency of the foreign customer, political occurrences that delay payment, cancellation of import or export licences, and the sudden introduction of exchange controls.

The British Overseas Trade Board also assists exporters: through its European Trade Committee it promotes awareness of export opportunities, in particular market segments. As well as the EC countries it has information on the EFTA countries – Iceland, Norway, Sweden, Finland, Austria and Switzerland.

Importing

To a large extent importing is the mirror image of exporting.

From an economic standpoint exporting tends to be treated as good for a country, whereas importing is bad, because of the effects on the balance of payments. This is simplistic, however, because a key question is whether the imports are to be consumed in the country or whether they are going to contribute to another product which is subsequently exported.

One may also take a wider international view. Within the EC, for example, each country has its own particular strengths in terms of climate, resources, skills, etc. It makes sense to take advantage of these strengths to further the common good through trade.

It is possible to buy goods to sell to consumers in this country, or to buy raw materials or components from which to manufacture other products.

One may buy machinery to use in the manufacturing process, or equipment (such as computers) to help control the business.

Increasingly there is a trade in products, such as stationery, packaging and power, that are consumed to keep a business running. Expertise and services are also increasingly international.

A buyer of imports is concerned to get a product or service of the right quality, at the right price, in the right quantity, at the right time.

Therefore, when is it advantageous to import rather than buy locally?

The answer is 'when there is a better mix of quality, price, quantity, and availability'.

Having identified a source, you need first to assess the costs of importing – taking into account the additional transport costs, paperwork, exchange rates, etc. and the reliability of a more distant source.

When buying from a local supplier 'just down the road' it may be efficient to buy small quantities as and when required. However, when importing goods, single, larger, periodic deliveries are the best way of minimising transport costs but then you will have to find storage space for the goods. Also, unless you can negotiate to pay for the goods as you use them, you must find a larger amount of money to settle the debt.

A supplier may be happy to offer a lower price to offset the cost of many smaller deliveries, having negotiated a long-term contract involving a steady supply. This involves anticipating future needs more accurately, introducing a financial risk if predictions are wrong.

As with exporting, there are several stages of internationalism.

The decision to import may arise as a result of an approach by an overseas company, or as a result of actively seeking overseas sources.

A proactive management is always actively researching for alternative materials and methods so that it can improve quality and reduce costs. It may also be concerned to avoid being tied to a single supplier if this adds to the risk of supply failure.

As a member of the buying team one would be constantly gathering information on market prices and trends, government policies, etc.

When embarking on importing, it would be useful to review the procedures for dealing with enquiries, selecting suppliers, negotiating contracts, preparing documentation, progressing deliveries, making payments, and checking the quantity and quality of incoming goods.

Activity 11.13   Investigate what you might expect to import directly if you were employed by a garment manufacturing company.

NEGOTIATING A DEAL

Interpersonal skills are important when negotiating and especially so when dealing with someone from another country.

Although it may be more difficult and time-consuming to arrange face-to-face communication, it enhances the chances of understanding because it is interactive (which a letter or fax is not) and body language can be observed (which is not possible in a telephone conversation).

These difficulties are magnified when negotiators are from different cultures and speak different languages, and may even be worse with an interpreter.

When communicating through an interpreter, it is important for the customer to make sure you watch the supplier as he or she speaks, and continue to look at them when listening to the translation.

Remember that the aim is to establish and maintain a good working supplier-customer relationship rather than to get the best terms in a single deal. By the same token, negotiating is about presenting your case in the best way possible. However, that does not mean telling lies. It is vital that both parties retain their integrity throughout negotiations.

Once a deal is concluded, it should be confirmed in writing, in wording that is clear and unambiguous, in both languages. The customer's version will be the definitive one if there are any inconsistencies arising from the translation.

Summary

1 Exporting is more complex than home trade because of the greater distances, different business practices and regional variation in culture and tastes.

2 An organisation may choose to export to prolong a product's life cycle, to avoid competition, to utilise excess capacity, to diversify geographically, to gain a bigger market.

3 Companies involved in trade between countries can choose to deal direct, or through third parties, and ultimately may choose to have their distribution and production organisations in each country.

4 Organisations often go through several stages in internationalism, beginning with disinterest, and progressing through unsolicited exports, active searching for export markets, establishing a foreign base, and becoming multinational.

5 A small business encounters greater difficulty as an exporter because of the commitment of management time, the exposure to risk, and the overheads of distribution.

6 Products may need different quality, packaging, and brand names to be successful in other markets.

7 Pricing will depend on market maturity and competition as well as export overheads, distribution methods and transport costs.

8 In choosing an export market, the business should initially select one that is psychologically close to the current market. Factors to consider are politics, market economics, business culture, and legislation.

9 The preferred methods of promotion vary from one country to another even within the 12 current EC countries and will be more diverse as the EC gains new members. The mix of advertising, direct selling, and use of agents must suit the country and local expertise is essential.

10 Government agencies, such as the DTI and ECGD, support companies entering export markets and offer some protection against the risks involved.

11 Importing is undertaken to achieve the best mix of product, quality, price, quantity and availability.

12 Negotiating is made more difficult by language and distance. The buyer should use his/her own language, the seller must be prepared to use the foreign language.

Assignment 11 **EXPORTING TO EUROPE**

Your organisation is the only one in the area that provides training in European awareness. As a result, locally-based businesses are beginning to turn to it for advice.

Two such enquiries are described below. Examine each and prepare a suitable response, outlining the facts, analysing the situation, and making practical recommendations. Each will be a separate formal report.

Task 1

Work individually.

Background

Pinkertons, a local medium-sized business, manufactures night vision equipment. It is an autonomous unit, but is part of a very large organisation whose head office is in the north-west of England. In the past its main customers have been British and other defence ministries. With the continuing fears of terrorist attacks, it is felt that private security firms, and the security departments of large companies, are potential customers for its products.

Two countries, France and Greece, seem to be most at risk, and hence the best prospects but Pinkertons are only prepared to enter one foreign market initially.

Activity

Assemble and present relevant facts about each country. Assess the attractiveness (or otherwise) of each country as the selected market. Make recommendations as to which country should be targeted and the method of market entry.

Task 2

Work co-operatively on the fact gathering; work individually on report preparation.

Background

CYA Holiday Homes is an agency that co-ordinates the letting of holiday homes throughout holiday areas of Britain. It has been very successful in attracting visitors from throughout the UK but the economic recession has had an effect upon business. The peoples of three EC countries – Belgium, Netherlands and Italy – are noted for their enthusiasm to spend holidays in European countries outside their own.

CYAHH is prepared to spend up to £200 000 on promotion.

Activities

Contact one or more organisations that might be able to provide information to help you (ensuring that no organisation is contacted by more than one student). Submit the information to the tutor who will ensure that it is made available to everyone.

Report on how you think the promotion should be carried out, apportioning the spending between the countries, and selecting an appropriate mix of methods in each country (agencies, media, etc.).

Part Five
Contemporary issues

12 Case studies in contemporary issues

Objectives
1 Trace developments in European contemporary affairs and the background to European Community integration in the 1990s.
2 Evaluate key current issues by using the case studies.
3 Carry out further investigation of current issues by building upon the case studies.
4 Understand the relationship between politics and economics at the European Community level and at the national level.
5 Analyse the importance of decision making at international summit meetings.
6 Identify the position of the British government on important economic, social and political matters and contrast these positions with those of Britain's EC partners.

Introduction

There is no doubt that Europe is at the centre-stage of politics in the 1990s. This is largely due to the startling changes that have taken place in the past decade that have altered the political, economic and social map of Europe. Before these changes took place we were used to a Europe that was stable but seemingly divided forever between an American-led 'Western alliance', NATO, and the Warsaw Pact in the east led by the Soviet Union. Forces for and against change showed themselves most often away from Europe in the Middle East with several Arab-Israeli wars and in the Far East with the economic rise of the Japanese and other 'Pacific Rim' countries.

Part Five of this book will introduce the changes that have taken place in Europe in recent years and then allow greater study of selected issues of importance in the case studies.

Europe: the coming of a new age

DEVELOPMENTS IN THE WEST In 1986 Spain and Portugal joined the European Community (EC), completing the process of enlargement of the Community from 6 to 12 members. This process started in 1969 when the original six member states of West Germany, France, the Netherlands, Belgium, Luxembourg and Italy decided to 'deepen, complete and enlarge' the Community.

As part of this process the United Kingdom joined in 1973, along with Ireland, Denmark and Greece, in 1981. Countries such as Austria and Sweden have also applied to become members of the European Community but it seems unlikely that there will be further enlargement in the near future.

At the same time as more countries were signing the Treaty of Rome as members of the 'European Club', the Community was moving towards the development of new policy areas such as foreign, security and environment policy and putting the finishing touches to existing strategies in areas such as agriculture.

By 1986 the 12 of the European Community were contemplating significant developments in the nature of the economic and political relationship that bound them together. The major one was the decision by each of the 12 to sign and ratify the Single European Act (SEA).

The Single European Act is of great importance. It means that by the end of 1992 there will be a Single European Market of 330 million people. The SEA brings a new era to all the countries of Western Europe when there will be one market in goods, services and capital. In addition the people of the Community will be able to live and work freely in any other member state.

The Single Market will be the biggest in the world and will enable businesses to make savings on economies of scale as they exploit the huge market and also compete more easily with American and Far-Eastern companies. From 1992 business and economics in Western Europe will no longer be on a national scale but instead on the scale of the large single market.

REACTIONS TO THE SINGLE MARKET

Because of the importance of the creation of the Single Market the countries of the European Free Trade Association (EFTA) – Austria, Finland, Iceland, Liechtenstein, Norway, Sweden and Switzerland – have signed an agreement with the European Community countries to create a European Economic Area in which most of the rules of the Single Market will apply. This is because the EFTA countries fear being left out of the benefits of the Single Market.

The companies of the United States and the Far East are rapidly establishing production and distribution centres inside the Single Market in order to exploit that market and also to avoid exclusion.

The newly independent countries of the old Soviet empire in Eastern Europe are anxious to conclude trade, aid and development packages with the Community for fear of greater economic and social divergence between Eastern and Western Europe. Even the states of what was once the Soviet Union are now looking for substantial trade deals with the Community on terms largely laid down in the West.

THE SINGLE MARKET AGENDA

The creation of the Single Market means the removal of barriers to trade between the 12 member states of the European Community and also with other states who agree to remove these barriers. Such barriers are k.... as fiscal or tax barriers, physical barriers such as border and customs posts and technical barriers. Technical barriers include such things as refusing to allow British beer to be sold in Germany because it is made from different ingredients than German beer. Another example is Germany refusing to allow French or British lawnmowers to be sold in Germany because they were said to be too noisy despite the fact that they were perfectly acceptable in France and in Britain!

1992 sees the completion of this process of bringing down the barriers. However the Single Market will not just be about making it easier to trade in Western Europe. The European Commission has determined, along with most national governments of the EC, that the development of the Single Market will involve important progress in terms of social and employment legislation. Much of this legislation is found in 'The Social Charter', the first case study in this section.

The Single Market is an important milestone on the road to economic and monetary union in Western Europe. Although there is still a good deal of negotiating and argument to come between the governments of the 12 over the nature and scope of this union there is little doubt that the economies of the 12 members are drawing closer together. The implications of this are discussed in the second case study.

Monetary union cannot be separated from political union, which is the subject of a case study (*see* p. 202). Within the development of a political union in Western Europe there are many individual policy issues that are currently being argued about. These include the environment, agriculture and the way the countryside is used as an economic and social resource. These issues are also the subject of case studies.

ALL CHANGE IN EASTERN EUROPE Whilst there have been very important changes in Western Europe in the recent past, there has been nothing to match the turmoil and upheaval that has overtaken the countries of Eastern Europe.

President Gorbachev of the Soviet Union came to power in 1985. He soon realised that it was no longer economically or politically acceptable for the Soviet Union to maintain a military, political and economic stranglehold on the countries that his predecessors had occupied in the 1940s.

These countries, Poland, East Germany, Hungary, Bulgaria, Romania and Czechoslovakia were dominated until 1989 by Soviet-approved Communist regimes but once President Gorbachev signalled his intention to let these countries develop outside of Soviet dominance, the fragility of the Communist system was exposed for all to see.

Between 1989 and 1991 the Communist governments in Eastern Europe collapsed, to be replaced by various forms of Western-style democratic institutions. Towards the end of 1989 the Berlin Wall, a potent symbol of the division between East and West Germany, came down as the two German states were united into one Germany.

Christmas Day 1991 saw the resignation of President Gorbachev himself.

He had tried and failed to introduce radical political and economic reforms in the Soviet Union. The heavily entrenched interests of the Communist Party of the Soviet Union, economic failure and mismanagement, continued disastrous food harvests and citizen frustration at a political system that clearly was not capable of reforming itself were all factors that combined together to lead to the demise of Gorbachev. The former Soviet Union has now split into independent states loosely allied together in the Commonwealth of Independent States but there is much argument over the powers of the states themselves relative to the powers of the Commonwealth. Russia dominates the other states in every sense – geographically, economically, politically and militarily – and a solution to the problems of the old Soviet Union will most likely come from within Russia. Without Russian approval and the backing of the charismatic Russian President Yeltsin, reforms are likely to fail.

The collapse of the Communist regimes in the East has unleashed a new problem for Western governments – the number of citizens of the newly freed Eastern European countries who want to come to live and work in the more prosperous West. This has put migration and immigration issues at the forefront of the political agenda. *See* case study on p. 207.

In the 1990s the countries of Eastern Europe will struggle to provide an adequate level of economic and social welfare for their citizens. In addition there are horrendous problems of pollution caused by 40 years of reckless disregard for the environment by the Communist regimes. The political institutions of Eastern Europe are only recently established and there will be further changes as the states adjust to new and dynamic circumstances.

The 12 members of the European Community are helping the governments of the East with loans and grants and also by supplying specialist advice and help. Presently, governments of East and West are agreed on the major goals of promoting democracy and economic growth in Eastern Europe but there are some disagreements about how to do this.

EUROPE IN THE INTERNATIONAL ARENA

The changes outlined above have not taken place in a vacuum. Europe has re-established itself as a main player in international economic and political relations. The changes in Europe are having an important impact on the international system.

The collapse of the Soviet-led Warsaw Pact has prompted a major re-think in Western defence strategy. The American-led NATO alliance of 16 leading Western countries remains intact but its major focus in the 1990s is no longer a Soviet military threat. Instead other long-standing issues such as military, political and energy security in the Middle East take priority. The decision of leading Western governments to restrict Iraqi expansionism in 1991 in the Gulf War illustrates this.

Instability in and around the Mediterranean is another concern to the West as international terrorism is often based in countries at the southern edge of Europe. The governments of the EC already co-operate together in an anti-terrorist alliance (the Trevi mechanism) but there is no agreement on the political dimension of terrorism when it comes to subjects such as trading Western hostages for arms or money.

Presently Western Europe cannot be said to be united on the international stage. It does not have a common foreign policy, although its major military structure is still with us. On certain international trade issues Western Europe does act together and this also happens at the United Nations on many issues. However, foreign policy has remained an area in which governments are unable to agree joint policies because of varying interests.

However it is becoming increasingly the case that much of the world treats Western Europe as one country. This is largely because the EC is now the world's largest economic organisation and has become a major voice in world economic affairs. The days are gone when the member states pursued their economic policies in isolation and co-operation, agreement and collaboration are now the order of the day.

In terms of security it has already been noted that America still leads a Western military alliance and there seems little real prospect of a challenge to this alliance. In this area where America leads, Western Europeans follow, sometimes reluctantly. However in the last couple of years the Western Europeans have begun to consider more seriously creating a military organisation of their own that could eventually replace NATO. This is an unlikely scenario.

Case studies

The case studies that follow focus upon some of the more important issues that confront governments and societies in the Europe of the 1990s. Every case study can easily be built upon as the issues are constantly evolving so the opportunity exists to use these studies as a starting point for further consideration. The final case study draws many of these issues together and takes a look at the complex decision-making, negotiating and bargaining that took place at the Maastricht Summit in December of 1991.

The Social Charter

In December 1989 all of the governments of the EC except for Britain agreed to the creation of the Social Charter. The Charter was developed as a result of negotiations between governments, employers, trade unions, the European Parliament, the Economic and Social Committee and the European Commission. In such a situation it is no surprise that the Charter is a compromise between the different interests of the bodies involved in the discussions.

The Social Charter is an important part of the 1992 Single Market programme because it tries to introduce social reforms alongside the economic changes that are being brought about by the Single Market.

The Social Charter as such does not have a legal status but parts of the Charter are being implemented by legally enforceable EC Directives. This means that they become part of the ordinary law of the member states and have to be obeyed.

WHAT IS IN THE
SOCIAL CHARTER?

The Charter is divided into 12 main areas of concern. The overall aim of the Charter is to improve the working and living conditions of all citizens throughout the EC by imparting certain basic rights backed by legislation.

1 Freedom of movement

All workers of the EC must have the right to legally work anywhere else in the EC and be treated the same as a citizen of the host country without discrimination. This applies to access to jobs, working conditions and social security (often called social protection).

2 Employment and pay

People have the right to choose which occupation they want, so long as they are qualified to do the job and satisfy any rules specific to it. They also shall be paid to enable them to have a 'decent standard of living'.

3 Improvement of living and working conditions

The aim here is to improve conditions for workers in terms of holidays, redundancy provision, compensation payments when a firm goes bankrupt, maximum lengths of the working day with rest periods and legal aspects of contracts of employment such as that all workers must have a contract of employment with their employer.

4 Social protection

All workers must have an 'adequate' level of social security benefits whether or not they are in a job.

5 Freedom of association and collective bargaining

This means that workers have the right to form and join a trade union and employers have the right to form and join their own organisation in order to promote or defend their economic and social interests. Equally there is the freedom not to join an employees' or employers' organisation.

There are also rights to collective bargaining contained in this part of the Charter. This means that employers and unions have the right to negotiate agreements on behalf of their members as a collective. The right to strike is included, subject to national law, but the Charter also wants to see mediation and arbitration procedures encouraged so as to reduce strikes.

6 Vocational training

Every worker in the EC should have access to vocational, i.e. job-related, training throughout their working life. This is seen as particularly important as technology rapidly develops in the 1990s and workers' skills need a lot of updating.

7 Equal treatment for men and women
There must be equal treatment for men and women and equal opportunities as well. This is to be applied to promotion and employment opportunities, pay and working conditions, social security, education, vocational training and career development.

8 Information, consultation and participation for workers
Workers must be kept informed of developments in their own company which will have an important impact upon their jobs. This is especially the case where the firm might be considering restructuring and redundancies could result.

9 Health and safety at work
Every worker must have 'satisfactory' health and safety provisions at work and must be trained properly to a level that enables the work to be carried on without harm if at all possible.

10 Protection of children
No child of under 15 years can have a job with few exceptions. Any young person must be properly paid and trained and not be allowed to work at night.

11 Elderly persons
Every retired person must be able to enjoy a decent standard of living and also have sufficient medical and social assistance for his/her needs.

12 Disabled persons
The aim of the Charter here is to ensure that the position of disabled people is improved in terms of mobility, training, housing and transport.

ANALYSIS   Unlike the economic aspects of the Single Market programme the Social Charter does not have to be in operation by the end of 1992. As the case study on the Maastricht Summit (*see* p. 211) shows there is very considerable controversy over implementing the Charter. Britain is against it.

However the Commission has come up with a Social Action Programme designed to put the Social Charter into practice. This action programme has two main features:
1 proposals for new laws that will implement the Charter;
2 where there are no proposals for new laws the Commission has issued advice to governments on what to do.

Proposals for new laws cover the areas of:
● working time;
● employment contracts;

- training;
- health and safety at work;
- part-time and temporary working;
- workers' rights to consultation and information;
- travel rights for disabled people;
- employing young people.

The Commission proposals have been welcomed by trade unions, especially in Britain where the unions say that British workers are treated very poorly compared to many European counterparts. The British government and many employers' organisations have been strongly opposed to the Charter and the action programme because they say it is costly to put in place and will lead to losses of jobs and productivity.

Activity 12.1

1 Contact a local branch of a trade union such as National and Local Government Officers Association (NALGO) – at your local council offices – or the General Workers Union (GWU) – local offices throughout the country – and obtain information on the Social Charter from the point of view of the union. If possible ask for material specific to a particular industry or job.

2 Contact a local employers' organisation, trade association, a regional branch of the Confederation of British Industry (CBI) or a local business club and collect information in the same way as you contacted the trade union.

3 Compare the approaches of the unions and the employers to the Charter seeing where there are points of agreement and where there are points of difference. You may be surprised at how much agreement there is between unions and employers!

4 Obtain from the Training Enterprise and Education Department (TEED) a copy of the government's 'fact pack' on the Social Charter and look at the views contained in that. Do these views coincide with those of (a) the unions; or (b) the employers?

The case study on the Maastricht Summit (*see* p. 211) also mentions the British government's position on the Social Charter at the end of 1991. Has the government's position changed since then?

Economic and Monetary Union

1992 sees the coming of the Single Market in Europe. This is an important step on the road to Economic and Monetary Union (EMU). What does this mean?

There is a lot of argument and debate over EMU. The argument concerns who should control key economic policies in Europe – individual governments or central institutions of the EC. Some governments, notably the British, are very cautious when it comes to EMU because they think that democratically elected national parliaments and governments should have the final say over economic decisions that affect the lives and jobs of their citizens. Those in favour of EMU argue that economic realities will force the economies of Western European nations closer together and so this should be recognised and built upon in a formal way.

What are these so-called 'economic realities'?

TRADE BARRIERS Trade barriers have been reducing steadily between the economies of Western Europe since 1945. The Single Market should abolish nearly all the barriers that remain. At the moment the economies of the members of the EC depend very heavily on trade with one another. Table 12.1 shows this.

Table 12.1

Country	% of total trade inside the EC (1985–90 average)	(1990)
Belgium/Luxembourg	70	72
Denmark	47	53
France	52	54
Germany	44	51
Greece	54	64
Ireland	69	72
Italy	51	54
Netherlands	67	76
Portugal	64	68
Spain	50	61
UK	44	48

Figures are for trade as a percentage of Gross Domestic Product (average 1985–90).
Source: XXIVth General Report on the Activities of the EC, 1990.

These percentages increase as every year goes by and therefore economic dependence between the countries also increases.

CURRENCIES The establishment of the Exchange Rate Mechanism in 1979, whereby the governments of the Community tied the rate of exchange of their currencies closely together, has been a success in reducing inflation across Europe. The value of one currency against another has stabilised and trade has been made easier because importers and exporters can now have more certainty that the value of the currencies they trade in will not be subject to sudden changes.

Current ideas for EMU aim to build on these past successes by integrating the economies of the 12 states even closer together. A key mechanism for doing this is by having a *single currency*. This will save the financial costs everyone incurs when changing money from one currency to another. It will also reinforce the stability of money across Europe and make business more profitable.

Some governments are not happy with the idea of a single currency because they fear that they will lose control of important economic decisions and think that their own nationals do not want to see familiar notes and coins disappear, to be replaced by a new currency called the 'Europa' or the 'ECU'.

ECONOMIC CONVERGENCE

Before EMU can become a reality the economies of the 12 EC countries will have to become more alike. Economists are calling this *economic convergence*. It means that inflation rates across the 12 states will have to be roughly the same, interest rates similar and government debt kept in check. This presents a difficult problem for countries like Britain because the British economy has not performed well in recent years in terms of inflation or interest rates and the government does not wish to see central EC institutions take control of these policy areas and impose harsh remedies on Britain.

A key European central institution will be the European Central Bank – ECB. By 1996, the ECB may have control of policies across Europe on prices, government spending, borrowing decisions and interest rates.

Summary

Those in favour of EMU see great economic benefits from more integration. This is not an area of controversy because in fact, most people agree that the EC will benefit from convergence. The real argument is a political one over who should control key economic decisions. Economic decisions have social and political consequences upon which governments can live or die at elections. Some European politicians, particularly the British, would rather keep control of the decisions that may cost them their positions of power than give the power to others in Europe.

Activity 12.2

1 In Chapter 5, you looked at the activities and powers of the institutions of the European Community. Discuss whether or not you think that these powers should be extended over key aspects of Britain's economic policy or whether the British government should resist losing some power. (Bear in mind that Britain's economic record since 1945 has been a poor one.)

2 Ask the local branch of your bank for a booklet on the ECU and ask when they expect to be using the ECU in everyday financial transactions.

Political union

When the European Community started life in 1958 the original six members signed the Treaty of Rome that committed them to move toward 'political union by economic means'. There was no definition then or now of just what political union is all about. The increase in EC membership to 12 has meant that getting any hard and fast definition is even less likely given the great range of national interests now represented in the Community. A look at the case study on Maastricht will enable you to look at how these interests clash and are sometimes resolved.

Political union is not about creating one, single European government. There is no realistic support for this. Instead political union is about greater co-ordination and co-operation between the EC states in the attempt to solve common issues. The argument over political union is whether or not this greater co-ordination and co-operation should lead to an increase in power for the EC institutions, notably the Parliament and the Commission, whether the co-ordination and co-operation should be formalised in a sort of treaty or whether it should be left to the governments of the Community to co-operate together outside of the formal institutions of the EC.

What are the common issues that are involved in political union?

A COMMON FOREIGN AND DEFENCE POLICY
This is discussed in more detail in a case study *see* p. 208. It is felt that because the EC is now the world's largest economic and trading bloc then it should also develop a security policy to match its economic strength.

LEGAL ISSUES AND JUSTICE
There are certain matters in the area of law enforcement that all the governments regard as being of common concern. These include, asylum and immigration policy (*see* p. 207); control of drug movements and combatting international fraud; customs and anti-terrorist measures; and information exchange between police forces and court procedures in criminal matters.

REGIONAL POLICY
In order to reduce the large gap between the rich states of northern Europe and the relatively poor ones of southern Europe the idea is to create a strong regional policy that will have its own funds to encourage development in the 'least favoured regions'.

CITIZENSHIP
Under a Spanish proposal of October 1990, every citizen of a member state shall also be a citizen of the union, be allowed to vote in the elections of any member state in which he/she lives, be able to live and work freely in any other member state and be supported by the host country if the need arises.

SOCIAL ISSUES
There are many items under this heading and they range from improvements to health and safety legislation to equal opportunities and the promotion of the Social Charter issues. In the future it seems likely that the European Commission will gain greater power over education matters, consumer protection, public health, cultural matters and programmes of social welfare.

Reform of the powers and functions of the European Community institutions is also included in discussions on political union as discussed in Chapter 5.

Summary
Political union is a complex subject because it covers a wide variety of issues on which there are many different viewpoints. What is certain is that the governments of the EC are being drawn closer together as they face more common problems and their economies become increasingly dependent on

Fact and fiction in the minefield of political union

SOCIAL POLICY

NOW: In December 1989, 11 member states – without Britain – signed the Social Charter on basic workers' rights. It envisages levelling out differences in employment conditions and giving 1992 a human face. Under the 1987 Single European Act, legislation relating to "health and safety in the workplace" can be adopted by majority vote, such as proposals for working hours and protection of pregnant women. All other proposals can only be passed by unanimity.

PROPOSED: The Maastricht draft would widen the scope of majority voting on social matters such as working conditions, worker consultation, equality between men and women. But more sensitive matters would always be dealt with under unanimous voting, such as social security provisions, protection from unfair dismissal.

MYTHS: The Social Charter does not spell the end of the Sunday paper round. Exemptions are always possible if national traditions are threatened. Sunday would not become an enforced day of rest, nor does the treaty foresee setting a minimum wage.

FOREIGN POLICY

NOW: EC foreign ministers meet regularly to co-ordinate action in world affairs under "European Political Co-operation", formalised by the Single European Act. It is a non-binding arrangement, where any decisions must be reached by consensus. Co-ordination of policies by the Twelve is in practice intense, although governments are free to pursue policies alone.

PROPOSED: A new mechanism for "common action" in foreign affairs. Heads of government would designate areas of policy as ripe for common action, such as US and Soviet relations. As a "general rule", detailed implementing measures would be agreed by foreign ministers by majority vote. Britain would be constrained from freelancing against the thrust of common policy. A European defence identity would be developed gradually, based at first on the Western European Union.

MYTHS: British troops could not be sent to war by a majority vote in the EC. Such decisions would remain for consensus. Nor could Britain be barred, for example, from defending the Falklands.

BRUSSELS' POWERS

NOW: The Treaty of Rome offers the possibility of developing EC powers over a wide range of areas from agriculture, foreign trade and industrial competition down to transport and energy. Some provisions are shallow and have barely been used.

PROPOSED: The Maastricht draft foresees a broader extension of competence by introducing new policy areas and reinforcing those already in the EC Treaty. New policy fields include development of cross-frontier communication networks, like roads and pipelines, health and education. Majority voting would be the rule in all competence areas and some would be subject to co-legislation between the Council of Ministers and the European Parliament.

MYTH: Brussels does not equal the Commission. EC powers are shared by all the institutions, though the Commission is the watchdog. When the Commission intervenes in a member state – as in Britain recently over the environmental cost of motorway building – it is usually ensuring implementation of laws agreed by member states themselves.

FEDERAL

NOW: Successive European treaties have always opened with a general statement of the aspirations of the member states. The 1957 Rome Treaty stated that the member states were "determined to lay the foundations of an ever closer union among the peoples of Europe". The 1987 Single European Act offers another variant by declaring that member governments will work to "transform relations as a whole among their states into a European Union".

PROPOSED: Last May Luxembourg suggested that the federal ambitions of most member states was spelt out in the new treaty. Thus a new phrase has been inserted in the proposed text's preamble: "This Treaty marks a new stage in a process leading gradually to a Union with a federal goal". On British insistence, all mention of the F-Word is likely to be erased from the treaty.

MYTH: Britain's perception of federal union spelling a United States of Europe is considered by member states to be a misunderstanding. For them, "federal" recognises the downwards gravitation of power to nations and to regions.

PARLIAMENT

NOW: The Parliament may call the Commission and the Council of Ministers to account by tabling questions; it is involved in drafting legislation in so far as its opinions are solicited; and in areas relating to the creation of a single market, its amendments are adopted if supported by the Commission. Most importantly, it has equal responsibility with the Commission and Council for drawing up the Community budget.

PROPOSED: The Parliament will have extra powers in limited areas: environment policy, establishing a framework for long-term research and development, trans-Europe integrated transport systems and internal-market laws. In these areas Parliament has potential to veto laws and may use this to pressure the Council into adopting amendments.

MYTH: Westminster becomes a parish council. False. Legislation in the areas proposed is now decided by majority of member states. Britain is thus already often forced to try to accommodate the consensus view. Additional power for the European Parliament would enhance the process of compromise.

IMMIGRATION

NOW: Each member state is responsible for its own immigration and asylum policy and for setting down visa requirements. Under single-market rules coming into effect next year, EC citizens will be able to move freely within the Community. Formal controls will be abolished but there will be spot-checks. In practice there will still be passport queues in airports to facilitate spot-checks, but EC nationals will probably be waved through in most cases.

PROPOSED: The Council will be able to standardise conditions under which non-EC nationals may be granted short-term visas. The document valid for one country will thus be valid for all 12.

MYTH: This is the thin end of the wedge: non-EC nationals armed with short-term visas will flood Britain, which will have no legal means of blocking their entry. False. The treaty specifically refers to the fact that these provisions will not interfere with a country's right to organise those procedures it deems necessary to maintain law and order and safeguard internal state security.

Figure 12.1 Fact and fiction in the minefield of political union

Source: The Independent, 29 November 1991

one another. It is unlikely that we will see a 'Euro-government' emerge in the near future but we will see more influence for the EC institutions.

Activity 12.3   In the 1992 general election the main political parties in Britain all said different things on the issues concerning political union.

1 Using the manifestos published by the parties compare the different approaches.

2 All the parties say that they are in favour of closer relations with the EC but they all approach the issue rather differently. Why do you think this might be?

The environment

Everybody wants a cleaner and healthier place in which to live. The numerous warnings on global warming, holes in the ozone layer and acid rain all add to the greater awareness that governments ought to do more to prevent pollution and clean up the environment.

Because pollution does not conveniently stop at national borders co-ordinated action is needed to cope with polluters and with cleaning up. For example it is little use Germany cleaning up the River Rhine if, further upstream, Swiss chemical companies continue to pollute the river. The European Community is in an ideal position to impose new, strict, anti-pollution laws on member states across Europe. There is little doubt that European-wide solutions are needed to European-wide problems.

European Community Directives and Regulations to prevent, reduce or eliminate pollution number over 300. This is a larger body of law than the whole of the Single Market programme which comprises 282 pieces of legislation. Examples of the legislation include:

- agreements to control car exhaust emissions;
- agreements to get rid of CFCs;
- Directives lowering pollution emissions from factory chimneys;
- Directives to clean up public drinking water;
- Directives to clean up public bathing beaches;
- Directives for governments to conduct 'environmental impact assessments' before major new works of construction or roadbuilding are undertaken.

In all of the above areas the British government has been criticised for failing to implement the law or for doing so too slowly. Some of this criticism is true and Britain has been before the Court of Justice in Luxembourg to explain the delay in cleaning up Britain's tap water and beaches.

One of the problems that all governments face is that whilst all electorates want to see a cleaner environment, the governments know that anti-pollution measures are not cheap. At the end of the day it is often the taxpayer who has to pick up the bill. Another issue boils down to politics and influence in Brussels. Take the following situation.

In Germany there is a law that says that only 28% of all beer and soft-drink containers can be disposable. The rest must be recyclable. Germany is accused of using this law to protect small Bavarian brewers who find it easier to reclaim their bottles in the locality than perhaps an importer would. It is said that Germany is using an environmental protection rule as a trade barrier. When Denmark was taken to the Court for doing something similar it won the case!

The point of this example is that governments are very quick to promote environmental protection when it suits their own national interests and equally quick to criticise when their economic interests are harmed. At the moment many EC manufacturers are worried that the political power of German industry will enable Germany to impose tough new environmental standards on the rest of Europe. The Germans argue that if they have to live with these high standards then so should the rest of us.

THE BRITISH POSITION
British environmental law is heavily influenced from Europe. For example the 1990 Environmental Protection Act, which was the major piece of legislation on the environment between 1979 and 1992, implements in part, four important EC Directives. The British government had no choice but to implement these Directives.

The Act introduces to British law the European concept of BATNEEC. BATNEEC stands for Best Available Technique Not Entailing Excessive Cost. Whilst this may at first sight seem complicated it is not. BATNEEC simply means that manufacturers must use the BATNEEC to reduce, eliminate or stop pollution. This means that manufacturers or other polluters must actively seek out the best solutions to their pollution problems. 'Available' means available anywhere in the world and cost must not be used, in the vast majority of cases, as an excuse not to take anti-pollution measures.

Most people see this Act as a positive contribution to making the environment better for all of us. The European Community can take much of the credit for this.

In Britain, environmental law is policed by a variety of bodies. These include Her Majesty's Inspectorate of Pollution, the National Rivers Authority and the Health and Safety Executive. Local councils also have environmental health officers with important responsibilities.

There has been much talk recently of establishing a European-wide anti-pollution force. At the moment the only example we have of European-wide inspectors is in the fishing industry where there are a small number of inspectors who travel around the ports of the EC checking fishing net sizes. This system has not worked well with many accusations of cheating as soon as the inspector has gone away and national interests being favoured in some states by their own inspectors. It does not seem likely that the near future will see the introduction of a Community pollution inspectorate.

Summary
There is a large volume of European environmental law and this influences the national laws of member states greatly. Despite national arguing there

is no doubt that governments take environmental issues much more seriously than they ever did before. In addition, Europe has the institutions in place to tackle the problems, Europe-wide.

Activity 12.4

1 If there is a beach near you, or if you take a holiday on or near any European beach see if there is a 'Blue Flag' flying. Find out what this means and why it is being flown and what the conditions are that must be met in order to fly the flag.

2 There will be a landfill site somewhere in your area. This is the place where rubbish is deposited. There are strict EC rules about this. Can you find out what these are from your local council, and how they might change in the next few years.

Agricultural reform

Agriculture is one of only two policy areas specifically mentioned in the Treaty of Rome (the other is transport). This means that the 12 governments are legally obliged to have an EC-wide agricultural policy. The policy that has developed has been a source of considerable argument and controversy ever since it emerged in the late 1960s.

There are several reasons for this. Part of the problem is that the original six governments of the Community all had problems with financing and developing their own agricultural industries and so wished to push the problem up to the European level. At this level the Commission has constantly struggled to bring together the conflicting national interests of the different member states.

Ever since 1968, when the Commission, in its Mansholt proposals, tried to get a thorough reform of agriculture culminating in the MacSharry reforms of 1991, there has been a struggle with a policy area that contains many contradictions and vested interests. What are these?

COMMON AGRICULTURAL POLICY: AIMS AND OBJECTIVES

- To improve agricultural productivity by making more efficient use of resources.
- To ensure a fair standard of living for everyone involved in agriculture.
- To stabilise markets.
- To ensure that food supplies are always available.
- To ensure that supplies reach consumers at reasonable prices.

On the surface these aims and objectives of the CAP appear rational and sensible. However, in practice they are contradictory and have led to an expensive mess.

The first objective, to raise productivity, could only be achieved by reducing the number of small farms in Europe, especially in France, Belgium and Germany. This would mean throwing people off the land, something that governments were not willing to do for political reasons as farmers are always valued for their votes.

The more farmers there were the more difficult it became to pay a fair return to the farmer, even if it could be agreed just what was a fair return in the first place.

The EC tried to achieve these first two objectives by having a 'Price Support Mechanism' that guaranteed farmers a market for their produce even if the consumer did not want to buy. Quite simply, the European Commission bought surplus produce and either stored it or destroyed it.

This meant that market stability, the third objective, was only achieved at the ridiculous cost of so-called food mountains – wine lakes, butter and beef mountains, peach swamps, etc. The combination of the first three objectives resulted in the taxpayer bearing the cost of the surpluses.

The fourth objective of ensuring that food supplies are always available, has been achieved but is largely irrelevant as Europe can always buy its food on a world market.

The last objective to have fair prices for consumers has obviously been in conflict with the second objective and in practice consumers have paid around 17% more for food with the Common Agricultural Policy than they would without it.

Overall, it can be said that the objectives of the CAP have not been achieved despite the policy taking up around two-thirds of the total EC budget. Politicians have grappled for over 20 years with the problems and contradictions of the policy and they are no nearer to a solution. The best that can be hoped for is that the issue becomes relatively less important as the EC develops other common policies through economic and monetary union and perhaps, political union. It is only then that the spotlight will be taken off agriculture.

Summary   Currently there will be no significant reform of agriculture in the EC whilst:
- farmers are a powerful political lobby;
- the politicians are unwilling to upset the farmers by undertaking more than minor reforms;
- agricultural policy is also taken to be a social policy to encourage small farmers to stay on the land and not move to towns;
- the CAP itself is full of contradictions;
- consumers remain willing to keep paying high food prices.

Activity 12.5   1 Research the latest reforms of the CAP as proposed by Commissioner MacSharry and use the resources of local and national newspapers to measure reaction to his proposals. Pay particular attention to the reactions of the British government.

2 In a local supermarket or greengrocer conduct a survey of how much produce (fruit and vegetables) comes from:
a within the EC
b from Africa
c from North America
d from South America
e from Eastern Europe.

Immigration

The plight of refugees is an important political issue in the 1990s: so important in fact as to prompt the British government into attempting new legislation, the Asylum Bill, in 1992, and to galvanise the EC into action towards a European policy on immigraton and refugees.

IMMIGRATION PROBLEMS

As more and more refugees have come into Europe since 1980 there has been an increase in racial tension. The numbers of refugees seeking asylum has risen from an EC-wide total of 169 000 in 1988 to 327 000 in 1990. Asylum means sanctuary from political, religious, racial, ethnic, social or other persecution and was being sought by people in the following countries of the EC at the end of 1991.

Germany	200 000 requests
France	48 000 requests
Italy	3 000 requests
Holland	21 000 requests
Portugal	100 requests
Britain	30 000 requests

Source: Guardian Extra, 12 November 1991

Attacks on refugees and asylum seekers has risen alarmingly. This is especially so in the newly unified Germany but there have been many serious incidents in France, Belgium, Austria and Italy. These incidents have been fanned by the re-emergence in some European countries – France, Germany, Belgium and Austria – of right-wing political groups in favour of nationalism.

Asylum-seekers and refugees try to come to Europe in order to improve their economic and political prospects, often from dictatorships with poor human rights records with little opportunity to participate in local politics or to advance socially. Many come from poor parts of southern Europe and the break-up of the Soviet empire in Eastern Europe has paved the way for a flood of refugees from those countries. There is also a fear that when the EC completes the Single Market there may be common rules of entry into the 12 states which will make it harder to enter than is currently the case.

There is a strongly held view in Britain, France and Germany that a large influx of asylum seekers will increase social tensions and put a large burden on social security systems in these countries. A counter argument is that the European Community can only benefit from having a fresh pool of labour to choose from as the Single Market creates more jobs.

EUROPEAN POLICY ON IMMIGRATION

The European Commission has been trying to get the 12 governments of the Community to act together to form a common policy on immigration. Britain is opposed because it thinks that only national governments should decide who enters each country. However the proposals of the Commission are actually similar to those in the Asylum Bill, and are as follows:

- developing a fast procedure for refusing asylum applications that are clearly without legal foundation;
- tough new fines on airlines landing passengers without the proper documents;
- stricter interpretations of the type of persecution that qualifies for sanctuary.

Currently, the governments of the EC co-operate on such matters outside of the EC framework. Britain wants to control its borders, not just to keep a check on immigration but also to enforce anti-terrorism, anti-drug and anti-fraud policies. The Commission would eventually like to extend its powers in these areas. All political parties in Britain oppose this move. The Labour party fear that a weakening of British border controls will mean the introduction of identity cards for all citizens, as happens in most other EC countries.

Activity 12.6

1 Throughout European history there has been fierce argument over immigration, whether it be from Eastern Europe, the Soviet Union or parts of the former empires of Portugal, Spain, Holland, France or Britain. Why do you think this is? Do you think that the debate has heightened recently and, if so, why?

2 Find out the meaning of the following terms: immigrant; refugee; dependants; right of abode; deportation.

Foreign policy

Until the European Community undertook its recent drive to develop economic and monetary union and political union, foreign policy was looked upon as strictly the business of national governments. This is yet another area where Community institutions are now challenging national governments for control of policy.

HISTORICAL BACKGROUND

The EC is now the world's most significant trading bloc, responsible for over 40% of all trade. During the last 30 years, the EC has developed a series of trade, aid and development packages with African, Caribbean and Pacific states known as the Yaounde and Lome Conventions. The EC also entered trade treaties with several Middle-Eastern countries, the USA and some nations of South America.

From the 1960s, the EC states have increasingly acted as one body on international issues at the United Nations and in the world trade barrier reduction talks – General Agreement on Tariffs and Trade (GATT). Such issues have included reducing the international tariff barriers to trade, forming a common position on disarmament talks between the USA and the former Soviet Union and the so-called 'Euro-Arab dialogue' where the EC countries tried to formulate a joint position on the long running dispute between the Arab states and Israel over the Palestinians.

In the 1970s, the Community developed what became known as the *political co-operation mechanism*. This was a system of co-ordination and consultation between the member states over foreign policy issues which resulted in some joint action. An example would be the EC-wide economic embargo imposed on Argentina after she invaded the Falkland Islands in 1982. *Political co-operatoin* was never actually seen as a joint foreign policy for all the member states but rather as an *ad hoc* affair.

The 1986 Single European Act formalised the process of *political co-operation* but did not make foreign policy an EC responsibility. This ensured that the institutions of the Community had no large say over foreign policy-making.

CURRENT DEBATES

The British government, with some support from Ireland and Denmark, has always argued that it is not realistic for the EC to develop a common foreign policy because while there are many things that unite the 12, there are also many factors which divide them.

Recent history

Britain, France, Germany and Italy have all been great powers in the twentieth century and have all had empires which are now gone. The break-up of empires, known as decolonisation, left the former colonial powers with very different outlooks on the world.

Britain took the view, after 1945, that she could no longer hold on to her empire but she hoped that the process of decolonisation would leave a number of former colonial powers newly independent but also sympathetic in outlook to Britain and the Western states in general.

For France retention of overseas colonies was seen as an important indicator of independent 'great power' status. In Algeria, for example, the French fought a bloody war to try and stay there and in countries of north Africa and the Pacific Ocean France maintained a military presence far longer than did Britain.

Both Germany and Italy had their colonies removed from them after world wars.

Anglo-American relations

Since the Second World War, Britain has always seen itself as being in a kind of 'special relationship' with the USA and having closer relations with American presidents than other European countries had. Britain always sought to preserve this relationship and with this, a different world view.

Defence

Both Britain and France possess arsenals of nuclear weapons. Neither country wishes the EC or any other organisation to have a say over the use of such weapons.

National character

Culture, history, language – those things that together make a feeling of citizenship or nationhood in a country – vary throughout the EC. This, it is said, should be recognised by maintaining separate foreign policies.

Community institutions

What is at stake is the ability or otherwise of the institutions to declare that matters involving foreign policy co-operation are 'actions of a joint nature' and therefore legally binding on the 12. This is a significant extension of the existing political co-operation mechanism. Some countries, notably Britain, maintain that it is unrealistic to expect there to be agreement on the issues and that what is needed is flexibility, not a legal statement.

DEFENCE Defence has always been specifically excluded from the powers of the European Community. Since 1949, it has been the American-dominated North Atlantic Treaty Organisation (NATO) that has provided for the defence of Western Europe against perceived Soviet threats. Now that these threats have gone, a new debate has opened about the defence of Western Europe.

No one is advocating that NATO should disband. This is a reaction to both instability in what was the Soviet Union and political uncertainty over the future of Eastern Europe. However, many people in Western Europe feel that Europe should take more responsibility for its own defence either, by giving the EC power over defence policies in conjunction with 'common' foreign policies or, by increasing the powers of the largely powerless Western European Union (WEU). The WEU has existed since 1955 but has not made a significant impact on European defence strategy largely because NATO was seen as a much more important body with the crucial membership of the USA.

Summary There is a lively debate over the future of European foreign and defence policies. This debate is a reflection of feeling among Western European governments that the success of the EC should be translated into defence areas. It is also a recognition of the huge changes that have taken place throughout Europe since 1989.

However, in the absence of a consensus among the members of the EC and NATO there is little possibility in the near future of important changes in Western foreign and defence policies or in the organisations that are responsible for them. For the present, it is therefore unlikely that the EC will gain significant powers over foreign and defence policy.

Activity 12.7   **1** On a map of Europe indicate which countries are NATO members and which countries used to be a part of the now disbanded Warsaw Pact.

2 Since 1991 there has been a bloody civil war in Yugoslavia between the Serbians and the Croatians. Can you find out why this war started and why the countries of

Western Europe have not been anxious to send their troops there to keep the peace? For information on this a good starting point is the weekly *Economist* magazine and a good quality newspaper.

Summit diplomacy

At the end of 1991, in the Dutch town of Maastricht, the 12 heads of government of the European Community countries met to decide on the future of many of the issues that have been discussed above. The Maastricht summit was the most important for many years though such summits take place at least three times a year. This final case study is about how issues are resolved at the top levels of government.

BACKGROUND
POSITIONS

All governments go to summit meetings determined to fight for their own interests. These interests sometimes coincide with those of other governments, and sometimes with what is often called the 'European interest' while on other occasions, no agreement can be reached. Often, the issues under discussion are very important to governments and the peoples they represent. Compromise will only come about when interests can be reconciled. No government gives anything away without something in return, so hard bargaining is common.

The European Commission can attend and speak at the summits but is not allowed to vote. Naturally enough it puts forward plenty of proposals to increase its own power and influence, but at summits it is the governments who decide. The Commission can be very influential in the run up to summits and behind the scenes but that is all.

Following, are the background positions of the 12 governments as they approached the Maastricht negotiations in December 1991.

Germany
It was agreed *before the summit began* that Germany, as the most powerful EC state, would design the treaty on economic and monetary union. This would contain Germany's objectives for EMU – a strong, independent European Central Bank, a firm timetable for EMU and plans for a common currency. It was also agreed prior to the summit that France would play the leading role in the development of political union but here too, Germany had its own objectives. These can be summarised as enhancing the powers of the European Parliament, developing an EC role in controlling immigration and moves towards a common foreign and defence policy.

France
The French took the pre-summit lead in discussions on political union. They were as keen as the Germans to see EMU, more as a device to control the strong German economy. President Mitterrand was under pressure in France

to achieve political union in order to reduce American influence in Europe, increase French influence in Eastern Europe and tie the EC countries even closer together so as to make permanent peace the norm.

Britain
The British position before Maastricht was not as clear as that of some of the other countries. However, it was clear that Prime Minister Major was opposed to the Social Charter; opposed to greater EC influence in foreign and defence policy and opposed to greater powers for the EC institutions. Major also said that no single currency could ever be imposed. Beyond this the British position was reserved. The strategy was to wait and see how the summit progressed.

Belgium
Belgium went to Maastricht enthusiastic about greater economic and political integration but also concerned to keep its economy in line with that of its powerful German neighbour. The Belgians also wanted to see the Social Charter implemented and more powers for EC institutions. This is not surprising as Brussels is the virtual capital of the European Community.

Denmark
The Danish economy is another one tied to the economic fortunes of the Germans. The Danes were in favour of greater monetary union. Denmark was cautiously in favour of political union so long as this did not mean less American input into Europe's defence. At the same time the Danes were prepared to see a limited increase in power for the European Parliament.

Spain
Spain's approach was dominated by money. She made it plain that at the summit she wanted to see agreement that she would pay less into the Community budget by 1993 and that more EC regional spending would be directed at southern Europe. Spain was against the implementation of any EC measures that could adversely affect her competitive position: she feared higher wage costs from the Social Charter proposals and greater costs if the EC institutions pushed for stronger policies to protect the environment.

Greece
The Greek economy is the poorest of the 12 and so Greece tends to be in favour of both economic and monetary union and political union in the hope of economic benefits, such as more European regional spending there. Greece was strongly in favour of a European defence policy, partly through fear of Turkey and also because of long-standing anti-Americanism. Greece supported the Social Charter.

Italy
Italy's main concern was not to be left behind, either economically or

politically, by anything decided at Maastricht. The Italians have for many years been enthusiastic about further economic and political integration, increased powers for the European Parliament and implementation of the Social Charter.

Luxembourg

As with Italy, Luxembourg can be described as enthusiastic about further integration before Maastricht. However a constant worry of the smallest EC state is that it will be ignored. This was why it agreed that a new European Central Bank should be sited in Luxembourg.

Ireland

Since joining the EC in 1973 Ireland has pinned its hopes for economic growth on the Community. It was in favour of closing the gap between richer and poorer EC states and therefore wanted to see greater EC spending in Ireland. Ireland has never been particularly enthusiastic about moves towards a European defence policy because officially she is a neutral country.

Netherlands

The Dutch were to play a key role at Maastricht because they would chair the proceedings as President of the Community in the last six months of 1991. Prior to the summit however, it became clear that the Dutch were having to bow to French and German pressure on the future shape of political union and EMU. Success of the summit as a whole was a major objective of the Dutch government so they always saw themselves as mediators between opposing views.

Portugal

Like Spain and Ireland, Portugal wanted to see more spending in the poorer EC regions but was wary, as a firm NATO member, of the EC having too big a role in defence matters. EMU was seen as being difficult for an economy as weak as Portugal's which could not compete with stronger EC economies in terms of levels of industrialisation, productivity, spending power, economic growth or keeping the currency stable. Generally the Portuguese could not be said to be the most enthusiastic supporters of greater political union but would have to go along with it in order to reap other benefits. These would come in the form of more EC aid.

THE NEGOTIATIONS   The talks at Maastricht lasted for two days. The bargaining was very tough and the Summit came close to failure throughout the second day. Most governments received something of what they wanted and were able to successfully defend special interests that were of little concern to others, e.g., the Danes got approval to stop Germans buying holiday homes in Denmark and the Irish received a guarantee that the EC would not interfere in Ireland's anti-abortion laws. These were however small decisions of little consequence to the success or failure of the Summit. It was clearly the actions of Britain, France and Germany that were the key to decision making at Maastricht.

THE OUTCOMES The outcomes were very complex, and in some cases unclear. This is because the effects of the decisions taken will take many years to become apparent. This is often a feature of EC summit meetings when politicians would rather not be around when the full consequences of their actions become plain for all to see. This is very true of Maastricht which charted a course towards both EMU and political union despite very obvious dangers along the way. What was decided?

The treaty

The treaty that was signed at Maastricht was an important development of the EC. The major countries all gained something. For France there was managing to get the Germans to agree to a single currency by 1999 at the latest. However the terms for EMU were largely dominated by Germany and they insisted that any country that wants to proceed to full economic union must be in a fit state to do so. (*See* Activity 12.8.) So German success was in shaping the further course of EMU and gaining some increase in powers for the Parliament. Both France and Germany were pleased that progress was made in the development of an EC foreign policy, but Britain insisted that all 12 countries had to agree on this first so that Britain's interests could not be ignored. Britain managed to avoid having the Social Charter applied to it and also won the right to opt out (not take part) in the single currency arrangement. Britain could not stop the other 11 moving forward on the Social Charter or on the single currency.

For Spain and Portugal there was the promise of more money from the EC. The Spanish were particularly pleased to see progress made on the idea of a 'Euro-citizen'. Soon a citizen of an EC country will be able to live anywhere in the Community and also vote in local elections.

Belgium, Italy, Denmark and Greece were all pleased to see an extension of the powers of the EC institutions into new areas. These included consumer protection and health, energy and transport projects, some environmental issues and communication projects. Germany's desire that the EC play a role in immigraton and asylum issues got nowhere. For Luxembourg there was the satisfaction that progress would be made on political union. The Dutch were widely praised for the way they had handled the meeting.

So, at the end of the two days all of the countries could claim they had gained something. This is often a feature of EC decision-making and reflects the fact that membership of the Community is a voluntary thing that is entered into because everyone benefits. If this was not the case then the Community would cease to exist.

Activity 12.8 **1** The following simple, but important, terms were used at Maastricht by the negotiators. Find out what they mean:
- cohesion

- competence
- convergence
- opting out
- subsidiarity
- unanimity.

2 It was decided at Maastricht that Economic and Monetary Union would proceed to the creation of a single currency. However certain important conditions were attached to this in terms of inflation, interest rates, debt and the value of currencies. What were these conditions and are they being brought about?

3 EC summits take place three times per year. Find out:
- when and where the next summit will take place
- what will be the main issues
- how the issues are resolved.

If you are to do this you must keep a close watch on newspapers and it is a good idea to start a newspaper file now of cuttings about the EC. This will prove invaluable as you try to answer the questions.

4 Now that you have read through this section you must decide for yourself whether or not you think that British membership of the European Community is a good or bad thing. Write 500 words for or against membership. You can use any material you have collected through the work you have done in this chapter.

Index